791.445   Nimmo, Dan D.
NIM   Nightly horrors : crisis coverage
       by television network news / Dan
       Nimmo and James E. Combs. --
       Knoxville : University of Tennessee
       Press, c1985.
         xiv, 216 p. ; 23 cm.

         Bibliography: p. [199]-205.
       Includes index.
       ISBN 0-87049-443-0

         1. Television broadcasting of
       news--United States. I. Combs,
       James E. II. Title.

PN4888.T4N5 1985   070.1'9

                             84-10464
                             AACR2 MARC

Library of Congress
01279 *66 11261   612617   5163

8c10
no last

Check in

NIGHTLY HORRORS
Crisis Coverage by Television Network News

Nightly Horrors

Crisis Coverage by Television Network News

Dan Nimmo and James E. Combs

The University of Tennessee Press
Knoxville

Library of Congress Cataloging in Publication Data

Nimmo, Dan D.
  Nightly horrors.

  Bibliography: p.
  Includes index.
  1. Television broadcasting of news—United States.
I. Combs, James E.   II.Title.
PN4888.T4N5   1985   070.1'9   84-10464
ISBN 0-87049-443-0

To

Walley Ballou

Real-Fictional Pioneer of Real-Fiction Journalism

Contents

Tables

Tables

Preface

This is a study of how the three major television networks in the United States reported six major crises in their nightly news programs, crises taking place from 1978 to 1982. A decade ago such a study, although not strictly impossible, would not have been and was not undertaken. The reasonant voices and flickering visuals that constituted nightly network television news were ephemeral. Once broadcast they were usually lost forever. No network or other organization recorded them for posterity on a regular basis. For scholars to examine televised network news coverage, months or years later, was largely unthinkable.

Now all of that has changed. In 1968 the Vanderbilt Television News Archive began systematic tapings of nightly newscasts. Also during the ensuing decade affordable VHS and Betamax recording and playback systems began to replace the often unwieldy reel-to-reel technology of earlier years. The systematic, empirical study of the full range of TV news—words, pictures, inflections, and even what former Vice President Spiro Agnew fretted about as "raised eyebrows"—became grist for the researcher's mill.

But archival and technological progress aside, the study of television news is still not an easy task. The often tedious content analysis of a medium that is visual as well as vocal, nonverbal as well as verbal, requires labor, patience, and support. In undertaking the analysis of videotapes pertaining to the six crises that form the basis of this study, we have had the assistance of several people. Four have been especially helpful and merit acknowledgment—Jay Felsberg, Ann Norris, Barry

Kolar, and Karen Johnson. It may well be that one or more now have an understandable reluctance to watch nightly network newscasts.

The support for this research came from several sources. A research fellowship from the Television and Politics Study Program of George Washington University, a summer grant from the University of Tennessee under the auspices of the Home Federal Savings and Loan Association fund, and a developmental grant from Valparaiso University provided much-needed funding. Professor Thomas D. Ungs, head of the Department of Political Science, University of Tennessee, Knoxville, was able to secure funding for purchase of state-of-the-art recording and playback equipment. Prior to that time Professor Tom Hood, head of the Department of Sociology, University of Tennessee, Knoxville, was generous in making his department's equipment available. Finally, we are indebted to the personnel of the Vanderbilt Television News Archive for their cooperation in filling orders for composite tapes and for opening their facilities to us.

NIGHTLY HORRORS
Crisis Coverage by Television Network News

Introduction
Crisis Coverage in
Television Network News

On Saturday, November 18, 1978, Congressman Leo Ryan, news reporter Don Harris, and cameraman Bob Brown were murdered as they were boarding a plane departing a small airstrip outside Jonestown, Guyana. Within hours mass murders and suicides in The People's Temple compound of Jonestown resulted in more than 900 deaths, a puzzling mystery regarding why, and widespread reports in the United States of the dangers of religious cults.

On Wednesday, March 28, 1979, in the early morning hours at the Three Mile Island nuclear plant outside Harrisburg, Pennsylvania, a series of pumps feeding water through the plant's cooling system shut down. What began as an "incident" became an "accident" that involved the evacuation of preschool children and pregnant women from a five-mile perimeter and, in weeks to come, was a major blow to the future of nuclear power in the United States.

On Friday, May 25, 1979, in the late afternoon, American Airlines Flight 191 took off from O'Hare Field in Chicago. Before clearing the airport, Flight 191, a DC-10 aircraft, crashed in flames, killing all 275 persons aboard. The worst domestic air crash in U.S. history, it resulted in repeated groundings of the DC-10 in this country and abroad and a massive financial loss to the airline industry.

Nightly Horrors: Television Network News

On Sunday, May 18, 1980, Mount St. Helens, a volcano in the Cascade Mountains hitherto dormant for 123 years, erupted, sending plumes of ash and steam 60,000 feet into the air. It was the first in a series of eruptions that killed 25 people; resulted in 40 persons missing and presumed dead; produced floods, mudslides, lightning fires, and ash storms; and caused $2.7 billion damage in southern Washington and northern Oregon.

On Sunday, November 4, 1979, a then unknown number of Americans were taken hostage at the U.S. Embassy in Teheran, Iran. Fifty-two remained hostage for 444 days. During that period eight American servicemen lost their lives in an aborted rescue attempt; a U.S. President and his nation were preoccupied with what many called a national "humiliation," even "defeat"; and there was an outpouring of joy and relief when the hostages were released minutes after the inauguration of a newly elected President in 1981.

On Thursday, September 30, 1982, three persons in the area of Chicago died after taking capsules of the pain reliever Extra-Strength Tylenol. The deaths led to nationwide concern about the sale of over-the-counter drugs, a coast-to-coast manhunt for the culprit, alleged "copycat" murders, the "stealing" of Halloween, the downfall of an elected state official, and federal guidelines for drug packaging.

Six events separated in space, time, and character. What had they in common? Beyond a loss—of lives, property, or office—seemingly very little. But there was one other thing. Each fell into the category of what the news media, especially nightly network television news, treated as a crisis. They were, to be sure, different kinds of crises: a human tragedy in Jonestown, a technological crisis at Three Mile Island, an industry's dilemma over what caused the crash of Flight 191, a natural disaster at Mount St. Helens, a political stalemate in Iran, and nationwide fears about the safety of over-the-counter drugs.

Notwithstanding these differences, however, there were patterns imposed upon these separate and diverse events by network television's coverage of them. It is the contention of this book that a close examination of these patterns reveals how television news networks define critical situations for viewers.

Whether such televised coverage does, in fact, directly determine how people cope with crises is another matter. But if
Thomas (1928) was correct in his view that what people define
as real can be real in its consequences, then television news as a
supplier of definitions may indeed be a key factor in how people
cope with their worlds. This is especially probable when we
recognize that two-thirds of Americans rely upon TV as a
source of news and that four in ten depend upon the medium as
their sole source. Moreover, TV news enjoys a two-to-one
advantage over newspapers among Americans as a believable
source of what is happening (Roper, 1983).

The view that news influences popular thought and action is
scarcely novel. Walter Lippmann (1922) argued as much with
respect to the newspaper's role in shaping readers' stereotypes.
More recently that argument has been extended to televised
news, by Frank (1973), Robinson (1981), Lemert (1981), and the
Langs (1968, 1983) among others. To describe how our study of
crisis coverage in television news complements that argument,
we turn to the current status of studies of the nature of TV news
in general and crisis news in particular.

The Study of TV News

Political scientist Doris Graber (1980) has noted that the mass
media perform an indispensable function during crises: "in
diffusing vital information to the public and officials, in interpreting the meaning of events, and in providing emotional support for troubled communities" (p. 239). Crucial though these
functions are, however, the ways news media actually report
crises have received relatively little study, either by working
journalists or communications scientists. In contrast, the newsmaking process (Roshco, 1975) as it pertains to coverage of
routine events has had considerable emphasis.

In exploring news content, for example, researchers have
been especially interested in how the press reports electoral
campaigns. The most notable has been in the alleged bias of the
reporting of presidential contests. Efron's (1971) controversial

"exposé" of 1968 presidential campaign coverage inaugurated a host of more careful analyses, including Frank's (1973) and Hofstetter's (1976) independent accounts of the news coverage in the 1972 presidential election. Other investigators have been less interested in news bias than in whether the information needs of the electorate are served by campaign reporting and if news coverage influences voters' decisions. In this respect Patterson and McClure (1976) provided a groundbreaking study of televised coverage of the 1972 presidential campaign, finding that candidates' spot advertising actually contained more information regarding contenders' issue stands than did televised news reports. Arterton (1978) and Patterson (1980) have investigated parallel questions about coverage of the 1976 presidential election, and Robinson (1981) traced shifts in the images of candidates as portrayed in the *CBS Evening News* during the course of the 1980 presidential contest.

Although these various analyses of TV news coverage employed, with varying sophistication and rigor, techniques of quantitative content analysis, other tools have been adapted to the study of television news as well. For example, drawing upon techniques of rhetorical criticism, Ernest Bormann and his colleagues developed the method of fantasy theme analysis for uncovering the latent themes, myths, and dramatic representations in TV news coverage not readily apparent in manifest symbols (see Brock & Scott, 1980; Cragan & Shields, 1981). Other analysts (Diamond, 1978; Adams, 1983) focus upon televised election coverage with a combination of quantitative and qualitative techniques.

Despite what seems to be an overarching emphasis upon televised coverage of elections, particularly presidential campaigns, researchers have delved into other questions. Exploiting a variety of analytical techniques, investigators have examined televised coverage of presidency, congress, and courts (Paletz & Entman, 1981); developments in the Middle East (Adams, 1981); and a variety of international matters, including relations of the U.S. to the Third World, the 1979 Camp David Summit, the 1980 Olympic Boycott, terrorism, and the war in Southeast Asia (Diamond, 1975; Braestrup, 1978; Adams, 1982).

Introduction: Crisis Coverage

In appraising the role of television as a news medium, free-lance critics, working journalists, and communications scholars have not restricted themselves solely to examining the contents of news reports. They have recognized that media content depends upon who does the reporting, what is being reported, to whom news is directed, the nature of the newsmaking process, and the likely effects of televised messages. It is not necessary to review the plethora of studies dealing with these questions. Rather, it is appropriate simply to note the general context within which the relatively few studies of crisis coverage have been undertaken.

Television networks are, of course, large-scale economic organizations whose interests go well beyond the altruistic motive of informing the public. Both political scientist Edward Epstein (1973) and sociologist Herbert Gans (1979) have examined how organizational factors influence news content. Epstein's focus drew upon organizational theory to explore how TV news reflects not only the circumstances of a reported event but, more importantly, pressures to satisfy the internal needs of the television news networks as large organizations. Organization concerns are frequently projected into, and imposed upon, news coverage. From a different perspective Gans explored the external pressures on news organizations, such as the search for profits, advertisers, and censorship. Like Epstein, he found that the urge to cope with such pressures are as significant a factor in shaping news content as the "objective" realities of reported events.

From the viewpoint of the working TV correspondent, reporting is something more than serving a large organization or an imagined public. It is a job, a way of working. This is the import of a variety of studies of TV news that argue the content of televised news is a "created reality" (Altheide, 1976; Tuchman, 1978). In performing their daily work, correspondents, camera personnel, editors, and producers develop standardized ways of doing things. These take the form of shared definitions of what is news, conventions of objective reporting, an aesthetic of visual presentation, an accepted grammar of news writing, and a logic of TV news, as distinct from other modes of reporting. These forms shape news content independently of the complexities of the events that trigger news stories (Berger, 1981; Zettl, 1981). We will see later that standardized ways of doing things play a prominent role in crisis reporting, regardless of the nature of the crisis itself.

Investigators have also examined how audiences for nightly news programs help define the content of the news itself. Robert MacNeil, now co-host of the widely acclaimed Public Broadcasting Service *MacNeil-Lehrer Report,* called attention to this factor in one of the earliest book-length analyses on the nature of television news (1968). MacNeil noted that the audience for public affairs news is one that commercial television built for other purposes, namely, to deliver prospective consumers to advertisers in order to charge those advertisers top dollar for the opportunity to sell products. Although the demographic makeup of audiences shifts over time (Diamond, 1975; Gans, 1979; Lichty, 1982) and regular viewers of nightly news grow more sophisticated, MacNeil's assessment of the impact of audiences on news content is still sound. Entertainment rather than information values guide all TV programming, including news: "For the journalist that means mixing show business with his journalism" (p. 13).

Finally, it is reasonable to assume that television networks, producers, editors, correspondents, advertisers, and politicians devote money, time, and energy to nightly newscasts because they believe people not only watch but will be influenced by what they see. Studies in the 1950s and 1960s regarding the actual effects of TV news on informing and guiding popular behavior did little to validate that belief. Research reinforced what was labeled a "law of minimal effects" (Klapper, 1960). But those studies were conducted during the early period of the development of TV news, in the 1950s when 15-minute newscasts reported what Diamond (1975) calls "fringe news" (correspondents simply reading wire service newscopy) and in the "headline service" years of the 1960s (quick looks at the top stories of the day without reports in depth).

With the advent of new technologies (satellite feeds, minicams, etc.) and audiences increasingly sophisticated in the nuances of TV news (and demanding in what they choose to believe) researchers are challenging the received wisdom of the "law of minimal effects." One set of scholars notes a close association between the stories emphasized in the news media and the issues and problems on people's minds. These researchers generated the "agenda setting" hypothesis of the role of news (Shaw & McCombs, 1971; Iyengar, Peters, & Kinder, 1982). Other scholars take what they call a "uses and gratifications" approach: i.e., depending upon why people follow the news media, what they seek, and what they do with media fare, their votes, opinions, and political socialization may be measurably influenced (Blumler & Katz, 1974). Robinson (1976), among others, provides evidence for a stronger hypothesis. He argues that TV news leads people to doubt their own understanding of politics; once that doubt begins, people begin to blame politicians for their perceived confusion. As a result, they grow increasingly cynical about and alienated from politics, and that sense of "videomalaise" contributes to the development of a feeling of political illegitimacy.

Current views on the impact of the news media, and of television news in particular, upon levels of information, emotional attachments, and popular behavior fall short of concluding with an "all power to the media" assessment. At the same time, however, researchers no longer dismiss TV news as having minimal consequences for the viewing public. Certainly the current verdict is consonant with Graber's view that during crises the news media do supply information, interpretations, and emotional support. But, as she goes on to suggest, the fact that the news media do play "a large part in public communication during crises" leads both officials and community members to ask how well the media "discharge their responsibilities" (p. 240). That depends upon the nature of crisis coverage.

The Study of Crisis Coverage

The bulk of research into crisis coverage of the news media falls into a general category of inquiry labeled "disaster reporting" by social scientists. Recognizing that "The mass communications media play important roles in disasters'' (Kreimer, 1980, p. vii), The National Research Council in 1978 formed The Committee on Disasters and the Mass Media to study issues surrounding disaster reporting. The Committee's point of departure paralleled that of Graber (1980) with respect to functions the press performs in crisis reporting: warning of predicted or impending disasters; conveying information to officials, relief agencies, and the public; charting the progress of relief and recovery; dramatizing lessons learned for purposes of future preparedness; taking part in long-term public education programs; and defining slow-onset problems as crises or disasters.

As part of its task, The Committee on Disasters and the Mass Media conducted an exploratory workshop in 1979. The published proceedings of that workshop provide a rare systematic effort to summarize the role and issues in crisis coverage by the news media (Kreimer, 1980). Unfortunately, however, relatively few of the papers delivered at the workshop focused in a detailed way on the content of crisis/disaster reporting. And, of those that did, the emphasis was on radio and newspaper coverage rather than television. It is nonetheless useful to summarize the major conclusions of the workshop, as they offer a context for the studies of crisis coverage by television that have been published.

A key question in any study of crisis coverage or disaster reporting is the precise definition of the terms ''crisis'' or ''disaster.'' In their respective reviews of the issues and the state of the art in disaster reporting, neither Krebs (1980) nor Larson (1980) distinguishes between the two concepts. Both use the terms interchangeably. Hence, the definition and characteristics of a disaster, as discussed in the Committee's workshop, are those of a crisis as well.

In summarizing definitions, Krebs begins with the oft-quoted characterization of Charles Fritz (1961, p. 655):

An event, concentrated in time and space, in which a society, or a relatively self-sufficient subdivision of society, undergoes severe damage and incurs such losses to its members and physical appurtenances that the social structure is disrupted and the fulfillment of all or some of the essential functions of the society is prevented.

Krebs properly notes that the Fritz definition is highly abstract. For one thing, it fails to distinguish between types of disasters. The most common distinction is between "natural" disasters (earthquakes, volcanic eruptions, floods, hurricanes, tornadoes, drought, famine, etc.) and "man-made" disasters (civil unrest, war, airline crashes, bombings, and other acts of sabotage, mass murders, etc.). This distinction is admittedly gross, but as Krebs points out, "as yet no definitive taxonomy of disasters has been produced" (p. 37).

The Fritz definition masks another problem. It specifies "severe damage" and "losses," along with social "disruption," as earmarks of critical situations. But, as Krebs argues, it is not always clear when a disaster has occurred. The devastation wrought by a hurricane or flood, loss of life and property during warfare, the strewn bodies of victims of air crashes—all are clear indicators of disastrous events. But sometimes no readily observable evidence is at hand. Consider the escape of toxic gasses from a waste disposal plant or industrial complex. Effects on humans, plants, and animals in the environs may go undetected, yet occur in critical proportions. Think also of people exposed to radioactive gasses. Physical illness may not follow until years later, but the individual and collective stress may take its toll despite the absence of confirming evidence of crisis.

Because, as Krebs says, "the determination of effects of any given event on a society or 'a relatively self-sufficient subdivision of a society' typically is uncertain in the short run and may be more perplexing in the long run" (p. 39), it is necessary to go beyond Fritz's characterization. Crises involve potentially disastrous events as well as actual physical damage. The potential—or more specifically the fear, stress, and anxiety which crises provoke—can contribute its own "severe damage" and "disrupted" life. Speaking of public crises, Doris Graber offers a useful addendum to standard definitions: "natural or man-made events that pose an immediate and serious threat to the lives and property or to the peace of mind of large numbers of citizens (1980, p. 225). To be sure, "peace of mind" is itself a slippery term, but at least it reminds researchers that crises occur even in the absence of direct threats of physical harm. Because "peace of mind" is a vague condition, let alone term, people's peace of mind often is what they are told it is. A key function of the news media in reporting crises, potential disasters, and physical disasters is precisely that of affirming, reaffirming, or subverting people's peace of mind. We return to this point in our concluding chapter after analyzing how nightly network television news covered six widely publicized crises between 1979 and 1982.

Let it suffice to say here that because the news media play a vital role in shaping or undermining peace of mind, to a large degree one answer to Kreb's question, "When, in fact, has a disaster occurred?" (p. 39) is when press reports say that it is or is not occurring (Lang & Lang, 1980). Certainly this is not always the case. When a skyscraper burns and topples to the ground, the disaster occurs independently of news accounts of it. But when news reports caution the elderly to take care in going to their mail boxes lest they be assaulted while pulling out their Social Security checks, residents of metropolitan areas against an epidemic of muggings, or subway riders not to stand too close to the edge of the platform for fear of being pushed onto the tracks, news definition and labeling plays a vital role in signaling that a problem has become a crisis. In sum, physical damage is surely one indicator of whether an event is critical, but so also is imagined harm provoking fear, be it justified or not. As James Carey (1969, p. 36) suggests, "All journalism, including objective reporting, is a creative and imaginative work, a symbolic strategy; journalism sizes up situations, names their elements, structure and outstanding ingredients and names them in a way that contains an attitude toward them."

In crisis/disaster reporting, TV news plays an increasingly important role in labeling and formulating attitudes toward what is happening. Leo Bogart, long a student of news media practices, points out the important role played by television in shaping how the public gets its news (1977, p. 82): "Consider those who remembered a major disaster—a jumbo jet collision in the Canary Islands, an earthquake in Rumania. Over half who mentioned this kind of story say they first found out about it on television."

Given the apparent importance of television as a news source and, if Bogart's research is accurate, of TV news as a source of recalled information about crises/disasters, we might assume considerable interest in exploring how TV news covers crises. Yet neither Krebs' nor Larson's separate 1980 surveys of studies of media content in disaster reporting indicate extensive analyses of the content of televised crisis coverage. Specific studies do include TV coverage of wars (Entman & Paletz, 1982; Rollins, 1982; Adams & Joblove, 1982; Muravchik, 1983), civil unrest (Saldich, 1979), and the oil crises of 1973–74, 1978–79 (Theberge, 1982). Moreover, as we shall see later, TV news coverage of two of the crises described in this volume, Three Mile Island (Chapter 2) and the Iranian hostage crisis (Chapter 5), has been examined, albeit in ways that differ substantially from those employed here.

As yet, however, there has been no systematic effort to compare televised crisis news coverage across a variety of events for purposes of discovering, as Krebs urges, "key patterns" in reporting (p. 58). Only Graber (1980) has hypothesized any such patterns, and she restricts herself to what she labels as three stages of crisis reporting: first, the news media transmit uncoordinated messages in response to a confusing, unexpected situation; second, as more information emerges, a coherent story can be pieced together; finally, there are efforts to put the critical events into a larger perspective in order to discern their long-range consequences. But Graber's stages are not based upon detailed examinations of specific cases of coverage, nor do they point solely to TV news as distinct from other news media.

This study shares Krebs' and Graber's efforts to discover patterns. The focus here, however, is specifically television news, namely, the content of nightly news broadcasts of the three major television networks in this country: ABC's *World News Tonight,* the *CBS Evening News,* and the *NBC Nightly News.*

The Nature of Television News

News is real. It is not imagined. It is not fantasy. News is not what might have been—it is the way things were.'' So wrote the editors of *TV Guide* in the "As We See It" commentary in the February 13, 1982, issue of that widely sold and popular weekly. The statement is reminiscent of how former CBS anchor Walter Cronkite signed off the *Evening News:* "And that's the way it is." The editors of *TV Guide* and Cronkite were far more confident about the realities underlying television news than many press observers have ever been about TV news or news in general. For example, in his classic work, *Public Opinion,* published in 1922, Walter Lippmann took great pains to distinguish between news and truth. They are "not the same thing," he wrote, for "the function of news is to signalize an event, the function of truth is to bring to light the hidden facts, to set them in relation with each other, and to make a picture of reality on which men can act" (p. 358). Hence, "journalism is not a first hand report of raw material," but a "report of that material after it has been stylized" (p. 347). And, unless it can be clearly demonstrated that news deals with "accomplished fact, news does not separate itself from the ocean of possible truth" (p. 340).

Lippmann's views remind us that news is a form of knowledge that is but tenuously related to some abstract notion of reality. But if news cannot be likened to truth, then what are the roots of its appeal? In recent decades the idea has evolved that the social roots of newsmaking are rhetorical, stemming from the ancient and universal impulse of human groups to explain reality by telling stories. The philosopher George Herbert Mead noted that since journalism reports "situations through which men can enter the attitude and experience of other persons," news possesses elements of drama that pick out "characters which lie in men's minds," then express "through these characters situations of their own time but which carry the individuals beyond the actual fixed walls which have arisen between them" (1934, p. 257). For Mead the bulk of news was not "information" journalism but "story" journalism that presents accounts to generate gratifying aesthetic experiences and to help people relate events to their everyday lives (Diamond, 1982).

As communications scholars have explored the nature of news in the electronic age, especially the character of television news, the distinctions made long ago between news and truth, and between information and story journalism, have proved useful. Scholarly literature increasingly refers to the "created reality" of the news media, particularly to the realities constructed by nightly network TV news (Epstein, 1973; Altheide, 1976; Tuchman, 1978; Hawkins & Pingree, 1981; Iyengar, Peters, & Kinder, 1982). The realities formulated through journalism conform to the logic inherent in each medium, or what Altheide and Snow term "media logic," i.e., the "format" of "how material is organized, the style in which it is presented, the focus or emphasis on particular characteristics of behavior, and the grammar of media communication." So conceived, write Altheide and Snow, "format becomes a framework or a perspective that is used to present as well as interpret phenomena" (1979, p. 10). Media logic suggests that different kinds of news stories can be told about identical events, depending upon which medium does the telling. It may not be that "The medium is the message," as Marshall McLuhan said (1964) but rather, to borrow Lippmann's phrase, the stylizer of the message.

In recalling Mead's emphasis upon the dramatic character of story journalism, media logic may be viewed as the logic of drama. The choices of format for reporting news in a given medium are choices of dramatic presentation. Certainly TV news exemplifies a logic that favors the portrayal of happenings in dramatic ways, making reported events sometimes larger than life (Berg, 1972). Reuven Frank, at the time executive producer for the nightly news programming at NBC, wrote a memo to his staff when they moved from a 15- to a 30-minute format in 1963. According to Epstein (1973, pp. 4–5) it read:

> Every news story should, without any sacrifice of probity or responsibility, display the attributes of fiction, of drama. It should have structure and conflict, problem and denouement, rising action and falling action, a beginning, a middle and an end. These are not only the essentials of drama; they are the essentials of narrative.

News accounts thus serve as what Walter Fisher calls "real-fictions," i.e., rhetorical compositions that concern the actual world of experience (they are about "real" things) but cannot be demonstrated true or false in detail (are fictional). Writes Fisher (1970, p. 132),

> Although its aim is to express a reliable guide to belief and action for one's daily deeds, it ultimately is a fiction since its advice is not, in the final analysis, susceptible of empirical verification. The fiction is not hypothetical; its author wants and intends that it be accepted as the true and right way of conceiving of a matter; and if he is successful, his fiction becomes one of those by which men live.

Real-fictions select and organize experience into an intentional unity that might not otherwise exist. Thus, the world evoked by TV news as a series of real-fictions is a dramatic pseudo-reality created from an ongoing flow of happenings "out there" but transformed into an entertaining story that conforms to the logic of the medium while assisting people to relate those events to their everyday lives.

Viewed in a dramatistic light, then, all news is storytelling, be it print or electronic (Darnton, 1975). Or, as Schudson (1982) contends, the accepted conventions of news in both print and television are narrative in form. The TV news format, as Sharon Sperry argues (1981), is a narrative employing imagery which is both verbal and nonverbal, both aural and visual, to construct a real-fictional world. In this sense the reporting process is a literary act, a continuous search for "story lines" that goes so far as to incorporate the metaphors and plots of novels, folk traditions, and myths (Knight & Dean, 1982; Breen & Corcoran,

1982). Indeed, Lawrence and Timberg (1979) argue that TV news stories often appeal to broadcasters and viewers alike precisely because of their "mythic adequacy," i.e., the degree that they are deeply rooted in cultural mythology and exploit appealing aesthetic qualities.

Drawing upon narrative theory, Sperry constructs a framework for exploring the nature of TV news. She notes that there are three elements in any narrative—teller, tale, and listener. The teller, or narrator, is an authority who relates the real-fiction; the ultimate narrator of any network's nightly news telecast is the anchor, assisted by correspondents of lesser stature. As Sperry points out, the anchor frames each story, reading brief reports, introducing and reviewing filmed, packaged reports from correspondents. The anchor-correspondent-anchor format, ingrained in nightly newscasts, identifies the anchor as clearly in command of storytelling. The anchor's words, says Sperry, "move the program along, linking story to story according to some larger pattern of meaning, as if the stories of the half-hour were thoughts from a single mind, ordered and moving in rational progression" (p. 299).

The anchor-narrator element of TV news links the other two, tale and listener. The tale is narrated not merely to provide information "but also to affect the listener in some way: to persuade or change him, to evoke an emotional response, or simply to interest him" (p. 298). The viewer-listener accepts the news-tale as only an approximation of truth but suspends belief willingly to share in the real-fiction spun by the narrator. The credibility of the tale, not truth or falsity as such, is the key; it increases to the degree that it conforms to standard mythic plots, especially that of a hero struggling against the odds.

Sperry quotes Av Westin, former president of ABC News, to the effect that he expected viewers to come to his news programs asking, "Is the world safe, and am I secure?" (p. 301; see also Westin, 1982). The hero motif, according to Sperry "man's simplest and most pervasive myth," offers a standardized news formula responding to Westin's question, namely, "Men muddle through life as best they can, but when tragedy strikes, they require and seek a leader, a single individual of superior worth and superior skill, who will meet the problem and conquer the evil'' (Sperry, 1981, p. 300). In TV news the heroic figures need not always be cast as saviors. Demonic hero, foolish hero, plain folk hero, even bumbling but well-intentioned hero—each enters the cast of televised news dramas.

The narrative logic of TV news directs TV anchors, correspondents, and producers to select (consciously or not) a melodramatic format, conforming to an heroic plot line, in their search for mythic adequacy (Bargainnier, 1980). Weaver (1976), for example, described how the ''melodramatic imperative'' informs and guides televised news coverage of presidential primary campaigns, a view developed even more systematically by Swanson (1977) in an analysis of press coverage of the 1976 presidential campaign.

Since news is only an aspect of the more general fare in television programming, it is not surprising that TV news draws from the same tradition of production values that pervades the entertainment medium. Adventure, mystery, romance, pathos, and nightmare fill children's programming, sports coverage, soap operas, situation comedies, docudramas, and other shows. We should not be surprised if we find variations on these formats adapted to crisis coverage as well. Crisis reporting offers opportunities for what is known in the trade as a ''continuing story,'' one that runs night after night, simplifies complex details around a few easily grasped symbols, and becomes almost a mini-series. When continuing stories strike a responsive chord among viewers, the possibilities for successful delivery of the audience to advertisers are increased.

Regardless of the values informing the content of nightly network television news, however, each narrative is a real-fiction contributing to the emergence of a symbolic reality created and transmitted by newsmaking, interpreted and shared by large audiences. Such realities Walter Fisher calls ''rhetorical visions'' (1970). Whether rhetorical visions grow out of televised crisis reporting and whether differing networks construct different visions are questions that this study addresses.

According to the conventional wisdom expressed in introductory textbooks in American politics and in mass communication, the three major networks transmit similar messages in similar styles. Dye and Ziegler, for instance, say, "There is very little diversity in television news. The three networks present nearly identical news 'packages' each evening" (1982, p. 133). Altheide's study of network coverage of the Iranian hostage crisis produced a similar view (1982). Yet Walter Karp (1982)— in an admittedly impressionistic examination of the 1981 crisis in Poland—charts provocative differences: NBC communicates interpretations in keeping with traditional Midwestern Republicanism, CBS transmits a view of Cold War liberalism, and ABC follows a style Karp associates with the political right wing. Confirmation that the major networks do not always package stories in similar ways comes from a more empirically based analysis, that of oil crises in the 1970s (Theberge, 1982). We believe that this study may shed more light on shared and contrasting patterns in TV news coverage of the rival networks.

If television news cannot be likened to truth, as Lippmann's seminal work before the dawning of electronic journalism implied, with what can it be associated? One answer is real-fictions and the rhetorical visions that derive from such real-fictions. This raises another question, how does one go about examining such real-fictions?

Analyzing the Content
of Crisis Reporting in TV News

As we have noted, this study focuses upon six crises covered by the three major television network nightly newscasts.[1] The crises selected represent a variety of natural and manmade

[1]We decided at the outset not to attempt content analysis of the emerging fourth network, Ted Turner's Atlanta-based Cable News Network (CNN). For one thing, CNN had not even started when one of the crisis stories occurred. And since Vanderbilt did not, and still does not, record CNN news, obtaining extensive tapes of their coverage was prohibitive. Further, comparing CNN to the other three "established" network news involved comparing oranges and apples: CNN does not have a nightly news program in quite the same sense that ABC, CBS, and NBC do; CNN is less tied to the evening news format and indeed has gone through several format changes in its brief history. So it proved impossible to analyze CNN. If CNN continues to develop, future research comparing network news coverage may well have to take this innovative news organization into account.

Nightly Horrors: Television Network News

disasters, i.e., situations either threatening potential damage—physical, psychological, political, economic, etc.—or actually producing clear-cut, measurable damage. We make no claim that the selected crises are a cross-section of all disaster coverage in nightly telecasts. However, since each crisis constituted the lead story of network newscasts for extended periods, these were prominent cases of continuous TV coverage.

Our original selection consisted of five crises for analysis:

1. Murders and mass suicides involving members of The People's Temple in Jonestown, Guyana, in 1978.
2. The accident at the Three Mile Island nuclear plant outside Harrisburg, Pennsylvania, in 1979.
3. The crash of an American Airlines DC-10 flight, Chicago to Los Angeles, on takeoff from O'Hare Field in 1979.
4. The 1980 volcanic eruptions of Mount St. Helens.
5. The Iranian hostage crisis, specifically the seizure of the American embassy in Teheran in 1979, the aborted rescue attempt of 1980, and the hostage release in 1981.

During the period of analyzing these five cases of crisis coverage, important changes occurred at each of the three television news networks. At CBS Dan Rather replaced Walter Cronkite as the anchor of the *CBS Evening News;* Cronkite had been the regular anchor during the network's coverage of all five crises. Moreover, Van Gordon Sauter replaced William Leonard as president of CBS News, a shift that had the potential to alter the network's existing news format. Also, in 1982 there were key changes at NBC. The anchor team of John Chancellor and David Brinkley gave way to Tom Brokaw and Roger Mudd. Reuven Frank, who had left the post of executive producer of NBC News in 1972, returned to it replacing William Small. Finally, at ABC News it was noticeable that Ted Koppel, regular anchor of the network's *Nightline* telecast, was "sitting in" with increasing frequency for anchors of ABC's *World News Tonight.*

To examine what, if any, changes in crisis coverage might derive from the shifts in personnel, we selected a sixth crisis, one emerging well after new anchors and executives had been installed. The Tylenol poisonings in late 1982 proved suitable.

That crisis too had received lead and continuous coverage by each network, coverage of events involving both physical and nonphysical damage over an extended period.

For each of the six crises, we obtained tapes of relevant nightly newscasts for each network from the Vanderbilt Television News Archive. Specifically, tapes for all evening network newscasts (weeknights and, where applicable, weekends) were analyzed:

1. The People's Temple—November 19, 1978, through December 8, 1978.
2. Three Mile Island—March 28 through April 30, 1979.
3. American Airlines Flight 191—May 25 through July 15, 1979.
4. Mount St. Helens—May 18 through June 26, 1980.
5. Iranian Hostage Crisis—the first week of the seizure (November 4–9, 1979; the rescue effort (April 25–28, 1980); and the hostage release (January 18–22, 1981).
6. Tylenol Poisonings—September 30 through October 31, 1982.

Thus, in each case we analyzed telecasts from the date of the initial breaking of the story through the time when it no longer received continuous coverage. The exception is the Iranian hostage crisis. Network coverage of those "444 Days" was not only continuous but almost an effort to saturate. To analyze the content of all reports from the beginning to the resolution of that crisis was beyond our resources. Moreover, there was some reason to believe from other analyses (Altheide, 1982) that coverage was repetitive, with patterns first established and then confirmed. (Our analysis, however, questions that supposition.) Therefore, we selected three key weeks of the crisis— seizure, rescue, release—for inquiry.

As leading texts on the technique indicate (Holsti, 1969a; Krippendorff, 1980), content analysis is a useful and sophisticated tool in communication studies. Content analysis of nightly network television newscasts has developed relatively recently and taken various forms (see Adams & Schreibman, 1978). Frank (1973) in his analyses of newscasts in 1969 and again in 1979 distinguished two such forms, the "hard" and "soft" approaches. The "hard" approach examines discrete and quantifiable items of data, such as seconds of airtime, story placements, and frequency counts of words. The "soft" approach is more subjective and evaluates entire news segments, stories, and broadcasts in keeping with selected criteria.

In this investigation we employ both approaches. As a result, depending upon the form of analysis employed, we define various units of analysis. Basically, however, we refer to two units, the story and the report. As Sperry (1981) indicates, a story is a narrative account introduced by an anchor. With the introduction complete, the anchor may then read the remainder of the story; cut to filmed, taped, packaged presentations by one or more correspondents; or follow the introduction with a live interview. At the conclusion of the story, the anchor returns to summarize, either concluding the narrative or bridging to another story of the same event. A report consists of a single presentation by an anchor or correspondent within the framework of the overall story. For example, if the *CBS Evening News* has a story on drought in the American Heartland, Dan Rather typically introduces and develops the story (the anchor report), which is followed by a packaged report from a correspondent in Des Moines and perhaps another from the National Weather Service; Rather concludes with a wrap-up. The drought story thus consists of four reports. Rather then may or may not introduce another drought story in the anchor-correspondent(s)-anchor pattern.

There are, of course, problems associated with using stories and reports as units of analysis. Holsti (1969b, p. 648) has pointed out that such "item analysis" presents "problems when items fall into two categories." If decisions on category placements are not cross-checked, the subjective choices of judges exaggerate differences between items. Granted those problems, however, there remain reasons for using a story/report focus. One lies in the narrative nature of TV network news. To achieve some understanding of the "story lines" in crisis coverage, it is appropriate to focus upon stories and reports as units of analysis. Moreover, as Lichty and Bailey (1978) point out, although the units in analyzing the content of TV news vary from entire programs to single words, most studies employ the story as an analytical unit, classifying as stories the reports of anchors, correspondents, and commentators. Also, Holsti (1969b, p. 648) posits that item analysis is useful when "gross categories will suffice."

Although we define stories and reports as units of analysis, we combine hard and soft approaches to analyzing the units themselves. Within each story and report we identify discrete, concrete data for coding. In addition to coding the length of each report and overall story, the number of reports comprising a story, and identity of the reporters, we quantify the following:

1. Locale of the report: network studio, government office, crisis site, private home or office, or other.
2. Source of the report: public official, technical expert/scientist, or average citizen.
3. Newsgathering mode: briefing by press officer or public official, speech or statement by public official, interview with press officer or other public official, interview with technical expert, interview with private spokesperson, interview with average citizen, or reporter quoting an unnamed source.

Such data involve newsgathering aspects of reporting, the "who, what, where, when, and how" of journalism. They do not distinguish TV news from radio or print journalism. Since much of the narrative of televised news involves visual presentation, that too must be taken into account. Coding for visual data involves the following elements (compare Frank, 1973; Doyle, 1982; Theberge, 1982):

1. Did the anchor read the story?
2. Was a slide, map, or other graphic used in the background? How many?
3. Was a still picture or graphic used on the total screen? With voice-over? How many?
4. Was a film rolled during the report? With voice-over or interview?
5. Was a second film rolled during the report? With voice-over or interview?

6. Did a correspondent take over with a packaged report? If there were interviews, how many?
7. Was a second packaged report used? If there were interviews, how many?
8. Was there a cut to a live report, microwave, or phone?

Depending upon coded responses to each of these questions, we calculated a visual prominence score for each story by assigning points to each response on a linear scale (see Doyle, 1982). Points were assigned to whether a given story contained one or more graphics, one or more stills, one or more rolled films, one or more interviews, and one or more packaged cuts. (Live cuts were so rare that they were deleted from the analysis.) For packaged stories points were similarly assigned, depending upon the presence of graphics, stills, films, and interviews. In all cases the number of points assigned consisted of the total number of graphics, stills, films, and interviews in the story. Although the lower limit of the scale is zero (for an anchor-read, "talking head," story without accompanying visuals), the total number of points possible for a story depends upon how many graphics, stills, and interviews comprise the story. The highest score was for a story about the crash of Flight 191 (73).

In addition to discrete data coded for individual reports and stories, we employed other categories for entire units. Following codes employed by researchers preparing *The Staff Report to the President's Commission on the Accident at Three Mile Island* in their study of news coverage of the accident, we coded all reports for crises as reassuring, alarming, or neutral. (The Task Force, however, used statements as units; see *Report of The Public's Right to Information Task Force,* pp. 182–218.) Also, employing content categories developed in another Three Mile Island study, this conducted by The Media Institute (Theberge, 1979, p. 3), we categorized all reports for each crisis as:

1. News: the factual "what, where, who, when, and why" of an event.[2]

---

[2]In the text readers will note two itemized listings of the elements of news. The first consists of those elements taken to be conventions in standardized wire

2. Peripheral: information or background not required to understand the event.
3. Perspective: information or background aiding understanding.
4. News/Peripheral.
5. News/Perspective.

A third coding set derives from a different form of "soft" analysis, that of rhetorical criticism. In particular, we have turned to what Brock and Scott (1980) describe as "the dramatistic approach." Dramatistic analysis, like many forms of rhetorical criticism, is what Krippendorff (1980) considers qualitative content analysis, "a method of inquiry into the symbolic meaning of messages" (p. 22). Examples of qualitative analysis abound in communication studies, including Gans' (1979) study of recurring values expressed in weekly news magazines and nightly network television newscasts. Qualitative analysis is particularly well suited to interpreting the latent messages contained in verbal and nonverbal materials. Although amenable to quantitative measurement, as in Bantz's analysis of selected broadcasts of ABC News (1979), rhetorical analysis favors message interpretation according to more subjective guidelines.

Dramatistic analysis borrows from the critical work of Kenneth Burke (1966). In Burke's perspective, human conduct takes the form of symbolic action, i.e., people know the world and relate to one another only through the creation, manipulation, and exchange of symbols. For Burke, symbolic action makes life dramatic; that is, life is not merely like drama but is in fact a series of unfolding dramas. This being the case, the major elements employed by a drama critic can be used to analyze human conduct. Various rhetorical critics have built upon Burke's teachings, extending his methods to the analysis of

---

service reporting. These are the "Four Ws and an H" common to wire service copy, newswriting, and broadcast journalism—i.e., news consists of who, what, where, when, and how. A second listing—that of what, where, who, when, and why—has been used by such writers and researchers as those involved in studies by The Media Institute (Theberge, 1979). Unless otherwise noted the second listing applies when we compare results of our analysis to those of The Media Institute and the first listing applies to more conventional newswriting.

presidential addresses (Fisher, 1980), television news (Bormann, 1972), and other messages.

For Burke the essential elements of dramatistic analysis appear in a pentad: acts, actors, agencies, scenes, and purposes. (Burke adds a sixth element, attitude, in later writings; however we will subsume that into the pentad.) Acts make up the script, plot line, or scenario of a drama, of any news event. Actors are dramatis personae—heroic, villainous, or foolish characters of a narrative. Agencies are the means actors use to achieve their aims and to attempt to legitimize their ends. The scene is the setting or locale of symbolic action. Purposes consist of motives, intentions, and meanings actors bring to and take from a drama, an event.

In analyzing TV news from a dramatistic point of view, the researcher seeks answers to specific questions regarding each element in the dramatic pentad. We examined each report and story addressing the following:

1. Acts
   a. Who is reported doing what to whom?
   b. What general plot line organizes these acts—tragedy, comedy, epic, elegy, satire, quest, or what?
   c. Is there a pattern in reported events, i.e., a repetition of accounts?
   d. Is there a resolution to the problem posed by the narrative?
2. Actors
   a. Who are the dramatis personae?
   b. Are there role types in the drama?
   c. If so, what types emerge—heroes, villains, fools, victims, objects of desire, incorruptible people, supporting actors?
   d. Are there role reversals?
   e. Does an abstraction personified as a character play a role—"The People," "The Hostage Families," "The Experts," etc.?
   f. How concrete and detailed are the role portrayals?
   g. Are insiders praised, outsiders/enemies damned? For what?

3. Agencies
   a. What reported source justifies and promotes the acceptance and promulgation of the narrative?
   b. What acts are performed by sanctioning agents—"The People," "America," "God," "Militants," "Diplomats," etc.?
   c. Which acts are praised, censored?
   d. What lifestyles are exemplified, praiseworthy, condemned?
   e. What metaphors are invoked and repeated?
4. Scenes
   a. What is the scope of the setting?
   b. What are the reported features of the locale?
   c. What props exist?
   d. Where is the drama set—wilderness, rural areas, urban ghetto, enemy territory, supernatural place?
5. Purposes
   a. What meanings do reporters give the drama?
   b. How does the event fit into the great scheme of things; i.e., of what is this a case?
   c. What emotions dominate—hate, pity, love, patriotism, indignation, resignation, etc.?
   d. What motives do reports ascribe to actors?
   e. What judgment of the present and prophecy of the future does the report imply?

Efforts to answer these questions informed all stages of our analysis of crisis coverage of nightly network television news. We do not treat each question separately in the chapters that follow but reconstruct network storytelling from what we found. In addition, we quantify gross patterns of storytelling. We derived a fourfold category of what we treat as real-fictions of TV news. Returning to Lippmann (1922, p. 347) we took seriously his view that "journalism is not a first hand report of raw material" but a "report of that material after it has been stylized." Our analysis suggested four ways the networks stylize accounts. Although these four categories derived from our ongoing analysis, much in the manner described by advocates of "grounded theory" (Glaser & Strauss, 1967; Glaser, 1978), we link them to four traditional styles of journalism for purposes of description.

POPULIST/SENSATIONALIST ACCOUNTS

Journalism has a long and honored tradition of stylizing accounts to maximize "human interest" in how ordinary people beset by seemingly unending and insurmountable complexities and problems are affected by events. This tradition has much in common with the melodramatic style that emphasizes fear and pathos, appealing directly to human emotions. Populist/sensationalist fare frightens and saddens, angers and provokes, even "tugs at the heartstrings." These are real-fictions of people threatened and endangered by what happens in a benign universe of chance, or perhaps a universe of evil intention. The problems faced by people in a crisis situation belong not only to them but to all TV viewers as well. Reality is unfriendly and ominous. Such perspectives yield accounts that are populist in that they are about ordinary people and appeal to popular feelings; they are sensationalist in their efforts to evoke emotional responses.

ELITIST/FACTUAL ACCOUNTS

A second journalistic tradition stems from an effort to confine accounts to what are the staples of wire service reporting, the "who, what, where, when, and how" that constitute the "objective facts of the event." Accounts consist of verified information (from "reliable sources") presented in the style of "serious, responsible journalism." Reality, though perhaps no less threatening than in other accounts, is made up of events that can be managed by responsible, trustworthy office-holders, experts, and insiders who know their business. Hence, such accounts are elitist in that they evoke a real-fiction of responsible people in charge of affairs acting on behalf of informed audiences; they are factual in their wire service-like, empirically-laden content.

IGNORANT/DIDACTIC ACCOUNTS

Didactic accounts assume that members of the news audience are ignorant of all, or most, of the specifics of a newsworthy event. Audience members are not stupid, just uneducated. Hence they must be instructed. So, in a style approximating that of an elementary school teacher, journalists teach. They break down complex ideas into simplified elements. Abstractions are explained in colloquial, not technical, language. Examples fill reports. There is an impression that journalists are talking down to their audiences. Such accounts tell how things work, how they are built, how things got the way they are, and what people can do about it. The resulting real-fiction is one of a complex world full of mysterious natural happenings and human contrivances. But once they are reduced to their basics through didactic instruction (diagrammed and memorized) they no longer threaten. Magic once understood is no longer magic.

PLURALIST/FEATURE ACCOUNTS

The rhetorical news style of the feature is one of context; it weaves current events into the fabric of a much larger framework. The feature looks at the "Big Picture" and formulates a real-fiction of events in the larger scheme of things—historical, geographic, and social. Accounts stand not alone but beside other accounts, each elaborating a different feature of an event's context. Whereas populist/sensationalist accounts threaten viewers with the awful, or elitist/factual accounts render the awful manageable, or ignorant/didactic accounts demystify the awesome, the pluralist/feature style blends sagacity with resignation. Accounts are pluralist as they address themselves to an audience assumed to be diverse in interests and information; they are features in that they attribute a multitude of causes for reported events.

To classify reports and/or stories into one of the four categories is risky. Over the course of a report or story, for instance, emphases may shift thereby rendering pigeon-holing prob-

Nightly Horrors: Television Network News

lematic. But an overriding manifest stylizing frequently is apparent; we have classified units of analysis accordingly.

Thus the content analysis on which this study rests includes quantification of discrete data regarding (1) newsgathering and (2) visual items united with classifications of reports and stories as (3) reassuring/alarmist, (4) news/peripheral/perspective, and (5) type of real-fiction. In the course of coding six persons examined all or portions of videotaped newscasts. Intercoder reliabilities were calculated between coder pairs since at least two coders, working independently, worked with identical materials. Reliability measures—namely, Scott's π^3 for nominal scale coding (1955)—were uniformly high with respect to the mechanical task of coding newsgathering and visual elements. The lowest intercoder reliability coefficient for a coding pair was .89 for newsgathering elements, .87 for visual elements.

[3]As this study employs both quantitative and qualitative means of analyzing the content of televised news programs, it is possible that various readers may find one or the other mode of content analysis more useful for their purposes. Moreover, readers primarily interested in the qualitative, rhetorical analysis of TV news may not be familiar with the statistical techniques employed in quantitative analysis. It is appropriate, therefore, to take this opportunity to define briefly the three such statistical devices used in this study: Scott's π, χ^2, and the F-ratio.

In content analysis it is frequently necessary to classify, or code, items of the material under study into one of several categories. To improve the accuracy of analysis and have a measure of the degree of agreement between persons coding the same material, pairs of coders may be assigned the task of classifying items independently. Scott's π is an index of the reliability of coding, i.e., the degree that people working independently with the same material and categories for coding agree in their judgments. The index, in effect, reports the percentage of agreement between coders, taking into account the number of categories available, the frequency each coding category is used, and the amount of agreement that might occur purely by chance. The index ranges 0.00 to 1.00. The higher the reported figure, the greater the reliability.

In each of the chapters reporting on a specific crisis there is reference to two measures. One of them, χ^2, is a statistical test that reports the probability of the difference between what is observed in a set of data and what could be expected by chance being *statistically* significant. Although tabular material in this study displays the χ^2 values, what is central to interpretation is the probability figure accompanying each reported χ^2. That probability ($p = $) reports the degree to which the differences between news networks could be due only to chance rather than being significant variations from network to network. A probability of $p = .01$, for example, indicates that there is only one chance in a hundred that differences are random; $p = .001$ indicates one in a thousand; and so on.

Reliability estimates were lower for report/story classifications. With respect to whether items were live, filmed, voiceovers, or talking heads, Scott's π was a minimum of .86. For coding items as reassuring/alarmist and news/peripheral/perspective, reliabilities were .66 and .62 respectively. Reliabilities for coding for stylized content did not fall below .63. Although we think all of these to be reasonable levels of agreement, given the complexities of the code (Holsti, 1969a, pp. 136–142), we urge readers to evaluate such findings within the larger context of dramatistic analysis which is the core of this study. Following Holsti (1969a, p. 142), we have sought to strike some balance between reliability and relevance of categories and units; "the coefficient of reliability cannot be the sole criterion for making such decisions."

We present our findings in a straightforward manner in keeping with the chronological occurrence of each crisis. Chapter 1 compares and contrasts network crisis coverage for the case of the mass murders and suicides at The People's Temple. We present a brief description of events surrounding the crisis, then analyze real-fictions of each network and compare coverage across networks. We continue this format through a discussion of Three Mile Island, the crash of Flight 191, Mount St. Helens, and the hostage crisis. We conclude with a summary of patterns in crisis coverage, an examination of the Tylenol poisonings to detect if earlier patterns persist, and an exploration of the rhetorical visions of network television news.

The F-ratio derives from a test to determine whether there is a statistically significant difference between two or more groups of data, or whether the groups of data were probably drawn from identical populations with differences between them due only to chance. In the chapters that follow, the reported figure of importance, as with χ^2, is not the ratio itself but the probability ($p =$) measure, which should be interpreted in the same way as noted above.

Finally, in tabular material there is reference to degrees of freedom, designated "df." In statistical calculations degrees of freedom refer to the maximum number of values of a variable free to vary under a given set of conditions. For example, when the sum of three values is fixed, only two of the three values are open to choice since after the two values are chosen the value of the third is determined by the sum. Hence, there are two degrees of freedom for three values of a variable. In general, the degrees of freedom are one less than the value of a variable. In a contingency table (such as a cross-tabulation on which the calculation of χ^2 is based) the degrees of freedom are one less than the number of rows multipled by one less than the number of columns.

Chapter One

The People's Temple: A Human Tragedy

The week of Thanksgiving Day, 1978, witnessed a news event that was strangely out of place for the festive season. Indeed, such an event would have been out of place during any time. For the event was one of the biggest mass suicides in history, certainly the most massive in the history of the United States.

It began in the late afternoon of November 18—eyewitnesses placed the time at 4:20 p.m.—on a remote airstrip called Port Kaituma. The locale was approximately 150 miles by air from Georgetown, the capital of the South American country of Guyana. Two miles from Port Kaituma was Jonestown, an agricultural community of some 900 residents. Jonestown had been founded by the Reverend Jim Jones, leader of a church called The People's Temple. The Temple's headquarters were in San Francisco, where Jones had located with a small congregation after coming, first, from Indiana to a rural area of northern California, then to San Francisco.

Although the congregation contained middle class whites and blacks, The People's Temple drew most of its members from a neighborhood of the poor. Nonetheless the church was prosperous. Through donations of money and property, Jones had been able to support a full range of social as well as religious services sponsored by the Temple. One such program was the agricultural project built upon land leased from the Guyanese government and called Jonestown. Temple members traveled to Jonestown, cleared the land, built dwellings, planted and harvested crops, and had visions of creating a self-sustaining utopia.

In 1978, however, U.S. Representative Leo Ryan, whose district included members of The People's Temple, received reports of Temple members being held against their will in Jonestown. Word of torture and other forms of mistreatment accompanied those reports. Believing that the only way to obtain full information on conditions at Jonestown was to witness them himself, Ryan organized a party to visit the agricultural project. In addition to staff members, he took along an NBC news team led by correspondent Don Harris, who had been researching the background of The People's Temple, its members, practices, and purposes.

The Ryan party flew to Georgetown, Guyana, and consulted with both Guyanese and U.S. Embassy officials. After some delays the party received permission from The People's Temple to visit Jonestown. The party flew to Port Kaituma airstrip, then traveled to Jonestown by motor vehicle. Ryan and members of his party were welcomed. They devoted their visit to talking with Temple leaders, including Jones, and to meeting with residents. On the surface all was apparently serene. It was not until days later, after the crisis at Jonestown was an accomplished fact, that reports surfaced of Ryan's being assaulted at knifepoint by one Temple official.

The Ryan party encountered relatively few Temple residents who desired to leave the compound. Ryan agreed to fly out those who desired to depart and to send transportation back for any who might change their minds. On Saturday afternoon, November 18, the Ryan party returned to Port Kaituma to board aircraft for Georgetown. But as they were preparing to leave, a tractor pulling a flatbed trailer arrived. Out jumped gunmen who began firing on the members of the Ryan party. Killed in the shootings were Ryan, reporter Harris, cameraman Bob Brown, photographer Greg Robinson, and People's Temple member Patricia Parks. Others were wounded, and many fled into the nearby woods.

Events did not end with these murders. Back in Jonestown,

Temple members engaged in acts that were to command the attention of this country's television news networks for days to come. As was later revealed, 912 residents of Jonestown either committed suicide or were murdered; 72 survived, along with Temple attorneys Mark Lane and Charles Garry. At People's Temple headquarters in Georgetown, Guyana, Temple official Sharon Amos and her three children were also murdered.

Such were the essentials of a story that the three television networks were to unfold during their nightly newscasts over the next three weeks. During the first week of that period, the networks carried accounts of the mass deaths at Jonestown as their lead evening stories. Total coverage over the three-week period was three hours and forty-five minutes, approximately one-fourth of the available newshole. And television was not the only medium to regard the story as newsworthy. Events at Jonestown became the basis of a best-selling book, *Guyana Massacre: The Eyewitness Account* (Krause, 1978); an acclaimed CBS docudrama, "Guyana Tragedy: The Story of Jim Jones;" a Hollywood movie, *Guyana: Cult of the Damned;* and a controversial series of audio tapes broadcast on National Public Radio and later produced as "Father Cares: The Last of Jonestown."

How, then, did the three networks portray the human tragedy of The People's Temple? Was coverage essentially the same, or did it differ? To answer these questions we turn first to a dramatistic analysis of each network's coverage as a means of discovering the real-fictions created through news coverage. Then we compare network coverage in a quantitative way by describing the results of content analysis.

NBC's Heroic Fallen Comrades

Simply put, *NBC Nightly News* scooped its rival networks in narrating accounts of events at Jonestown. The reasons are clear. First, because it broadcast the only evening newscast on the networks on Sunday, November 19—one day following what was happening at Jonestown—NBC had the only televised reports of what was happening. Second, since NBC News had a correspondent and camera crew traveling with the party of Congressman Leo Ryan, the network was well positioned to cover the breaking story. Third, and most importantly, NBC newsmen not only covered the story, giving firsthand, eyewitness accounts, but were also a key part of the story. Two NBC newsmen, correspondent Don Harris and cameraman Bob Brown, were murder victims of the ambush at Port Kaituma. NBC technician Steven Sung, who aided Brown with the minicam, was wounded during the ambush. And field producer Robert Flick narrowly escaped the airstrip shootings. That NBC newsmen were as much the story as reporters of it was to shape the nature of the network's coverage of the crisis.

The style and tone of that coverage was set in the network's broadcast of November 19. Eighty percent of the evening's newscast concerned events surrounding the murders at Port Kaituma. Anchor Jessica Savitch, using film that had been flown from Guyana to Puerto Rico, then fed by satellite to NBC studios, narrated. The film had been shot by slain cameraman Bob Brown. Savitch began with the fact that there had been shooting deaths in the Guyanese jungle of members of a party leaving the area with unhappy members of a "religious sect." She identified those killed as Ryan, Harris, Brown, photographer Greg Robinson, and Temple member Patricia Parks. (This was to be the only reference to Parks in this or later NBC newscasts; similarly Parks's death received only single mentions on the other two networks.)

At this point Savitch began narrating the rolling film. Pictured were Representative Ryan and diplomat Richard Dwyer moving toward one of two small aircraft preparing to receive departing passengers. Savitch misidentified Dwyer as Ryan when the former walked over to the aircraft to shake hands with the pilot. The camera then panned across others preparing to board, catching Don Harris walking slowly about. Savitch then noted the arrival of the tractor-trailer. At that point the camera caught one man jumping from the tractor and opening fire, then others jumping from the trailer and doing the same. The film ceased to roll, apparently at the moment cameraman Brown was hit. The shooting portions of the film were rerun in slow motion, again with Savitch narrating. "Unbelievable," said Savitch as the film ceased.

The Savitch report continued with a satellite interview with field producer Robert Flick, who had been flown to San Juan, Puerto Rico, following his escape. This was the first eyewitness description of the Port Kaituma slayings. Although portions of the interview were repeated in rival network newscasts the following evening, this showing of the Flick interview was the most extensive description of events. In addition, Steven Sung, Brown's camera technician, provided a description of his personal experience, but this appeared on nightly network newscasts the following evening (NBC running longer versions of his statement than either ABC or CBS).

Two things about NBC coverage to this point were noteworthy: visual coverage existed at all because there was an on-the-scene NBC camera crew, and the only eyewitness accounts were those of NBC news personnel. In this respect, then, NBC News was apparently in a better position to describe events at Port Kaituma than was the U.S. State Department's spokesman, Tom Reston, in a report filed from the State Department by NBC correspondent Bob Kur. This report was the first to mention the possibility—which State Department officials refused to confirm—that there had been mass suicides at Jonestown. Reston noted only that there was a report of 200 suicides. What he dwelt upon was the possibility that if such reports were true, it might well be that People's Temple members in the United States—he estimated 3,000—might start taking their own lives.

By this point in the broadcast, then, viewers had received hard information only from NBC news correspondents, not from public officials. Moreover, what was rumored and reported by an NBC correspondent regarding events at the Jonestown compound was not yet confirmed by public officials. News personnel were thus emerging as the principal dramatis personae of the narration, or certainly at least coequal with government officials. This billing was emphasized when anchor Jessica Savitch noted in a brief report that President Carter had expressed regret at Congressman Ryan's death and that NBC President Lester Crystal had done the same with respect to the deaths of Don Harris and Bob Brown, pointing out that the two newsmen represented the finest traditions of journalism. Three accounts comprised the remainder of this first NBC newscast on the tragedy of The People's Temple. The first was a background report on Representative Leo Ryan in which the NBC correspondent noted that Ryan possessed the "instincts of an investigative reporter." Like any such reporter, he learned about things firsthand—becoming a school teacher in the Watts district of Los Angeles to learn about conditions there after riots in the 1960s; entering Folsom Prison as an inmate, again to experience conditions for himself. His scrutiny of The People's Temple was but another instance of investigative reporting.

In sum, a pattern had begun to emerge in NBC's coverage of the Jonestown crisis. The motif of "journalist as hero," understandable under the circumstances, continued to be emphasized in the remaining two reports of the November 19 newscast. And it was returned to repeatedly over the course of later broadcasts. We can best illustrate this motif by examining how newscasts portrayed NBC journalists as prominent actors in the unfolding real-fiction of The People's Temple and of Jonestown. In doing so we are not saying that NBC reported markedly different events than its rival networks. Rather, we are suggesting that even though similar events are reported, the narration shows NBC news personnel as leading personae in the drama, not simply recorders of it.

Begin with correspondent Don Harris. In NBC's November 19 coverage reporter Don Oliver provided a five-minute packaged report on the backgrounds of the three newsmen slain at Port Kaituma. Oliver narrated material as film rolled, showing each newsman in various settings. Harris appeared in combat garb and helmet on Highway 1, reporting from Viet Nam. There followed a clip of his award-winning documentary on California prison gangs. Finally, Harris' interview with Temple member Debbie Blakey—filmed prior to the trip with Ryan to Jonestown—probed whether or not Temple members possessed guns. Harris' work, said Oliver, proved him to be "tough and careful," certainly an "investigative reporter in the truest sense of the word."

Harris continued to play a leading role in NBC's coverage throughout the crisis, even though he was no longer alive. Harris' filmed interviews with Temple members and officials recorded prior to the Jonestown trip appeared prominently in background stories on events. That thrust began on the newscast of November 19. In a profile of Jim Jones, Harris appeared in a filmed interview with Jones; in an account of how Jones mistreated Temple children, Harris interviewed a Temple member; and, in an interview with Temple attorney Charles Garry, viewers saw the lawyer assuring Harris that there were no armed guards in Jonestown, that indeed Garry hoped that Harris could go and see for himself.

The "journalist as hero" motif continued to revolve around the persona of correspondent Don Harris throughout NBC's coverage, not vanishing from the screen until after the newscast of November 30, almost two weeks following his death. NBC, like competing networks, covered the return of Harris' body to his hometown and his funeral. All networks did the same for murdered newsmen Bob Brown and Greg Robinson. But within the context of the general plot line of NBC's unfolding drama, Harris' persona took on added significance. Two examples are noteworthy.

On November 20, NBC again repeated its showing of the film taken by cameraman Bob Brown at Port Kaituma. This time reporter Richard Hunt did the "voice-over" narration. Hunt described film of Harris walking around the aircraft, calmly smoking a cigarette. Then, noted Hunt, it was Harris who turned, looked over his shoulder, and saw the approaching tractor-trailer. With the background of Charles Garry's earlier assurance that there were no armed gunmen at Jonestown, a viewer could infer a tragic premonition on the part of Harris.

The second example involves film taken by cameraman Brown of a confrontation in Jonestown between Don Harris and Jim Jones. Prior to this encounter, the NBC narrative suggested, the Ryan party was treated with utmost hospitality by Temple members. Film even showed Congressman Ryan addressing Temple members, to audience cheers and applause, and assuring them that he had found no unhappiness, no dissatisfaction. Then, said correspondent Gerald Harrington in his narration of the film, Don Harris questioned Jim Jones about a note received by Harris from a Temple member desiring to leave the compound. Jones nodded, agreed to the contents of the note, but said that the member still wanted to leave his son in Jonestown. Harris then inquired if such an expression of dissatisfaction concerned Jones. Jones replied, "People play games, friend. They lie." Jones pled with Harris to go away and "leave us alone, we don't bother nobody."

Here, narrated Harrington, the "carefully orchestrated production begins to fall apart." Jones's "mood changed abruptly." The film then showed Representative Ryan, with bloodstains on his shirt, confiding to Harris that the congressman has been the victim of a knife attack. It was at this point that decisions were made to leave the compound and to take as many Temple defectors with the Ryan party as possible. Throughout the film, as with many other filmed accounts of the days preceding— whether filmed at San Francisco, the Guyanese capitol of Georgetown, or Jonestown—the portrait of the journalist as hero appears.

That portrait is not confined to Don Harris. The narrative account of field producer Robert Flick's escape from the Port Kaituma ambush and Jessica Savitch's satellite interview with him—weary, exhausted, concerned—intensifies the image of the dedicated journalist. Steven Sung's account of his close brush with death while his partner Bob Brown had "his brains blown out" does the same. As for Brown, Don Oliver's November 20 tribute said of him that "with the camera he was an artist." The NBC correspondent covering Brown's funeral reminded viewers that Brown kept his camera rolling "up to the moment of his death" and "died a hero." Again the sense of selfless dedication appears in Oliver's description of photographer Greg Robinson: "he loved every picture he ever took."

The slain NBC correspondents—"they were among NBC's finest," said Oliver.

There was one other instance—almost totally ignored by other networks—in which NBC called special attention to the role of journalists in the Jonestown tragedy. This time, however, the journalist was not dedicated hero but misguided believer. On November 23 three men were arrested in connection with the murders at Port Kaituma. One was charged, and he therefore became the focus of later news accounts on all networks. The other two were not. Yet NBC found something newsworthy about one of them, Michael Prokes. What was newsworthy was that Prokes had once been a television newsman in Sacramento. Doug Kriegel of NBC narrated a packaged report on the background of Prokes, noting that he had at times become "involved" in his stories, especially in coverage of a farm workers' strike. Interviews with friends, Proke's football coach, and his assignment editor rounded out a portrait of a dedicated but confused former journalist.

In focusing upon NBC's "journalist as hero" motif, we of necessity do not detail the network's coverage of each item in the Jonestown story. However, from the standpoint of dramatistic analysis we have identified what emerges as the real-fiction of NBC coverage, the recurring theme that unifies the narration of events seemingly beyond comprehension. Other networks, however, imposed other themes.

ABC's Account of Demonic Horror

If the real-fiction portrayed in NBC's coverage of The People's Temple was one of heroic conduct, ABC's depiction was of villainy demanding a valorous response. That villainy took several forms—the overriding horror of the tragedy, the character of Jim Jones, the bizarre mystery of the missing bodies, and a suggestion of conspiracy. The perspective taken on such villainy was not that of the honor of investigative journalism but of the victims of the villainy—Temple members, survivors, and distraught relatives.

ABC's *World News Tonight* began coverage of events in Guyana on Monday evening, November 20. By that time the Port Kaituma murders had been reported extensively by NBC. Moreover, both ABC and CBS were at a disadvantage because neither network could compete with NBC's film footage or on-the-scene reports. Not able to match NBC's filmed coverage, ABC turned elsewhere. Anchor Frank Reynolds set the early tone, noting that the murders of Representative Ryan, two NBC news staff people, and others resulted from Ryan's investigation of a "religious cult," the People's Temple, headquartered in Jonestown (NBC's initial report had used the less pejorative "religious sect").

ABC's Bernard Shaw in Georgetown, Guyana, followed with two packaged reports, one utilizing a film of the Guyanese information minister reporting the suicide/murders in Jonestown. Shaw's second report introduced a character who was later to play a key role in suggesting conspiratorial motives behind events, Mark Lane, an attorney for The People's Temple. Lane's controversial background in probing the assassinations of President John Kennedy and Martin Luther King, charging U.S. atrocities in Viet Nam, and involving himself with the widely publicized Indian protests at Wounded Knee in 1973 made him a readily recognized news source. Lane was at the Jonestown compound when the mass suicides and murders began. His filmed description of events, confined primarily to his rendition of Jim Jones' last words—"Mother, Mother, Mother, Mother, Mother"—symbolized what anchor Frank Reynolds spoke of as the "incredible but true" tragedy.

With respect to what had actually taken place in Guyana, ABC then confined itself to but one report during its November 20 newscast. That report consisted of an edited film of NBC's Robert Flick's account of events (which had appeared on NBC the preceding day) and a second edited film of NBC's Steven Sung describing what had happened at Port Kaituma (which NBC ran the same evening but in a much longer version).

Aside from accounts by Lane, Flick, and Sung, ABC's coverage devoted the bulk of its reporting on November 20—as it was to do for the next three weeks—to reactions to the events rather than to the events themselves. First, relying upon interviews with Temple members in San Francisco, ABC narrated an account of the "suicide pact" planned by Jones and agreed to by Temple members. An unidentified man, seen in the interview only from the rear, spoke of his fear of retaliation should he say too much. Insisting that the "Government" should bring his people out of Guyana, he said of Jones, "They stopped Hitler, didn't they? Why can't they stop him?"

This was not the last time a symbolic "They" was evoked in interviews held with Temple members or survivors. From the standpoint of dramatistic analysis, a drama often includes a sanctioning agent, a symbolic character that can either resolve or exacerbate the conflicts underlying dramatic action. For ABC News coverage of The People's Temple, "They" served as such an agent. For example, on November 22 the wife of the man identified as making the knife attack on Leo Ryan prior to Ryan's murder at the airstrip spoke of the danger her husband posed to all surviving Temple members: "They" would have to kill him to stop him. In the ABC News telecast of the following day, Bernard Shaw interviewed a mother newly arrived in Guyana to search for her children. "Where are your children now?" he asked. Mrs. Janaro did not know. But she did know that people had escaped into the jungles surrounding Jonestown, where snakes and jaguars preyed upon them. Why, she asked, could not the "marines who fought in the jungles of Viet Nam" (another "They") save the survivors and end the "holocaust"? Shaw closed his report noting that, in effect, there was no hope, for "They" (in the person of a U. S. military official) had announced that searching for survivors in the jungle "isn't part of our mission."

That "They" were not doing enough to help victims cope with the crisis was a repeated theme in ABC coverage. On the first evening of the network's reporting on November 20, correspondent Ted Koppel reported from the situation room of the Guyanese Task Force in the U. S. State Department on the "aftershock that made its way through the building" following the events at Jonestown. Koppel noted in closing that "questions" were being asked, "Did government do all it could" to prevent the tragedy?

Indeed, as the ABC narrative unfolded, viewers would have been justified in asking whether "They" ("Government," the "Federal Bureau of Investigation," or other agent) were a sufficient match for the crafty and evil James Jones. In its background story on Jones (November 20) based primarily on interviews with Temple members in San Francisco, ABC made the following points: First, in founding the Temple, Jones may have counseled love and tolerance, but he came to inspire fear. Second, real estate records revealed that property deeded to the Temple by its members was being sold by Jones to finance his operations. Third, when members protested his rule by threat and intimidation—and the criticism became public—Jones fled with devoted cult members to Guyana. Fourth, in Jonestown Jim Jones drilled Temple members in a death ritual, of willingly drinking a poisoned liquid, for purposes of enforcing discipline and dealing with any outside threats to the community. And, noted ABC in closing, Jones during his successful days in San Francisco had friends in high places and was even appointed head of the local housing authority.

With Jones dead one might think that the demon posed no threat to people trying to cope with the tragic consequences of the Jonestown suicides and murders. But for ABC there was no certainty of this. Frank Reynolds noted that "even though James Jones is dead" the fear he inspired continued among Temple members. One reason for this was the "hit squads" allegedly formed by Jones to kill all defectors and detractors of his cult even after his death. In an ABC interview a former Temple official, Mike Cartmell, revealed that funds were set aside to support an assassination team. He told ABC correspondent Irv Chapman not to be surprised to discover Cartmell's obituary in the near future. James Cobb, who had witnessed events in Jonestown, said in an interview that anyone trying to expose what Jones had been should fear for his or her safety.

Claims of the existence of hit squads and assassination teams were a common theme among ABC interviews with Temple members and relatives. Adding to the fear were the claims of Mark Lane. On November 28 anchor Frank Reynolds reported that Lane had stated that he had been told by Jones's "second in command," that leaders of The People's Temple had made elaborate assassination plans. In a follow-up interview with Barbara Walters of ABC, Lane noted that the Secret Service had questioned him about those plans. Lane pointed out that his concern was for the mid-term Democratic convention to be held in Memphis. There President Jimmy Carter and Vice-President Walter Mondale would be open targets for Temple assassins. Reynolds closed the story with a report confirming Secret Service interest in Lane's information. Two evenings later in an unusually long interview for a nightly newscast (five minutes), Barbara Walters added more plausibility to Lane's claims by reviewing his previous involvement in controversial causes.

Hence, the death of the demon was not sufficient cause for Temple members or government officials to believe "They" could cope with the crisis with confidence. As ABC's narrative developed, however, it might not be from a coffin that James Jones was directing a scenario of assassinations and murders. Anchor Max Robinson introduced the ABC's *World News Tonight* of November 23 with a disturbing question, "Is cult leader James Jones really dead?" Two facts cast doubt on reports of Jones's demise. One was that a boat allegedly owned by The People's Temple was missing from its dock near Jonestown. (As in the case of Adolf Hitler's alleged escape from Berlin at the end of World War II, had another demon fled his fate?) Second, as Frank Reynolds reported, Jones had in the past used doubles to impersonate him. An interview with one such double, Wayne Pietila, lent credibility to the possibility that Jones was still alive. Jones had fooled people in the past— why not now? (It was not until the following evening's newscast, November 24, that ABC reported confirmation by an autopsy that the body flown to Dover, Delaware, the receiving center for Jonestown victims, had been identified as that of James Jones by the FBI.)

But adding to the earlier speculation that Jones might still be alive was another mystery. First reports from Jonestown at the time of the discovery of the mass deaths estimated approximately 400 victims. Since Guyanese officials had passports for more than 900 Jonestown residents, all three networks assumed that hundreds of Temple members had escaped into the neighboring jungle. Military officials planned to send helicopters into the air above the jungle to broadcast messages that it was "safe to come out now." But the messages were not broadcast. Four days passed, and all three networks spoke of the discrepancy. Frank Reynolds calculated that with 400 dead and 72 survivors "several hundred are unaccounted for." Until the evening of November 24 there was speculation that Jones and Temple leaders might comprise a good number of those "unaccounted for."

On November 24 the mystery was solved. A U. S. Air Force press officer revealed that because bodies had been hidden under bodies, early estimates of the number of victims were in error. NBC News put the onus for the error—which anchor John Chancellor had earlier called a "mathematical puzzle"— on "Guyanese troops" who had made the first estimate. CBS reported the discrepancy without comment. But for ABC there was a strong suggestion that, once again, "They" had not been able to deal with crisis efficiently.

To be sure, both NBC and CBS reported each of the elements that combined to make ABC's real-fiction of The People's Temple a demonic tale. Both networks reported packaged stories based upon interviews with Temple members, survivors, and their relatives. Both took note of Mark Lane's presence and claims. Both discussed the possibility of hit squads and assassination teams. And both reported (though NBC scarcely in passing) that some Temple members feared Jones to be still alive. But neither of the other two networks gave these elements the emphasis apparent in ABC's *World News Tonight*. Victims trying to cope in a crisis with unseen, unnamed forces without the benevolent intervention of "They" (indeed, coping with obstacles frequently produced by unidentified agents)—such was the Guyanese tale of ABC.

CBS and the Distasteful Aberration of Jonestown

For the *CBS Evening News*, the story of The People's Temple was neither a story of journalistic valor nor one of demonic threat. Instead, the CBS narration presents the mass deaths at Jonestown and the story of their aftermath as an incident when something went wrong in the natural order of things, even though what went wrong is never made clear.

As with ABC News, CBS did not report the events that took place in Guyana until two full days after they had occurred. On November 20 anchor Roger Mudd led off the CBS newscast with a report that Guyanese troops had discovered the bodies of as many as 400 persons in a jungle compound. Like ABC, the network identified the bodies as those of members of a "religious cult," The People's Temple. Only after establishing this lead did Mudd turn to an account of the preceding Saturday's events at Port Kaituma, noting that Representative Ryan and "three American newsmen" had been killed. Mudd then switched to the filmed interview with NBC soundman Steven Sung that appeared on other networks. There was a difference, however, in the CBS presentation; the network edited out of Sung's statement an obscenity yet left in details of Sung's escape glossed over by rival networks.

The remainder of CBS coverage on November 20 (which totaled only seven minutes in contrast with NBC and ABC, which devoted twice as much air time) consisted of two reports. Both dealt with governmental officials' response to The People's Temple rather than the events themselves. Correspondent Ike Pappas from Washington, D. C., recited in detail Pentagon plans for evacuating bodies, listing the military bases from which HU-10 helicopters would be transferred and the possible air fields to be used in Guyana. From Los Angeles Bill Stout reported that both the office of Vice President Walter Mondale and the State Department had been approached earlier by Temple members' families claiming "human rights violations." Affidavits had gone to Secretary of State Cyrus Vance and "five other State Department officials." Other "documents" had later gone to Vance and to the Guyanese Prime Minister. Yet all such "affidavits," "documents," and "communiqués" (many appearing on the TV screen as Stout narrated) did no good. We take note of the content of *CBS Evening News* coverage on November 20 to illustrate three points. First, all reports were from locales in this country, not Guyana. Second, CBS accounts emphasized factual details and printed materials—air fields, helicopters, letters, communiqués, documents, and affidavits. Third, coverage of events at Port Kaituma or Jonestown occupied less time than official responses to them. These traits, combined with one other, characterize the real-fiction evolving from CBS coverage of the crisis of The People's Temple.

Let us begin with the additional item. It consists of the labeling applied to the crisis by CBS correspondents, especially by anchor Walter Cronkite. That labeling suggested how distasteful an aberration the crisis was. Acts that "U. S. military personnel" were to perform, according to Cronkite on the evening of November 21, included the "gruesome task" of removing the bodies of members of a "fanatic religious cult." It "assaults the senses" and "defies description." It all added up to "a macabre story," observed Cronkite. The description of the scene of the drama was similarly oppressive: "a dense, snake-infested rainforest," said Cronkite on November 21, and "filled with poisonous viper snakes, man-eating piranha fish, malarial mosquitos, and quicksand" (November 22). Another element in the dramatic pentad, agencies, appeared in the "foul play" reported by Cronkite on November 22, the "shattered faith" (November 24), and the "suicidal carnage" (December 6). As for the actors, CBS characterized them as "religious zealots" and "blind followers" led in the end by a "drug addicted, paranoid, power-hungry fascist" (all labels applied by Cronkite during nightly newscasts).

The full distaste for the crisis and its aftermath is captured in Walter Cronkite's account of the unfolding plot: a "macabre story" of a "jungle commune" turns into a "nightmare," then "a nightmare that just won't quit," and "the horror of Jonestown that will not go away." Only on December 10 did the plot line finally resolve itself; "Jonestown is dead," concluded a report on the return of the first victims of Jonestown to San Francisco.

How did CBS endeavor to make sense of this distasteful aberration? For one thing, the network confined its reporting efforts primarily to viewing the crisis from afar. It was not until November 22 that CBS placed a correspondent in Guyana, David Dick, who reported from Georgetown. Thereafter three CBS correspondents reported from Guyana, but in only one instance did a reporter go to the scene of the mass suicide and murders, Jonestown, and that was not until ten days following the events. Instead, CBS emphasized reports from network studios or from locales in California in interviews with Temple members and their relatives.

Secondly, CBS focused upon another set of actors, not participants in the crisis but people who could be called upon to understand and clarify what had taken place. These actors bore various titles but were generally referred to by correspondents as "government spokesmen," "experts," or "specialists." For example, correspondent Bruce Morton reported from Washington, D.C., on Jim Jones's alleged connections with ranking government officials. Morton noted that offices of Vice President Mondale, Senator Henry Jackson, and Representative Philip Burton could not locate letters of endorsement Jones had claimed such officials wrote to him. Even if they did exist, noted Morton, such letters are "the small change of politics." They would scarcely tie official Washington to the Jonestown events.

"What kind of person joins a religious cult and blindly follows the commands of its leader?" asked Walter Cronkite as an introduction to a CBS feature on cults. In that feature "experts" and "specialists on cults" explained cult psychology: the yearning to follow a charismatic leader, dependence upon fellow cult members making it impossible to leave, peer pressure, a tendency to regress to infantile status, and an experienced feeling of isolation. Throughout this report and others like it, "experts say" served as the designation that what Cronkite had said "defied description" might, with expert and specialist assistance, be described after all.

In addition to categorizing the Jonestown crisis as an aberration, reporting on its aftermath rather than events on the scene, and relying upon expert clarification, one other characteristic marked the real-fiction of *CBS News*. That was the painstaking detail, both verbal and visual, in correspondents' reports. We have already noted this to be the case with reports of Pentagon plans for evacuating bodies. Similarly, CBS accounts of the discrepancy between numbers of bodies found in Jonestown and numbers of residents known to have been there were marked by detailed accounting. (This accounting was in marked contrast to Walter Cronkite's introduction of the report that finally resolved the discrepancy: the story took a "quantum leap in horror.") Reported details did not always prove to be accurate, yet in first reports statistical data were a prominent feature.

Detailed presentation extended beyond facts and figures—aircraft, body counts, how many people join cults, the assets of The People's Temple, and other subjects of CBS reports. For example, NBC and ABC reported that the poisoned drink consumed by Jonestown residents was a Kool-Aid mixture. CBS' Cronkite was far more informative. "There was a meticulous precision to the ritual," reported Cronkite. It was "a flavored drink laced with potassium cyanide," but also contained "sedatives, a tranquillizer, a painkiller, and other chemicals all prepared by a 30-year-old doctor." Similarly, CBS reported removal of bodies from Guyana to Dover, Delaware, as a problem in "processing the dead" and described a step-by-step procedure for doing so.

Visual portrayal of documented detail also marked CBS accounts. In addition to official documents, affadavits, etc. displayed on the screen, CBS, unlike its rival networks, took careful note of letters written by Temple members to Jim Jones. In the only CBS story originating from the Jonestown compound, reporter David Dick leafed through and read letters written by church members to "Dear Dad" (noting that to be the title Jones demanded). Dick not only read the letters—including a painstaking rendition of grammatical errors—but held several of them so that viewers too could inspect the contents in detail.

Again, as with the other networks, CBS covered many of the

basic elements of the Jonestown crisis (although only Walter Cronkite ever used "crisis" as a designation). The perspective brought by CBS, however, was more impersonal. Procedures, processes, details, expertise dominated as correspondents tried to make sense of where and why things seemed to have "gone wrong." For CBS, then, Jonestown was not a narrative dominated by actors—be they heroic newsmen, demonic forces, or helpless victims—but one featuring the dramatic scene (Jonestown) viewed from afar in an effort to clarify motives, intentions, and, above all, purposes.

Comparative Coverage

Dramatistic analysis permits a researcher to contrast differences in the narratives of nightly network news. But news networks narrate their stories by employing a variety of technical devices common to the journalistic enterprise generally and to television news in particular. As noted in the Introduction, we have focused upon four sets of such news devices that provide an opportunity to compare crisis coverage of TV news networks in a systematic fashion: newsgathering techniques, visual devices, journalistic styles, and news types.

In presenting the findings of this portion of our content analysis of network news reports and stories concerning the crisis of The People's Temple, we rely upon quantitative rather than dramatistic data, upon "hard" rather than "soft" content analysis. We reiterate that in examining coverage of The People's Temple crisis (and this holds also for other cases of crisis coverage described in this book, with the exception of the Iranian hostage crisis) we analyzed all televised network news accounts of the crisis over the extended period of the continuing story. For that period we have, in effect, canvassed the entire population of news accounts respecting the life of the crisis. Hence, any differences between networks revealed by quantitative analysis are actual differences, not differences produced by chance out of having analyzed only a sample of accounts from the entire population defined as coverage of The People's Temple crisis.

However, as Selvin (1957; 1960), Kish (1959), Coleman (1956), and others pointed out when quantitative studies were emerging as staples of the social sciences, there is considerable controversy regarding the appropriateness, or lack thereof, of taking the statistical significance of findings based upon a population canvass for granted. Certainly we cannot resolve that controversy. Rather, in the tabular material that follows, we report all of our findings but, in addition, specify which network differences prove significant at the .05 level or better.

Having provided this background, we turn first to a comparison of the newsgathering techniques employed by the three news networks in their coverage of The People's Temple crisis. As the Introduction mentions, we analyzed three elements of such techniques. To begin with, the locale of news reports, that is, the setting for network narratives, should be considered. As Table 1.1 indicates, more than half of all reports concerning the crisis originated from network studios. Relatively few of all reports (6%) originated from the crisis site of Jonestown, Guyana. That studio reports dominated network coverage is not surprising, of course; it but illustrates the vital narrative role played by anchor personnel in TV news, a role confirmed by data to be considered later. Although the differences are not measurably significant, by considering the non-studio reports, one can get a sense of how the three networks covered the crisis in different ways. NBC, the network that broke the story, originated most of the crisis site reports, for example, in the opening account on November 19 when anchor Jessica Savitch conducted her satellite interview with field producer Robert Flick. It should also be noted that NBC's reports from government offices included Guyanese locales; ABC and CBS, in contrast, featured State Department reports. The networks differed little in their emphasis upon locating their respective narratives in private homes (those of friends and relatives of Jonestown victims), but here too NBC included reports from private locales in Georgetown, Guyana, which the other networks did not.

As for news sources, the networks relied upon the same types of persons. Public officials were primary news sources; relatives and friends of victims constituted sources for reaction

Nightly Horrors: Television Network News

Table 1.1
Newsgathering Modes for The People's Temple News Reports: by Network

Modes	ABC	CBS	NBC	Combined
Locale				
Network studio	32 (67%)	34 (56%)	43 (54%)	109 (58%)
Government office	2 (4%)	6 (6%)	10 (10%)	16 (10%)
Private home/office	13 (27%)	20 (33%)	22 (28%)	55 (29%)
Crisis site	1 (2%)	1 (1%)	4 (5%)	6 (3%)
Source (when identified)				
Public official	36 (51%)	46 (50%)	54 (51%)	136 (59%)
Technician/scientist	4 (5%)	5 (5%)	6 (6%)	15 (7%)
Interest group leader	6 (8%)	5 (5%)	8 (7%)	19 (6%)
Average citizen	25 (33%)	37 (40%)	38 (36%)	100 (37%)
Means				
Briefing by public official	33 (40%)	30 (33%)	20 (18%)	83 (29%)
Speech by public official	10 (12%)	7 (8%)	15 (14%)	32 (11%)
Interview with public official	7 (8%)	11 (12%)	30 (28%)	48 (17%)
Interview with technician/scientist	4 (6%)	4 (6%)	5 (4%)	13 (6%)
Interview with average citizen	26 (32%)	34 (37%)	37 (34%)	97 (34%)
Reporter quoting a source	2 (2%)	5 (4%)	2 (2%)	9 (3%)

$\chi^2 = 24.427$ with 10 df; p = .01

stories. What differs, as we have seen, is not sources per se but how networks depict those sources—ABC showing public officials as failing to prevent the tragedy, CBS describing them as processing events, NBC picturing them as caught up in a larger heroic drama.

The networks differed most sharply in newsgathering techniques, however, in the means by which they acquired their news items. For ABC and CBS the preferred means of newsgathering from official sources was through public briefings, either direct briefings by policy officials or, in most cases, by press officers. In either case the scheduled briefing was central to each network's coverage of what government was doing about the crisis. Combined with interviews with friends and relatives of victims, more than 70% of each network's coverage stemmed from official briefings and lay interviews. In contrast, NBC relied significantly more upon interviews with public officials rather than merely upon scheduled briefings. That emphasis reinforced the network's contextual, feature-oriented coverage. Although speeches by public officials, when used as sources for news, did not set the networks apart from one another in this crisis, a word is in order about the term "speech." We use it in an all-inclusive sense, not merely for formal oratorical presentations but for less formal, hastily called public gatherings (say, a President's impromptu remarks walking out of the Oval Office, prepared remarks before boarding or after deboarding airplanes, comments at "photo opportunities," or merely asides while responding to a crowd).

Although television is a visual medium, news stories via TV contain much less visual richness than one might suspect. As we have already indicated, we distinguish between reports and stories. A story consists of an anchor introduction (a report), one or more follow-up reports, and (but not always) a closing anchor report. In Table 1.2 we display the various visual elements involved in network stories of The People's Temple, along with visual attributes of individual reports. (Since stories and reports are different content units, the total numbers of each will not be the same.) As indicated in Table 1.2, a majority of 55% of news stories about The People's Temple were strictly anchor stories. That is, the anchor alone—with or without the aid of graphics, still photos, or film—narrated the whole of the story. In the case of ABC, 60% of stories were narrated by Frank Reynolds, Max Robinson, or a weekend anchor. Packaged reports by another correspondent constituted the remainder. Anchors of the two rival networks narrated 54% of each network's crisis coverage. If one recognizes that packaged reports, with the exception of ABC's, seldom contained interviews, then combined anchor talking heads and packaged standuppers accounted for almost nine of every ten stories.

Nor did graphics, still pictures, or rolled film add a great deal of visual prominence to network coverage. In graphics CBS led the way, usually with some form of art work displayed over anchor Walter Cronkite's shoulder. The networks differed only slightly in use of still pictures occupying the entire screen as either anchors or reporters narrated accounts. Whereas graphics were contained in one-third of the stories, stills appeared in less than 10%. Rolling film constituted the networks' basic visual device, with almost half of the stories rolling

Nightly Horrors: Television Network News

Table 1.2
Visual Elements in The People's Temple Stories: by Network

Visual elements of story	ABC	CBS	NBC	Combined
Anchor read story	27 (60%)	32 (54%)	42 (54%)	101 (55%)
Cut to packaged report(s)				
One or more, without interview	8 (18%)	24 (41%)	29 (37%)	61 (34%)
One or more, with interview	10 (22%)	3 (5%)	5 (9%)	18 (11%)
$\chi^2 = 10.071$ with 2 df (anchor/packaged); p = .01.				
Graphic over anchor/reporter shoulder				
None	39 (87%)	31 (53%)	54 (69%)	124 (68%)
One	5 (11%)	22 (37%)	22 (28%)	49 (27%)
Two or more	1 (2%)	6 (10%)	3 (3%)	9 (5%)
$\chi^2 = 14.191$ with 4 df; p = .01.				
Still picture/graphic on total screen				
None	42 (93%)	53 (90%)	71 (91%)	171 (93%)
One	1 (2%)	3 (5%)	1 (1%)	5 (3%)
Two or more	2 (5%)	3 (5%)	7 (8%)	6 (4%)
Film rolled during story				
None	19 (42%)	32 (54%)	44 (56%)	94 (52%)
Film, without interview	14 (31%)	18 (31%)	19 (24%)	51 (28%)
Film, with interview	12 (27%)	9 (15%)	16 (20%)	37 (20%)
Second film during story				
None	28 (62%)	41 (70%)	55 (70%)	123 (69%)
Film, without interview	7 (16%)	6 (10%)	11 (14%)	24 (13%)
Film, with interview	10 (22%)	12 (20%)	13 (16%)	35 (18%)

at least one film, almost a third using two films. But most such films were voice-over presentations, that is, the anchor or reporter narrated without employing any form of interview.

Only one-fifth of the stories involved at least one filmed interview; a slightly smaller proportion carried a second film with interviews. And, recalling from Table 1.1 the role played by interviews with average citizens in overall coverage, it is clear that across networks the crisis of The People's Temple was primarily one of the reaction of victims' friends and relatives. Although there is no contrast between networks regarding the use of films, it is apparent that networks differ in whether filmed reports involve interview material. ABC used at least one film with interviews in over one-fourth of its stories and in almost as many stories included a second filmed report with an interview. CBS and NBC, although using film as much as ABC, were not so likely to incorporate interviews into filmed reports.

We remarked in the Introduction that, on the basis of visual elements, it was possible to construct scores of visual prominence. Points were assigned according to whether a given story contained one or more graphics, one or more stills, one or more rolled films, one or more interviews, and one or more packaged cuts. For packaged stories points were similarly assigned. In the case of The People's Temple, the highest score was 43, with a mean of 17 and a standard deviation of 10. Means between networks were not significantly different (as measured by the F-ratio). Thus, the general assessment emerging from Table 1.2, that of marked similarity across the networks in visual emphasis given the crisis, is reinforced by taking note of visual prominence scores for network stories.

Although there was visual similarity in network presentations of the crisis of The People's Temple, there were marked stylistic variations between the networks. As we pointed out in the Introduction all crisis reports have been coded in one of four categories: populist/sensationalist, elitist/factual, ignorant/didactic, or pluralist/feature. Table 1.3 presents the resulting data in two ways. First, Table 1.3 presents the total number of reports in each category for the three networks, for each network, and for each network's anchor and correspondent reports. The modal proportion of network accounts (42%) were of the elitist/factual category, emphasizing the hard facts of the news. Populist/sensationalist accounts, stressing human interest elements, constituted another one-third. Accounts attempting to teach the uninformed or place the crisis in a larger context (ignorant/didactic and pluralist/feature reports, respectively) shared the remaining proportion.

Underlying this overall pattern, however, were marked differences between and within the networks. ABC's emphasis was clearly upon human interest accounts, a point revealed in the overall dramatistic analysis of that network's coverage. Moreover, it is apparent that both ABC's anchors and its correspondents emphasized that style; 62% of all anchor and of all correspondent reports were classified as populist/sensationalist. In contrast, CBS set the pace of combined coverage, that is, emphasizing elitist/factual reporting. It is also noteworthy that

Nightly Horrors: Television Network News

Table 1.3
Coverage Styles in The People's Temple Crisis:
by Networks, Anchors, Correspondents

Reports	ABC	CBS	NBC	Combined
Total number	48	61	79	188
Anchors	32 (67%)	34 (56%)	45 (57%)	111 (59%)
Correspondents	16 (33%)	27 (44%)	34 (43%)	77 (41%)
Style (by number of reports):				
Populist/sensationalist	30 (63%)	18 (30%)	16 (20%)	64 (34%)
Anchors	20	13	8	41
Correspondents	10	5	8	23
Elitist/factual	10 (21%)	33 (54%)	35 (44%)	78 (42%)
Anchors	10	18	19	47
Correspondents	0	15	16	31
Ignorant/didactic	1 (2%)	3 (4%)	14 (18%)	18 (9%)
Anchors	1	1	12	14
Correspondents	0	2	2	4
Pluralist/feature	7 (14%)	7 (12%)	14 (18%)	28 (15%)
Anchors	1	2	6	9
Correspondents	6	5	8	19
Total time of coverage (in minutes)	51	59	92	202
Anchors	20 (39%)	18 (30%)	28 (30%)	66 (33%)
Correspondents	31 (61%)	41 (70%)	64 (70%)	136 (67%)
Style duration (in minutes)				
Populist/sensationalist	21 (41%)	20 (34%)	18 (20%)	69 (34%)
Anchors	11	6	4	21
Correspondents	20	14	14	48
Factual/elitist	5 (10%)	32 (54%)	31 (34%)	68 (34%)
Anchors	5	9	8	22
Correspondents	0	23	23	46
Ignorant/didactic	0	3 (5%)	12 (12%)	15 (7%)
Anchors	0	0	6	6
Correspondents	0	3	6	9
Pluralist/feature	15 (49%)	4 (7%)	31 (34%)	50 (25%)
Anchors	4	3	10	17
Correspondents	11	1	21	33

Significant differences are as follows:
1. Between networks for number of reports per style is not significant.
2. Between networks for duration of reports per style $\chi^2 = 40.960$ with 6 df; p = .001.
3. Between networks for number of anchor reports per style $\chi^2 = 26.536$ with 6 df; p = .001.
4. Between networks for number of correspondent reports per style $\chi^2 = 18.342$ with 6 df; p = .02.
5. Between networks for duration of anchor reports per style $\chi^2 = 18.258$ with 6 df; p = .001.
6. Between networks for duration of correspondent reports per style $\chi^2 = 41.766$ with 6 df; p = .001.

we find some confirmation of a point hinted at in our dramatistic analysis of CBS coverage. Anchor Walter Cronkite's richly descriptive accounts of the Guyanese and Jonestown setting help "hype" follow-up stories which, in turn, tend to be more low-keyed in language. Hype, as defined by Stephen M. L. Aronson (Yardley, 1983, p. 18) is "the merchandising of a product—be it an object, a person or an idea—in an artificially engendered atmosphere of hysteria, in order to create a demand for it or to inflate such demand as already exists." In perhaps a less strident sense Cronkite's introductory reports for CBS stories constitute hyping. Whereas 38% of his reports have a human interest style (still much lower than the 62% of ABC anchors), only 18% of follow-up reports fall into that category.

NBC also provided an elitist/factual accounting of the crisis of Jonestown. Where CBS and NBC differ, however, is in the latter network's tendency to offer more reports in a teaching, professorial style associated with anchor reports. If anything, NBC's *Nightly News* reports on the crisis of The People's Temple tend to be more evenly distributed among stylistic categories than those of rival networks. It is a pattern we shall encounter again in examining other cases of crisis coverage.

The Introduction presented cautions pertaining to coding entire reports in one of the four stylistic categories. A report may well contain elements that could justify placing a report in more than one category. Coders in this project were instructed to make their judgments on the basis of dominant report emphasis. In the case of the Jonestown crisis, intercoder reliability for such classifications provided a Scott's π of .68. Partly to overcome this problem, we also coded styles by duration of time. Hence, if a packaged report, for example, contained one film of a populist/sensationalist style and another of a pluralist/feature mode, we calculated the total air time devoted to each. As the data also reported in Table 1.3 reveal, coding by duration rather than number of reports provides a different distribution across networks. However, the principal patterns outlined above remain: ABC's coverage was of a populist/sensationalist style, CBS emphasized a factual/elitist approach, and NBC's reporting was even more evenly distributed across styles. Overall

Table 1.4
News Content of The People's Temple Reports: by Network

Content Types	ABC	CBS	NBC	Combined
News value				
News	11 (23%)	17 (28%)	10 (13%)	38 (20%)
Peripheral	23 (48%)	14 (23%)	31 (39%)	68 (36%)
Perspective	7 (15%)	14 (23%)	25 (32%)	46 (24%)
News/peripheral	3 (6%)	12 (20%)	7 (9%)	22 (12%)
News/perspective	4 (8%)	4 (6%)	6 (7%)	14 (8%)
$\chi^2 = 17.988$ with 8 df; p = .05.				
Emotional content				
Reassuring	2 (4%)	8 (13%)	24 (30%)	34 (18%)
Alarming	21 (44%)	19 (31%)	14 (18%)	54 (29%)
Neutral	25 (52%)	34 (56%)	41 (52%)	100 (37%)
$\chi^2 = 20.056$ with 4 df; p = .001.				

coverage, however, was equally distributed in main emphases between populist/sensationalist and elitist/factualist accounts.

Finally, for each crisis under study, we coded reports according to two types of content described in the Introduction—whether news, peripheral, or perspective and whether reassuring, alarming, or neutral. There are, of course, identical problems in such a coding scheme to that in coding reports for style. Yet, as noted in the Introduction, we deem intercoder reliabilities sufficiently strong to warrant reporting those findings. As Table 1.4 indicates, there were differences between the networks. In keeping with the human-interest theme of its tale of demonic evil, ABC stressed reports peripheral to the "what, where, who, when and why" of events (Theberge, 1979). In conformity with its elitist/factual style, the highest percentage of CBS reports were in the news category and 55% of reports involved news, perspective, or a combination thereof. NBC devoted a higher proportion of its reports to perspective than did either other network but also included considerable peripheral material in its tale of fallen colleagues. Finally, neither ABC nor CBS was very reassuring about events surrounding Jonestown, filing reports that tended instead to be alarming (more so ABC) or neutral (CBS). For viewers searching for reassurance, NBC was the network most likely to provide it.

To summarize, in this our first examination of crisis coverage we can draw a tentative conclusion: Each network, although covering largely identical events in approximately the same visual ways and relying on modes of newsgathering that did not differ substantially, narrated different real-fictions in contrasting styles and with differing news values and emotional content. Whether this working proposition, either in general or in its particulars, will survive scrutiny when network news coverage of other crises is examined, remains to be seen.

Chapter Two

The Technological Fables
of Three Mile Island

The Three Mile Island (TMI) nuclear power plant went into operation on March 28, 1978, at 4:38 a.m. One year later, almost to the minute (36 seconds after 4:00 a.m. on Wednesday, March 28) there began a series of events which made TMI "one of the most heavily reported stories of 1979" (*The Need for Change: The Legacy of TMI,* 1979, p. 104). When it was over, the fallout from TMI turned out to be less radioactive than economic, social, and political fallout, producing a major setback for the nuclear power industry in this country.

In the aftermath of the crisis at Three Mile Island, President Jimmy Carter appointed a special commission to examine what caused the accident at TMI, how it was handled, and what could be done to prevent similar events in the future. The report of that commission fills ten volumes. The summary volume alone consists of more than 170 pages. Hence, any brief compilation of TMI events must of necessity be superficial. The essentials are as follows.

The Three Mile Island nuclear facility has two plants, TMI-1 and TMI-2. In the early morning of March 28, 1979, a series of pumps supplying water to the steam generators at TMI-2 "tripped," i.e., shut down. The trip triggered a second shutdown, that of the plant's steam turbine. Since steam runs the electric generator, the shutdown of the turbine stopped the plant's electrical production. But steam also helps cool the intense heat built up in water circulating in the nuclear reactor. With steam cut off, the water expanded, building up pressure. As the pressure increased, a valve opened, releasing steam and water, but pressure continued to rise and, as designed, the reactor "scrammed," with the result that nuclear fission ceased. The elapsed time from pump trip to scram was but eight seconds.

To this point the plant was performing as intended. What happened next was not. The valve that opened to release steam and water should have closed automatically after 13 seconds. Instead, it stuck in the open position. Unknown to plant operators, it remained so for almost 2½ hours, draining water needed to cool down the reactor and producing a "loss of coolant accident." The loss of coolant uncovered the reactor's core of nuclear fuel. Rods containing the fuel ruptured, releasing radioactivity into the cooling water and, subsequently, into both the building containing the reactor and an auxiliary building. Some radioactivity then escaped into the outside atmosphere. Moreover, rod casings contained an alloy that reacted with steam to produce hydrogen, which later in the day collected in a large gas bubble.

Following the release of radioactivity, officials of Metropolitan Edison declared a site emergency, then a general emergency. Among other things, local police and fire fighting units were contacted in accordance with the emergency plan. "Captain Dave," traffic reporter for a Harrisburg, Pennsylvania, radio station heard the alert as he was monitoring traffic for his regular morning reports. He informed his news director, who followed up on the report. In its 8:25 a.m. newscast the radio station broke the story that there was a problem at TMI-2.

The accident itself was brought under control at TMI-2 on the day it occurred. The following day, plant and public officials declared the crisis over. But it was not. On Friday, March 30, in an attempt to transfer radioactive water and gases between storage tanks, radioactivity was vented into the atmosphere. Moreover, the hydrogen bubble formed two days earlier was discovered and became a source of concern. Because of the vented radioactivity, the Governor of Pennsylvania issued an evacuation advisory recommending that pregnant women and preschool children within a five-mile radius of the plant leave the area. And, because of the hydrogen bubble, there was concern that it might not be possible to cool the reactor; if that should be the case, a meltdown—a melting of nuclear fuel through the floor of the containment building, ultimately releasing radioactive gases into the atmosphere—might occur.

Over the weekend private and public officials engaged in a technical debate over threats posed by the hydrogen gas bubble. One side argued that the bubble would continue to grow in size and ultimately explode, thus increasing the likelihood of melt down. The other maintained that the bubble would stabilize and slowly decrease in size. By late afternoon Sunday, April 1, the size of the bubble was diminishing, and scientists of the Nuclear Regulatory Commission concluded that there was no possibility of explosion. By Monday the reactor had stabilized, the bubble continued to shrink, and the crisis subsided. But it was days before the advisory evacuation ended and weeks before TMI-2 reached cold shutdown. The cleanup still continues amid doubts that the plant will ever return to operation.

Much has been written about the accident at TMI and its consequences. Surveys of public opinion have charted changes in attitudes toward nuclear energy as a result of the widely publicized accident (Schulman, 1979; Vogel, 1980). Practitioners of public relations employ TMI as a leading case study of corporate failures to design and execute an adequate program of public information (Bernays, 1979; Friedman, 1981). And Farrell and Goodnight (1981) have explored what TMI teaches students of rhetorical discourse about "accidental rhetoric."

Among the efforts to understand what happened at Three Mile Island have been studies of news coverage of the accident. Two journalists have described the problems of covering such a highly technical crisis and the relationship between press, private, and public officials (Sandman & Paden, 1979). Scholars associated with The President's Commission On The Accident at Three Mile Island have published both public documents (*Report of the Public's Right to Information Task Force*, 1979) and scholarly articles (Stephens & Edison, 1982) describing how newspapers, the wire services, and television networks reported events surrounding the accident. Of particular interest for our purposes is their analysis of the content of nightly TV news coverage for the first week of the accident. The researchers coded the content of statements about the accident as "reassuring or positive" and "alarming or negative." Employing that scheme, Stephens and Edison report that the ratio of reassuring to alarming statements was 70:30 for CBS, 59:41 for ABC, and 66:34 for NBC.

Finally, The Media Institute (Theberge, 1979) examined nightly television network news coverage for the period between March 28 and April 20, 1979. That study coded all reports on TMI as news (the "what, where, who, when, and why"), peripheral (insignificant color, background, or opinion material not necessary for understanding the event), perspective (explanatory information contributing to understanding), a combination of news-peripheral, and a combination of news-perspective. Two-thirds (67%) fell into the news category, 7% were news-peripheral, 11% peripheral, 12% news-perspective, and 4% perspective.

Such studies either do not find or do not examine differences between the three television news networks in their coverage of Three Mile Island. Is it possible, however, that from a dramatistic perspective the three networks narrated differing real-fictions? We find that they did.

CBS's Danger at Three Mile Island

During their coverage of the crisis at TMI all three networks presented special programs on events surrounding the accident. Although our focus is upon nightly news coverage rather than these specials, the title each network used in its special program says a great deal about how it approached the story in its regular newscast. CBS called its program "Danger at Three Mile Island." NBC labeled its as "Crisis at Three Mile Island." For ABC it was "Three Mile Island: Nuclear Nightmare."

A standard dictionary definition of a danger is an exposure or vulnerability to harm, a source or instance of risk or peril. A way to avoid danger is, first, to understand that it exists, and second, to identify its source and deal with it. "Warning: The Surgeon General Has Determined That Cigarette Smoking is Dangerous to Your Health" is such an effort. A warning says danger exists; a statement identifies its source. Nightly CBS coverage of TMI followed precisely such a pattern: nightly warning, nightly explanation.

The CBS warning each evening emanated from the news cast's anchor, Walter Cronkite, during weekdays, Bob Schieffer or Morton Dean during weekend telecasts. The warning came in the form of metaphorical introductions to subsequent reports. The result was akin to what Herzog (1973, p. 166) has called "thermopolitical rhetoric," a language device that presents things as "hotter, flatter, mushier, massier, messier" than actually is the case. The first hint of the pattern to unfold came in the CBS newscast of March 28, the first following the 4:00 a.m. accident. TMI was not the CBS lead story that evening, as it was on the other networks, but followed accounts of a government loss of a vote of confidence in Great Britain and a bombing incident in the American embassy in Moscow, and commercials for "Mrs. Goodcookies Cookies" and Chrysler.

"It was the first step in a nuclear nightmare," warned Cronkite. Then, with more assurance, "But as far as we know at this hour, no worse than that." Yet, he continued, "a government official said that a breakdown in an atomic power plant in Pennsylvania is probably the worst nuclear reactor accident to date." Thus the warning narrated by Cronkite. Correspondent Gary Shepard's follow-up report then provided what would be the characteristic response to the anchor's thermopolitical lead. Without detracting from the danger at hand, Shepard led viewers through a data-based, technical report of how a nuclear power plant works (using filmed graphics similar to those found in Nuclear Regulatory Commission technical manuals) and what had gone wrong. The plant would remain closed until further notice, he ended. With danger warned of and identified, Cronkite warned again, but in subdued fashion, citing a parallel of the

TMI accident and fictional events in the film *The China Syndrome*. But once more there followed a data-rich report, this time from Robert Shakne in Washington, D.C., on radiation levels and cooling rates. The source of danger had again been laid bare.

This tale of viewers alerted, viewers informed was basic to the content of CBS coverage throughout the crisis, but examples drawn from the opening week make the pattern clear. On "Black Friday," the March 30 venting of radioactivity, revelation of the hydrogen bubble, and evacuation advisory, Cronkite began the broadcast:

> The world has never known a day quite like today. It faced the considerable uncertainties and dangers of the worst nuclear power plant accident of the atomic age. And the horror tonight is that it could get much worse. It is not an atomic explosion that is feared. The experts say that is impossible. But the spectre was raised of perhaps the next most serious kind of nuclear catastrophe—a massive release of radioactivity. The Nuclear Regulatory Commission cited that possibility with an announcement that, while it is not likely, the potential is there for the ultimate risk of a meltdown at the Three Mile Island atomic power plant outside Harrisburg, Pennsylvania.

Correspondent Robert Shakne's report identified the "problem" stated by "the Government's top nuclear specialists" as "a 15- to 20-foot-wide bubble of trapped radioactive gas at the top of the damaged reactor, gas that cannot be removed." Shakne went on, "One of the dangers is meltdown." There followed a technical explanation by NRC spokesmen of efforts to void the bubble. "The experts say that the risks of catastrophic disaster are very small," but "the experts say they're not absolutely sure."

With that danger identified and explained, Cronkite turned to another, the danger of confusion. Said Cronkite, "Earlier on this incredible third day of the accident, confusion, contradiction, and questions clouded the atmosphere like atomic particles." Viewers then learned that radiation would continue to leak for five more days, a million residents would not be evacuated from four counties, children and pregnant women were advised to leave a five-mile radius, all 23 schools were closed, 20,000 residents within ten miles were to stay indoors, and care centers were set up 15 miles from Harrisburg. Fallout there was, but a fallout of numbers from the lips of CBS correspondents.

The warning-identification exchange between anchor and reporters continued throughout Black Friday's newscast. Cronkite asked rhetorically, "Just what is the meaning of all those confusing dose levels we've been hearing about?" A packaged report from Mt. Sinai Hospital in New York gave the answer: the average American absorbs 100 millirems of radiation per year; a normal chest x-ray adds ten more; 5,000 millirems per year is "considered allowable by the Government"; and 200 yards from TMI radiation was measured at 30 millirems, "equivalent to three chest x-rays." And, faced with "waves of confusion that reached tidal proportions," Cronkite turned to another correspondent who reviewed technical details and data of the March 28 accident, identifying the source of the confusion, this time Metropolitan Edison spokesmen.

By Monday, April 2, NRC representatives had announced that the size of the gas bubble had diminished and the reactor had stabilized. Cronkite was not so sure. "Like doctors reporting from the bedside of a seriously ill patient, the nuclear authorities gathered at Pennsylvania's crippled Three Mile Island atomic power plant were cautious in their announcement today," he reported. But, he went on, "the tone is optimistic," even though "the convalescence promises to be dangerous, long, and costly." Why? True to the CBS narrative, a packaged report followed with the data-laden answer: "The $600 million structure is 365 feet high and contains two steam generators, four pumps, and a pressurizer" and "the troublesome bubble is inside this eight-inch-thick, carbon-steeled pressure cooker" but was reduced from 1,800 cubic feet to an estimated 47 cubic feet, even though the 2.6% concentration of hydrogen was not too far below the 4% level at which hydrogen burns. The correspondent closed by explaining that technicians were coping with the problem.

Over the course of the crisis, CBS warned of other dangers, identified their sources, and detailed how "experts," "scien-

tists," "officials," or "technicians" were dealing with them—
"catastrophic economic costs," reactor "design problems,"
and "psychological problems," to name but a few. By April 4
Walter Cronkite had lumped them together as the "eighth day of
the Harrisburg Syndrome" which he defined as the "economic,
psychological, and health costs of the cleanup." No one knew,
he said, what the precise costs would be, for there were only
"guesses." Yet, in painstaking detail, CBS offered viewers a
nightly parade of facts and figures pertaining to each and every
portion of the syndrome. It even extended to an upbeat report on
how to make a "Radiation Cocktail," a drink popularized in a
local bar as a sales gimmick: "For $2.25 you get a shot of vodka,
lemon-lime soda, and a luminescent swizzle stick for people
who really want to get a glow on."

In keeping with its emphasis upon technical, data-based
coverage of TMI, CBS provided viewers with numerous reports
concerning nuclear power plants in other parts of the country
either built by the same manufacturer as TMI or of similar
design. Reports from Cleveland, Ohio, Crystal River, Florida,
Rancho Seco, California (all on March 31), Zion, Illinois (April
1), Green River, Utah (April 21), and Oconee, South Carolina
(April 25), as well as several studio reports, provided "experts"
with opportunities to detail how technical points of plant de-
signs differ, thus making it unlikely that an accident similar to
TMI would occur again.

Although the CBS narrative was one of detail, data, design,
and technique, featuring experts grappling with danger, the
network did not ignore the human interest content of the news;
it simply placed much lower priority on such accounts than the
other networks. And although CBS did report the fears of local
residents and evacuees, even those fears took on a technical
ring. For example, CBS reports covered potential problems
residents might have in selling their property as a result of the
reputation of TMI. When reporting health fears, CBS covered
the exact symptoms of radiation poisoning, even to the point of
filming one mother bringing her child, who displayed the symptoms, to her local doctor (the child was diagnosed as having a
virus, much to the mother's relief). And on two occasions CBS

filmed students in classrooms discussing their fears about TMI but also included their science teachers' data-based, technical explanations minimizing any direct threats.

Finally, on April 9, Walter Cronkite decreed that the danger at Three Mile Island was over; the accident had, after all, been an accident. "The 'All Clear' sounded, in effect, in Middletown, Pennsylvania, today," announced Cronkite. "The Governor," he said, "declared that life could now return to normal in the area of the stricken Three Mile Island nuclear plant." It was "the official end of twelve days of terror." The story of TMI did not thereby fade from CBS newscasts, but only two more times during the remainder of the month did it lead, and it never again followed the pattern of warning-identification that had been the CBS trademark for the previous twelve evenings.

Viewed dramatistically, then, CBS coverage of Three Mile Island had overtones of an adventure tale in the tradition of "disaster averted" movies (for example, Walt Disney's films of men conquering forest fires). In such dramas responsible people take concerted action to bring an unfortunate situation under control. That they were able to do so in the case of TMI—at least from the CBS perspective—resulted from knowing that dangers existed, discovering their technical sources, and coping with them skillfully. That was the story CBS narrated, a tale filled with metaphors of danger, data of explanation.

ABC's TMI: Nuclear Nightmare

Theodore Gross, provost of Pennsylvania State University's Capitol Campus, located in Middletown, the community but a few miles from the Three Mile Island nuclear power plant, wrote the President's Commission investigating the accident (Report, 1979, p. 81):

> Never before have people been asked to live with such ambiguity. The TMI accident—an accident we cannot see or taste or smell . . . is an accident that is invisible. I think the fact that it is invisible creates a sense of uncertainty and fright on the part of people that may well go beyond the reality of the accident itself.

In the face of such ambiguity and uncertainty, CBS alerted viewers to the danger, then explained it. CBS told of a threatening situation and how governing and technocratic elites dealt with it. ABC took a different approach. Its news reports also narrated a story of a threatening reality, but one with which elites could not cope. The ABC drama is one of farm and factory, cottage and castle, little people haunted by a nightmare of forces set in motion by insensitive rulers. ABC's narrative revolved about the theme of a technological nightmare created by scientific elites, a monster—much like Frankenstein's—out of control. Unlike CBS (or NBC, as we shall see) there was little effort to educate viewers with "a crash course in nuclear physics" (as CBS anchor Morton Dean described his network's reports), no automatic assumption that ruling elites were honest or responsible, and only scant encouragement that things would turn out all right.

ABC's image of TMI can be illustrated by the themes the network developed in the early days of the crisis. The thrust of the verbal, visual, and sound imagery conveyed the basic elements familiar to fans of nightmare melodramas: a Gothic setting, a populist leaning which stressed sentimental values, and unrelenting threat.

The tradition of fear contained in many popular melodramas has long favored a Gothic setting wherein the threat to peace, tranquility, and happiness is embodied in a forbidding structure overlooking the community of simple folk. It may be the despot's castle, the smokestacks of the robber barons' mills, or the guard towers of a prison. Dr. Frankenstein's castle in Transylvania, in a bucolic countryside above a quaint village, is the classic setting. Romantic literature favors the juxtaposition of Castle and Cottage: the arrogance of educated aristocrats against peasant pleasures, urbane sophistication against rustic simplicity.

ABC's filmed reports of TMI captured such imagery. Visuals of the nuclear plant possessed a Gothic quality, especially on days when ABC correspondents did stand-up reports with the plant's massive cooling towers, enveloped in mist, looming in the background. Frequently the network's films cut from such a plant setting to panoramic views of farms, cattle grazing in fields, and school busses departing the area. While ABC correspondents narrated accounts of school closings, evacuations, worried farmers and housewives, lead-ins and summations took place before the turret-like cooling towers, the icons of a Frankensteinian castle. Aerial shots, too, captured a technological intruder in a rural setting.

It is not possible to say what the cumulative impact of such visual fare is on viewers. But with audio added they may be striking, as they were in ABC's treatment of "Black Friday," March 30. First came anchor Frank Reynolds' lead, one that rivaled Walter Cronkite's announcement of danger:

> The news from the Harrisburg, Pennsylvania, nuclear energy plant is worse tonight. For the first time, an official of the Nuclear Regulatory Commission said today there is the possibility, though *not yet* the probability, of a meltdown of the reactor core. In plain language, that would be a catastrophe!

As correspondent Tom Jarriel narrated the follow-up, a shot zoomed in on the plant's cooling towers, then back to houses and children's bikes in the foreground. A day earlier Jarriel had included interviews with concerned residents in his accounts, remarking that their main "concern is over wind direction to answer the question, 'Is it blowing my way?' " Now as on-site anchor he introduced reports on the meltdown danger. In one such report, correspondent John Martin in Middletown interviewed an eight-year-old girl wearing a leg brace. "She rode home from school early today," he reported, "to find her mother, brother, and sister packing clothes to leave their home." The girl then expressed her fears, ones the reporter did not bother to inform viewers were scarcely plausible: "When the radiation goes on I'm afraid all the houses will fall down and my mother will be in there and I'm afraid she'll get locked in." Martin did go on to report that the family had no car and so a friend drove them away. The camera caught the mother in the right front seat of the car, the girl on her lap. The car had a rear-view mirror outside the right front door. Reflected in it were the plant's cooling towers.

Even after the crisis had started to ebb, ABC did not abandon its Gothic portrayal. On April 3 as a correspondent hinted at "new problems," a camera panned back from a close-up of the towers, across the river to houses, abandoned bikes and an abandoned little red wagon. Radioactive iodine was showing up in milk, said the reporter (actually it did not). The camera, with the cooling towers still visible in the background, focused upon grazing cows. Off camera came the cry of a baby and the crackling of a Geiger counter.

Nightmarish drama appeals to many people not only because of its ominous setting but also because it casts as heroes and victims the people who live near the castle and who are threatened by what goes on inside. In the tale of Frankenstein's monster, for example, it is the creation of science and technology that threatens the townspeople: the scientist is villain, the villagers are victims. Family, community, and the simple life (centerpieces of ABC's narrative) must prevail over large-scale organization, wealth, complex technology, and sophisticated scientific data (precisely what was prized in a CBS account).

This populist leaning in ABC news reports is illustrated by the types of interviews contained in packaged accounts. For instance, it was not to any official spokesman that ABC turned on March 28 for its first report of the accident but to a farmer living across the river from the plant. He said that he had heard "an explosion" that morning and witnessed "smoke coming out of the plant." ABC featured another farmer on April 3. As he walked up a country path (cooling towers visible in the background), he spoke of his fears of radiation and how since the plant was built he had experienced problems with his sheep and goats ("loss of the young" or young that were "deformed"). His cows' milk, he said, was "definitely, no doubt" contaminated. The farmer's dream, concluded the ABC correspondent, had been destroyed by the plant, "a place that looms over his home, his dream, his life." The Machine had destroyed Eden.

The populist leaning is also manifested in reporters' characterizations of what people think of public officials. Here are samples from the reports of four correspondents:

March 30:   "People frightened by the unknown invisible rays of escaping radiation are not reassured much by officials who try to explain the potential in technical terms, like millirems."

March 30: "The last two days have demonstrated that when it comes to nuclear safety, there are no certainties."

April 1: "The President came and went, and while most people here give him high marks for coming, they'd prefer some straight answers."

April 2: "Of course, those people who live in this area, they do not wear dosimeters. And they don't have much faith in experts or their gadgets."

With a third theme of ABC coverage, the persistence of threat, the network was unrelenting. According to the tradition of nightmare, the people of the village have more to fear than immediate danger. There is no "All Clear" to be sounded, for once the monster lives, it cannot be destroyed; it can always return to work its evil ways. Howard K. Smith in his ABC News commentary on April 5 reminded viewers that the remnants of nuclear power, such as plants and buried wastes, might "like some secret monster break their chains and return to destroy life later."

On the evening of April 2, anchor Frank Reynolds introduced ABC's *World News Tonight* by saying, "Good Evening. It is at last possible to say 'Good Evening' tonight and mean it, for there is relatively good news now from Harrisburg and the nuclear energy crisis that has seized the world's attention for the past few days." Such an introduction was as rare for ABC as it was short-lived. For a theme of persistent threat was carried in the message that "Things are bad, but they may get worse" underlying many ABC reports. On March 29 correspondent Bettina Gregory concluded, "There are many questions, few answers about why and how this accident occurred." But, she said, "In the sobering aftermath officials of Metropolitan Edison have admitted that if this happened, it's possible for a much more serious accident to occur." ABC correspondent John Martin reported that doctors treating evacuated pregnant women "could not say what might happen later" following exposure to radiation. Bill Zimmerman concluded on April 1 that "People around here aren't sure what to do, and no one is telling them." Max Robinson reported the next day that "there are still many engineering unknowns." And, just as things seemed to look brighter on April 3, Bettina Gregory pointed out that "before anyone could breathe a sigh of relief, the shadow of a new problem appeared" (radioactive iodine).

But the most anxiety provoking feature of ABC coverage over the long haul was narration of a real-fiction of multiple monsters. CBS, as noted above, had featured reports about plants similar to TMI-2 in other parts of the nation. But the general CBS message was that there were technical differences which obviated the likelihood of a recurrence of the TMI accident elsewhere. ABC, however, portrayed other plants as clones of TMI, reporting on April 10 that 42 had the potential for disaster. Even on April 27, when TMI finally reached "cold shutdown," there was no rejoicing. ABC noted "still another malfunction" in a California plant. Moreover, the NRC suspected eight other reactors of significant problems.

We do not say that ABC's *World News Tonight* is a product of the New Romantics, since we know nothing of the corporate attitude toward technology that prevails in that organization. But we do suggest that ABC's Three Mile Island narrative had clear themes that differentiated it from CBS. In fact, at one pole stood CBS, alerting viewers to danger but implying technological problems had technological solutions. At the other was ABC, presenting a nightmare for which there was no solution. Between the two was NBC News, treating a crisis as a crisis.

NBC's "Crisis at Three Mile Island"

In covering events at Three Mile Island *NBC Nightly News* took almost literally the dictionary definition of crisis, that is, an unstable condition in which an abrupt or decisive change is impending. Unlike CBS's warning of danger in order to avert disaster or ABC's unfolding a nightmarish tale, NBC's approach to TMI was low key, almost resigned. A crisis is something people must live with until change has occurred and stability is restored. And people can do that if the mystery surrounding the unstable condition is removed and the course of likely change charted. Hence, for NBC the basic themes of coverage were demystification and debate. Through didactic instruction and placing events in context, NBC demystified TMI, rendering ABC's monster a "tea kettle." Through unedited discussions NBC presented a calm but Great Debate over the future of nuclear power.

Anchor David Brinkley set the low-key tone of NBC coverage from his first report. "In a nuclear power plant near Harrisburg, Pennsylvania," he began, "the cooling system broke down this morning, some radioactive steam escaped into the air, radiation passed through the four-foot-thick concrete walls, and was detected a mile away from the plant." But, he continued, "the radiation was said to be at a very low level, and not dangerous." Mentioning that "some workers may have been seriously contaminated" and that "the plant is shut down," Brinkley introduced three reports.

The three reports established a pattern which NBC was to make a ritual in the days to come. The first told what happened and why. The second reported how the populace was adjusting to unstable conditions. The third narrated what company, government, and other personnel knew and were doing. The *Mr. Wizard, Real People, Today* triad of stories formed NBC's functional equivalent of CBS's warning-identification and ABC's persistent-threat coverage styles. It is a style particularly well suited to NBC's penchant for multiplying the number of brief reports it packages for a single event, in contrast to rival networks' use of fewer, longer accounts. (Thus NBC presented 138 reports averaging 55 seconds in length, CBS 135 averaging 66 seconds and ABC but 97 averaging one minute, from March 28 through April 30). The result is a pluralizing of correspondents, sources, and points of view on the *NBC Nightly News*.

Given its pluralist news format, NBC covers a crisis like TMI from a host of different angles. No single angle dominates. Hence, analysis of NBC's coverage at TMI included, to name but a few topics, accounts of the accident proper, safety hazards, evacuations, dislocated families, the future of nuclear power, long-range health problems stemming from the accident (both physical and "psychological fallout"), unemployment rates in the area, and economic consequences (even presenting one report speculating that people might not buy Hershey's chocolate bars since they are manufactured close to TMI). Some of these items were carried by competing networks, but not all. NBC reported all and more.

NBC's demystification efforts differ substantially from the informative model employed by CBS (and from ABC's tendencies to mystify rather than clarify). CBS's coverage of TMI was in the tradition of print journalism—based on technical explanations and data, and documented with printed reports used as visuals. The *NBC Nightly News,* in contrast, went out of its way to simplify the complex, minimize technical jargon in reports, eschew numbers and statistical measures, and present readily understood visuals: diagrams, graphics, and films. The NBC model of demystification was that of the calm, professorial classroom lecture, almost a "chalk talk" on the complexities of nuclear power generation.

The NBC approach is best illustrated by how that network covered "Black Friday." Anchor John Chancellor's lead-in on the evening of March 30 was quite different from the way Walter Cronkite of CBS and Frank Reynolds of ABC had introduced the day's events:

> There was serious trouble today at the Three Mile Island nuclear plant in Pennsylvania, trouble serious enough to cause the evacuation of small children and pregnant women from a five-mile area around the endangered plant. The problem is that it is more difficult than had been thought to cool the radioactive fuel inside the power plant, and until it is cooled, it is very dangerous. The situation was described this afternoon as stable, but the experts are going to have to decide in the next day or so just how to cool the nuclear material, and there's no option they have that's guaranteed to be safe.

With that calmly, almost flatly, delivered introduction, Chancellor went on, using diagrams, to explain, "Here's the problem. The building in which the nuclear fuel is located is filled with very radioactive gas, xenon and helium, which is too dangerously radioactive to release into the atmosphere." But, he continued, "the gas in there is intensely hot, so hot that it is making it difficult to use normal methods to cool the nuclear fuel." Then, adding a note of resignation, Chancellor concluded, "So for the moment they're stuck with the gas. They can't release it into the air, but as long as it's there they can't cool the nuclear fuel." And, "If they can't cool it, the risk of a meltdown, of turning the nuclear fuel into a molten mass, increases."

After introducing a packaged report which further simplified for viewers what was going on "inside the plant," Chancellor then returned to close the "what and why" report. "What is a total meltdown and why are people so afraid of it happening?" asked Chancellor of his viewer-students. He provided an answer: "If the nuclear fuel is not cooled, it will get so hot that it begins to melt and turn into a molten mass with enormous heat and radioactivity. In this fluid and highly dangerous state, it could burn through the walls of the building and spill out on the ground, venting radiation." But, instructed Chancellor, "More likely is that a total meltdown would melt through the foundation of the building and sink into the ground below. There it would slowly cool emitting radiation and causing just all kinds of difficulty."

In five consecutive evenings of coverage from March 29 through April 3, *NBC Nightly News* presented a total of nine reports of this nature, consuming eleven minutes of coverage. On the day before "Black Friday," for instance, Chancellor described how a nuclear power plant operates. "A nuclear power plant is really just a big tea kettle," explained Chancellor. Using a simple, uncluttered diagram, Chancellor went on, "Nuclear fuel in a chain reaction produces heat. The heat turns water to steam. The steam moves turbines. The turbines produce electricity." No mystery about that. He continued, "The nuclear fuel has to be cooled or it will get so hot that it melts down. Water is used for cooling." Chancellor pointed to "a regular system and an emergency system." At TMI, he noted, the regular system broke down, automatically shutting down the plant. Then the emergency system "should have kept the fuel from getting too hot.'' But that system was not on ''for a while'' and ''the fuel began to heat up.'' This, he said, turned the water in the building into radioactive steam. Now, ''some of that radioactive steam had to be released into the air, vented, or the pressure would have blown up the tea kettle.''

This pattern of demystification, of reducing the awesome to an everyday occurrence, repeated itself for other topics: Robert Bazell lectured again on the operations of a nuclear power plant for weekend viewers (Saturday, March 31) and diagrammed the bubble problem as well (Sunday April 1); Andrea Mitchell placed the TMI accident in historical context (April 1); Bazell reviewed the entire accident, with diagrams, on April 2, then reviewed the entire history of the TMI plant on April 5.

Each of these ''show-and-tell'' reports was followed by reports on how residents around TMI were responding. Like CBS and ABC, the NBC network took note of the confusion produced by conflicting reports from company and governing officials. And NBC reported fear. But it was not the confusion and fear of the panic-stricken. It was the fear of the resigned. ''The people here in Goldsboro,'' reported correspondent Steve Delaney, ''don't seem to know whether the nuclear power plant is more beneficial or dangerous; some are scared, some are not.'' Then, shifting from the lecture model to a seminar one, NBC presented two elderly ladies talking in the back yard of one's home. ''I'm not scared, and I'm not scared of that over there'' (pointing in the direction of the plant), said one. Delaney, noting she had ''lived with it a long time,'' asked whether she had ever been afraid something might happen. ''No!'' she responded. But her neighbor said, ''Yes, I have.'' The two women then debated whether there was any reason to be afraid. ''They aren't goin' to hit just us, Mabel. If it goes up, it's goin' to take more than just us, so why worry about it?'' concluded one. Delaney closed the one-minute seminar that captures the NBC view of a resigned citizenry: ''This village is not out of danger, but the people who live here don't seem to know what they can do to make the danger any less.''

The third feature in the tripartite NBC format of what-and-why, popular response, and official action was markedly different from what was carried on other networks. For CBS, official action consisted of the highly technical workings of a technocratic elite. For ABC it was the victimizing of beleaguered masses. NBC, although reporting how company and regulatory officials were dealing with the crisis, focused more on debates emerging from what had happened at TMI.

The debates took two principal forms and covered a range of topics. The first form was debates between local officials about how to deal with evacuations. Again a note of resignation prevails. A typical report, filmed in a civil defense office in Middletown, was one of three constituting three minutes of coverage, each report essentially repeating the message of the others, a feature characteristic of *NBC Nightly News*. The report carried a filmed exchange between the fire chief and civil defense director, debating about what was to be done to assure evacuation. "What can we do? I'm not acceptin' responsibility of all them people. I will if a state of emergency is declared," said one. "They talked until the sun came up," reported the correspondent, "with comments like 'The power company says one thing, the federal and state governments say another.' And they said a lot of people here don't know who to believe, if anybody." Hence, the officials stayed put and did nothing.

The second debate forum covered by NBC was the U. S. Congress. Here the focus was the Great Debate over the future of nuclear power. In largely unedited exchanges between congressional members of investigating committees and both company and regulatory officials, NBC informed viewers that a major change in the nuclear industry was about to take place. Indeed, the problems of safety, health, and costs raised by TMI, opined one correspondent, might lead to the end of the industry itself. In ten separate reports over a two-week period, NBC covered the Great Debate from various angles but frequently featuring the same pros and cons. In the end, for NBC, the debate, like life after TMI, went on.

The *NBC Nightly News*, then, presented a different real-fiction of the crisis at Three Mile Island from its competitors. It was a version that said crises will always happen and there is not a great deal people can do about it. But things at least seem less critical once their sources are revealed, once it is clear, as the Wizard of Oz said to Dorothy, "I'm not a bad man, just a bad wizard." Perhaps David Brinkley best exemplified the NBC attitude the evening before "Black Friday" when he said, "These plants are designed with numerous safety systems, backup systems, emergency systems, and so on. Even assuming all the systems always work, which is an assumption, there's still the possibility that some human in the plant will do something wrong and cause a disaster."

Contrasts in Newsgathering and Style, Similarities in Presentation and Content

Compared with The People's Temple crisis, that of Three Mile Island was a much bigger story. From the journalistic perspective, events surrounding Jonestown were newsworthy for little more than two weeks, even though more than 900 persons had died. No one died at TMI, and the crisis itself abated within but a few days of the original accident, yet Three Mile Island received prominent coverage for almost six weeks. In fact, from the time the Vanderbilt Television News Archive began recording evening newscasts in 1968, through March 27, 1979, the networks had devoted a little less than eight hours total time to reports about nuclear energy. In the next six weeks the TMI story alone ran for 6.4 total hours on evening newscasts.

Just as the networks did not treat the continuing story of TMI in similar dramatistic ways, they also varied in technical aspects of their coverage. One of the most notable differences was in newsgathering modes. We have already noted that each network's narration had a differing scenic background: ABC's motif (indeed almost a filmed logo) was the stand-up report with a correspondent framed by the cooling towers of the plant in the background—Max Robinson, Tom Jarriel, or Bettina Gregory; CBS concentrated on stand-ups outside the Washington, D.C., offices of the Nuclear Regulatory Commission, Department of

Nightly Horrors: Television Network News

Table 2.1
Newsgathering Modes for TMI News Reports: by Network

Modes	ABC	CBS	NBC	Combined
Locale				
Network studio	58 (56%)	41 (30%)	65 (54%)	164 (47%)
Government office	17 (17%)	70 (59%)	23 (19%)	110 (32%)
Private home/office	10 (10%)	15 (11%)	25 (21%)	50 (14%)
Crisis site	17 (17%)	0	8 (6%)	25 (7%)
$\chi^2 = 72.423$ with 6 df; p = .001.				
Source (when identified)				
Public official	70 (62%)	91 (58%)	81 (62%)	242 (60%)
Technician/scientist	6 (5%)	12 (8%)	9 (7%)	27 (7%)
Interest group leader	0	0	2 (2%)	2 (1%)
Average citizen	34 (30%)	55 (34%)	37 (28%)	126 (32%)
Means				
Briefing by public official	12 (10%)	23 (12%)	26 (20%)	61 (14%)
Speech by public official	12 (10%)	37 (19%)	7 (5%)	56 (13%)
Interview with public official	9 (7%)	15 (8%)	15 (12%)	39 (9%)
Interview with technician/scientist	14 (11%)	15 (8%)	17 (14%)	46 (10%)
Interview with average citizen	22 (18%)	43 (22%)	23 (18%)	88 (20%)
Reporter quoting a source	55 (44%)	59 (31%)	39 (31%)	153 (34%)
$\chi^2 = 28.923$ with 10 df; p = .01.				
Source of reporter's quotations				
Public official	41 (87%)	44 (79%)	32 (82%)	117 (82%)
Technician/scientist	1 (2%)	0	2 (5%)	3 (2%)
Interest group leader	0	1 (1%)	0	1 (1%)
Average citizen	5 (11%)	11 (10%)	5 (13%)	21 (15%)

Energy, or Congress; NBC was true to its conversational motif, filming neighbors in backyards or patrons in bars. The data in Table 2.1 lend credibility to such a dramatistic analysis.

Particularly noteworthy is the locale of CBS reports: government offices dominate, with almost a two-to-one margin over the studio; and few private settings; and none from the crisis site itself, the plant. For CBS TMI was primarily a Washington story, not a localized one. Washington means two things, reports either originating from the nation's capital or about federal officials on the ground at Harrisburg and/or in local communities. Not so for ABC. As high a proportion of that network's locales were at the crisis site as in government offices, although ABC's penchant for studio reporting (noted also in the case of the Jonestown crisis) is pronounced (Table 2.1). And it is NBC that concentrated more on private settings, such as homes, offices, and businesses.

In turning to the sources preferred by the networks, these differences do not appear so pronounced. All three networks relied to a large degree on public officials, and each based a substantial percentage of citations on the words of average citizens. It is worth noting that if we combine the categories of public officials and technicians/scientists as sources, i.e., what CBS staffers might label "experts," the overall emphasis is indeed one of a technological tale.

When it comes to how the networks claimed to have derived their information, it is clear that in more than one-third of the instances reporters simply cited an unnamed source, for example, "a spokesman for the Nuclear Regulatory Commission" (unidentified) or "a farmer residing near the crippled plant" (again unidentified). It turns out that these unidentified sources were usually public officials. There are, however, network differences. In contrast with its rivals, NBC preferred the official briefing as a newsgathering technique. The formal statement of a public official served as a primary device for CBS. All three networks made use of interviews with citizens.

That interviews with average citizens constituted the highest percentage of CBS newsgathering techniques indicates that raw quantitative data can, if taken solely at face value, be misleading. The findings in Table 2.1 are based upon specific mentions of or films of locales, sources, and newsgathering devices. Although a higher percentage (22%) of devices specified for CBS than for either other network were average citizen interviews, what is crucial is how those interviews were used. The CBS citizen interview normally involved persons expressing confidence in how things would turn out (for example, expressing appreciation for President Jimmy Carter's visit to Middletown). ABC's average citizen interviews focused instead upon personal fears and anxieties. In fact, if one examines reports based solely on interviews with average citizens for each network and controls for whether reassuring, alarming, or neutral (although the number of such cases is small), the ratio of reassuring to alarming reports for CBS is 3:1, for NBC 2:1, and for ABC 1:1.

From the standpoint of visual presentations—at least as measured by variables such as those listed in Table 2.2—the contrasts between the networks are not of statistical significance even though a pattern revealed in Jonestown stories is repeated. ABC is the network of the anchor-read story to a greater degree than its rivals, which rely upon a higher percentage of cuts to packaged reports. And, as in the case of The People's Temple crisis, CBS anchors were more prone to dress up their talking-head approach by having one or more graphics displayed in the background, although full-screen stills or graphics again played no major role in reporting. Unlike the Jonestown crisis, TMI did lend itself to several full-screen visuals, notably diagrams of the workings of nuclear power plants. In a majority of stories for each of the three networks, no film, with or without interviews, rolled on the screen.

In fact, as in the case of the coverage of the Jonestown crisis, one is again struck by the nonvisual quality of the visual medium of television news. This is particularly noteworthy if we recognize that across all three networks a majority of stories were read by the anchor; of those, only a few were accompanied by illustrative graphics or stills, and less than a majority were augmented by rolling films. Furthermore, packaged reports were frequently without films or interviews as well, and almost three-fourths of stories on the crisis of TMI were essentially talking heads or stand-uppers.

As in the case of all crises examined, we calculated visual prominence scores for each of the three networks. The lowest score was again zero (any talking head anchor report) and the highest was 65 (in contrast with 43 for The People's Temple crisis). But whereas we found no differences of note in Table 2.2, we do find significant differences in visual prominence scores between the networks. NBC is the most visual of the three networks, with a mean score of 24 for its stories compared to 20 for CBS and 17 for ABC. Means between networks all have F-ratios where $p = .05$. Thus, from the standpoint hinted at but not demonstrated solely by date in Table 2.2, NBC's coverage

Table 2.2
Visual Elements in TMI Stories: by Network

Visual elements of story	ABC	CBS	NBC	Combined
Anchor read story	57 (61%)	71 (55%)	56 (52%)	184 (55%)
Cut to packaged report(s)				
One or more, without interview	15 (16%)	23 (18%)	23 (21%)	61 (18%)
One or more, with interview	22 (23%)	36 (27%)	29 (27%)	87 (27%)
Graphic over anchor/reporter shoulder				
None	66 (70%)	74 (57%)	66 (61%)	206 (62%)
One	24 (26%)	42 (32%)	37 (34%)	103 (31%)
Two or more	4 (4%)	14 (14%)	5 (5%)	23 (7%)
Still picture/graphic on total screen				
None	77 (82%)	113 (87%)	87 (80%)	277 (83%)
One	11 (12%)	7 (5%)	12 (11%)	30 (9%)
Two or more	6 (6%)	10 (8%)	9 (9%)	25 (8%)
Film rolled during story				
None	54 (57%)	73 (56%)	56 (52%)	183 (55%)
Film, without interview	29 (31%)	38 (29%)	41 (38%)	108 (33%)
Film, with interview	11 (12%)	19 (15%)	11 (10%)	41 (12%)
Second film during story				
None	66 (70%)	87 (67%)	72 (67%)	225 (68%)
Film, without interview	11 (12%)	21 (16%)	16 (15%)	48 (14%)
Film, with interview	17 (18%)	22 (17%)	20 (18%)	59 (18%)

of TMI relied less than the other networks on talking heads and stand-uppers, and on stories without stills, films, or interviews.

As with coverage of the crisis surrounding events at Jonestown, the most notable differences between networks involve not newsgathering or visual techniques but reporting styles. Limiting ourselves first to the number of network reports for each journalistic style as reported in Table 2.3, we see two patterns familiar from the Jonestown crisis. One is that ABC retains its distinct emphasis upon human interest accounts, this time in keeping with its overall narrative of a nuclear nightmare. Educational and contextual reports played little role in ABC coverage, although a higher proportion of ABC reports fell into the category of elitist/factual journalism than had been the case with The People's Temple (one-third instead of one-fifth).

CBS too followed a pattern we found apparent in coverage of the earlier human crisis. A majority of CBS reports were of the elitist/factual type. There were, however, differences from the Jonestown coverage. Instead of anchors frequently reporting in

Nightly Horrors: Television Network News

Table 2.3
Coverage Styles in TMI Crisis:
by Networks, Anchors, Correspondents

Reports	ABC	CBS	NBC	Combined
Total number	97	135	118	350
Anchors	37 (38%)	71 (52%)	55 (47%)	163 (47%)
Correspondents	60 (62%)	64 (48%)	63 (53%)	187 (53%)
Style (by number of reports):				
Populist/sensationalist	56 (58%)	27 (20%)	7 (6%)	90 (26%)
Anchors	17	12	0	29
Correspondents	39	15	7	61
Elitist/factual	33 (34%)	71 (53%)	8 (7%)	112 (32%)
Anchors	19	43	1	63
Correspondents	14	28	7	49
Ignorant/didactic	7 (7%)	19 (14%)	48 (40%)	74 (21%)
Anchors	1	13	36	50
Correspondents	6	6	12	24
Pluralist/feature	1 (1%)	18 (13%)	55 (47%)	74 (21%)
Anchors	0	3	18	21
Correspondents	1	15	37	53
Total time of coverage (in minutes)	102	149	128	379
Anchors	17 (17%)	28 (19%)	23 (18%)	68 (18%)
Correspondents	85 (83%)	121 (81%)	105 (82%)	311 (82%)
Style duration (in minutes)				
Populist/sensationalist	65 (64%)	32 (21%)	12 (9%)	109 (29%)
Anchors	8	5	1	14
Correspondents	57	27	11	95
Factual/elitist	28 (27%)	65 (44%)	10 (8%)	103 (27%)
Anchors	8	16	1	25
Correspondents	20	49	9	68
Ignorant/didactic	6 (6%)	18 (11%)	37 (29%)	61 (16%)
Anchors	1	6	15	22
Correspondents	5	12	22	39
Pluralist/feature	3 (3%)	34 (24%)	69 (54%)	106 (28%)
Anchors	0	1	6	7
Correspondents	3	33	63	99

Significant differences are as follows:
1. Between networks for number of reports per style $\chi^2 = 191.847$ with 6 df; p = .001.
2. Between networks for duration of reports per style $\chi^2 = 173.419$ with 6 df; p = .001.
3. Between networks for number of anchor reports per style $\chi^2 = 116.346$ with 6 df; p = .001.
4. Between networks for number of correspondent reports per style $\chi^2 = 82.060$ with 6 df; p = .001.
5. Between networks for duration of anchor reports per style $\chi^2 = 44.024$ with 6 df; p = .001.
6. Between networks for duration of correspondent reports per style $\chi^2 = 128.911$ with 6 df; p = .001.

a populist tone to be followed by correspondents' factualism, common in the Jonestown crisis, anchors set the elitist/factual pattern. Moreover, whereas CBS had little interest in didactic accounts about Jonestown, the network did devote 14% of reports to explaining the workings of nuclear plants, evacuations, etc.

From the standpoint of sheer number of reports per journalistic style, it was NBC whose reports on TMI contrasted most strongly with its People's Temple coverage. For the Jonestown crisis, NBC, like CBS, emphasized the elitist/factual. At TMI, however, the bulk of NBC reports were either directed at teaching the uninformed or placing the crisis in a larger context. NBC did not exaggerate the story in the tradition of populist/sensationalist journalism nor limit itself to wire service accounts of the alleged facts. And although NBC's reports are almost evenly divided between the categories of didactic and feature journalism, it makes a difference who is doing the reporting. Anchor reports are primarily didactic; correspondents respond with a contextual style. Hence, the complexities of the nuclear age were broken down into their essentials, then recombined in a larger social, political, and economic context.

Table 2.3 reveals that across the three networks the proportion of reports were fairly evenly distributed among the four journalistic styles. It is clear, however, that depending upon what network one tuned to during the crisis, one received not only a different narration (and in the case of NBC a different visual emphasis) but also a different style. Similar patterns appear when we examine the duration of reports per style. ABC becomes even more populist/sensationalist in coverage. CBS becomes more feature-oriented but is still primarily factual. Not so high a percentage of NBC accounts are didactic; a greater proportion of time is feature reporting. There is, of course, a reason. Because anchor reports are shorter, they account for less of the networks' total air time; hence, anchor didacticism declines when compared to packaged reports of longer duration. In any event, the overall picture of coverage that is balanced across networks but styles that are differentiated among them holds, regardless of measures employed.

Table 2.4
News Content of TMI Reports: by Network

Content Types	ABC	CBS	NBC	Combined
News Value				
News	27 (27%)	33 (24%)	26 (21%)	86 (24%)
Peripheral	39 (38%)	64 (48%)	44 (37%)	147 (41%)
Perspective	8 (8%)	14 (10%)	20 (16%)	42 (12%)
News/peripheral	23 (22%)	19 (14%)	24 (20%)	66 (18%)
News/perspective	5 (5%)	6 (4%)	7 (6%)	18 (5%)
Emotional content				
Reassuring	21 (21%)	25 (18%)	23 (19%)	69 (19%)
Alarming	45 (44%)	49 (36%)	53 (44%)	147 (41%)
Neutral	36 (35%)	62 (46%)	45 (37%)	143 (40%)

In the news content of network reports (Table 2.4) no differences reach acceptable levels of statistical significance. However, if the categories of news content are combined, there are a few differences deserving of comment. Peripheral material constituted some aspect of 60% of ABC reports, 62% of CBS reports, and 57% of NBC reports. Perspective, however, was some aspect of almost one-third of NBC reports, only one-fifth of CBS reports, and but 13% of ABC reports—again suggesting the educational and contextual style of NBC.

As we have mentioned, an earlier study conducted by Stephens and Edison (1982) of TMI reporting by the nightly networks employed data generated by The Public's Right to Information Task Force. In that study individual statements in news reports were coded as reassuring, alarming, or neutral. Stephens and Edison reported that a majority of such statements for each network fell in the reassuring category. Since our coding units for this portion of the analysis were entire reports rather than statements (with all the problems attendant in using such content units) the findings reported in Table 2.4 are not comparable. We merely note that overall the networks were more neutral or alarming in their reports than reassuring. Differences between networks are not significant but do, in one respect, compare well to the contrasting network narratives: the ABC "nightmare" could well have been alarming (44%) and certainly NBC reported a potentially alarming "crisis"; CBS's "danger" was, if not more reassuring, at least less alarming.

Chapter Three

The Disaster of Flight 191

From the time it went into service, the DC-10, an aircraft built by McDonnell Douglas Corporation and in service with both domestic and foreign airlines, had been in the news. In 1972 an aft cargo door on a DC-10 blew off as the plane was taking off from Detroit. The plane landed safely without casualties. In 1974, however, an aft cargo door blew off another DC-10 near Paris. This time 346 persons died.

But the DC-10 became the subject of a story of continuing crisis in 1979. On May 25th of that year Flight 191 departed from O'Hare Field in Chicago bound for Los Angeles. Within seconds of take-off, the craft rolled to its side, lost power, and crashed into a mobile home park adjacent to the airport. The final death toll was 275 persons, the highest death toll from any domestic airline crash in this nation's history.

Fortunately air disasters are not frequent. Yet they do occur. Under normal circumstances the crash and its attendant casualties make headline and lead story news, but only on the day of the disaster and for a brief time thereafter. Days, weeks, months later—following extensive investigations—an official report on the cause of the accident attracts momentary news interest once again. After that, the event joins the almanac list of "notable aircraft disasters," an item of historical interest no longer newsworthy.

Such was not so with the crash of American Airlines DC-10, Flight 191. The disaster itself and its aftermath were a prominent story in television news for two months. As reported, the essentials of the story are as follows. Besides coverage of the accident and casualties and speculation regarding causes—all staples of news accounts of air disasters—TV news networks included another fact. As we mentioned in the Introduction, Av Westin, former president of ABC News, remarked that news audiences come to a story with the question "Is the world safe, and am I secure?" (Sperry, 1981, p. 301). The question was particularly relevant to coverage of the crash of Flight 191, for the accident happened on a Friday afternoon, the beginning of the long Memorial Holiday weekend. Countless Americans had holiday trips planned, many via air travel. And, since thirteen percent of domestic passengers in the U.S. were booked on DC-10s during that period, large numbers of people might be asking, consciously or not, about the safety and security of their world.

But the potential for the flight and plight of DC-10s to affect vast numbers of viewers directly was not the only element setting the story apart from those of other air disasters. As events developed, those people's lives were indeed affected. On Monday afternoon, May 28, following the May 25 disaster, the Federal Aviation Administration (FAA) announced a grounding of all DC-10s in the U.S. for inspections of engine mounting bolts. It was clear, however, that once inspections were complete, airlines could put their DC-10s back into service. Since many airlines had anticipated such a call for inspections, they had already completed them. Hence, the FAA order was at first but an inconvenience.

That, however, was not to be the end of it. Because of problems uncovered in requested inspections on May 28, the FAA mandated a regrounding of all DC-10s the following day for "comprehensive inspections." This time the aircraft could not be put back into service until the FAA so authorized. Inspections followed, but this time at considerably more cost to airlines forced to cancel and reschedule flights, shift to other aircraft, and placate passengers. Once again, however, with inspections completed, the FAA certified DC-10s for flight, and they were back in the air on May 30.

Over the course of the next week, however, questions regarding the safety of the DC-10 did not abate. Members of the National Transportation Safety Board criticized the FAA for recertifying the DC-10 before discovering the cause of the crash of Flight 191. Congressional investigating committees joined in the criticism. The Airline Passengers Association sought a court order grounding all DC-10s. Then, on June 6 nightly network TV news returned the DC-10 story to lead status: the FAA had again grounded all 138 DC-10s operated by U. S. airlines and prohibited all DC-10s in service with foreign airlines from entering this country.

It was Friday, July 13, 1979, before flights of DC-10s were resumed in the United States. Over the period leading to resumption of DC-10 service, network television's nightly news reported a story of conflict between and among governing officials, interest groups, major corporations, and foreign governments; of a search for the cause of the disaster of Flight 191; of disrupted lives, travels, and schedules; and of economic losses. But each news network did not narrate the same real-fiction.

ABC and the Bungled Search for a Missing Bolt

Unlike NBC's coverage of the crisis of The People's Temple, no network had a clear jump on its rivals in reporting the disastrous flight of American Airlines Flight 191. Only by foregoing the anchor's introduction on its *World News Tonight* of May 25, 1979, did ABC begin its report but seconds before coverage began on NBC and CBS. Over the course of the next two months, ABC devoted less time than other networks to the DC-10 crisis (only 57 minutes compared with NBC's 63 and CBS' 73). But in that shorter period ABC packaged a clear, dramatic portrayal of events.

In his report, joined in progress at the opening of the nightly newscast, ABC correspondent Ron Miller reported the crash of the "holiday-crowded DC-10" that "fell into a mobile home park in the Chicago suburb of Elk Grove." (The aircraft did not in fact fall in the park.) An eyewitness reported the appearance of fire in one engine and a "white streamer" behind it. Miller did not report the number of casualties nor the fact that the number was the highest in domestic airline history—items reported in the other two nightly network newscasts. Anchor Max Robinson in his wrap-up took note that "word of the Chicago air disaster came on a day of dramatic news developments, an unusual beginning for a normally quiet Memorial Day weekend."

ABC's opening reports on the crash of Flight 191 thus offered minimal information or background; in fact, they were more confusing than enlightening. But as ABC developed the story, the onus of confusion was transferred from the network to other dramatis personae. The transfer began the next evening when anchor Sam Donaldson unveiled "The Case of the Missing Bolt." In a packaged report, ABC Science Editor Jules Bergman pointed to an assembly of a DC-10: "This fitting is where disaster began," he said. The fitting consisted of a bolt and collar joining the aircraft's engine to the wing. Discovery of the bolt from the Flight 191 DC-10, implied Bergman, would assist investigators in discovering the cause of the crash. But Bergman was not optimistic that the bolt would be recovered. He narrated for viewers the sequence of events causing the accident: because of metal fatigue, bolts holding the engine to the wing broke; the engine "ripped off," and its pylon assembly fell away, cutting hydraulic lines in the wings of the aircraft; "without hydraulic lines you just about lose control," reported Bergman; hence the crash.

Throughout the remainder of its coverage of the DC-10 crisis, ABC continued to attribute the crash of Flight 191 to a single cause: the broken bolt. With cause clearly identified, the ABC narration shifted to whether those in charge knew the cause and, if so, were they doing, or failing to do, anything to correct it. The plot line developed quickly. When the FAA first grounded all domestic airline DC-10s on May 28, anchor Frank Reynolds specified the reason: "unless or until they have been reinspected to make sure the wing engine bolts are not defective." Said Reynolds, "It's now believed the faulty bolt was the cause of the crash last Friday."

ABC follow-up reports on May 28 hinted at the scenario that

was to unfold. First was a packaged report of FAA administrator Langhorne Bond's announcement grounding all "134" DC-10s in domestic service (the actual number turned out to be 138). The ABC correspondent asked, rhetorically, why the grounding order would not take effect until 3:00 a.m. the next morning. Bond's filmed response cited practical reasons and—a remark that would be recalled later—the fact that "the risks seem sufficiently small" not to impose an earlier deadline. Ending the packaged report, the ABC correspondent raised questions not only about the deadline but about the effectiveness of the grounding. Since many airlines had "anticipated" Bond's order, they had already inspected their aircraft and would have them back in the air. Moreover, the order had no effect on aircraft owned by foreign airlines, "more than 150" DC-10s.

Again ABC called on Jules Bergman for a packaged report on what the required inspections were all about. Bergman reported that the "potentially fatal bolt" could be easily replaced; "a relatively simple procedure, it can be done in a couple of hours." But was the bolt the cause of the crash? Bergman asked an official of the National Transportation Safety Board. His response: "Negative. The bolt might not have anything to do with the cause of the crash. The bolt has something to do with the loss of the engine." Bergman, however, was undeterred. His second reconstruction of the accident to Flight 191 was like the first he had delivered the previous evening: the bolt "cracked from fatigue and pieces went flying," thus "causing the rest of the engine to shake loose." "Disaster was underway"; when the engine broke loose, hydraulic lines were cut, "causing" loss of control. Since "the missing bolt" might never be found, "federal investigators may never know for sure." But what "federal investigators" might not know, ABC seemed sure about, i.e., the bolt was the cause of a chain reaction of events leading to the crash.

The "cause and cure" plot line was the leading motif of ABC coverage, but there was a second. This subplot involved the impact of the crash upon ordinary people and of how officials were dealing with it, or failing to do so. The impact motif was also introduced on May 28. Anchor Max Robinson reported that "as the investigation into the crash slowly proceeds, many people across the country are adjusting to the sudden loss of relatives and friends." This lead—which contrasted the slow pace of the investigation with ABC's recognition of a known cause—introduced correspondent Julie Eckert's report about a "collie named Charlie." Showing film of the dog barking beside a backyard swing set where children had once played, Eckert reported that the dog had lived with "the Sutton family." With all four members of the family, including seven- and nine-year-old sons, killed in the crash of Flight 191, the "horror of such proportions" had "left neighbors in a state of shock" and Charlie in their care. Eckert closed her report with a film of the memorial service for the "hundreds of crash victims" (it was to be yet another evening before ABC News ventured a precise number of fatalities).

These two ABC plot lines of, first, cause and correction combined with, second, human consequences were sharply defined on the newscast of May 29. On that date the FAA again grounded all DC-10s, this time for "comprehensive inspections" in light of what FAA had labeled "grave and potentially dangerous deficiencies in many of the pylon mountings." "Now all 137" DC-10s "have been grounded effective immediately" (again the actual count was 138). Correspondent Bill Zimmerman reported that "Bond admitted that the FAA shares the blame." Zimmerman's report closed with Bond saying on film, "There's no question that somewhere along the way we didn't do it right." In short, ABC introduced a more basic cause than a fatigued bolt, namely, bungling public officials. The bungling was still going on, for, noted anchor Frank Reynolds, "there was one sign of confusion in today's FAA action," specifically, the grounding of another aircraft. The FAA, believing that the A-300 Airbus had engine mountings like those of the DC-10, ordered their grounding, only to learn they were not the same. The FAA rescinded the order.

Again Jules Bergman recounted the problems leading to the second grounding. This time it was the discovery of a series of cracks including some in the linkage where "fractured bolts led to the engine falling off." Bergman repeated that this led to the slashing of hydraulic lines, then loss of control over slats governing the pitch of Flight 191's wings. In Bergman's scenario, the "plane tilted so sharply it was beyond recovery." This view that the technical cause of the DC-10's crash resided in a faulty bolt was by this time influencing how ABC covered the international implications of the disaster. Peter Jennings at the network's overseas desk reported that European airlines had already checked "the suspect bolt," but nonetheless would also engage in more comprehensive inspections.

The human interest subplot of ABC coverage took on another aspect with the regrounding of the DC-10. Given the potential disruptions of airline schedules, ABC took its cameras to airports to cover how disruption of lives would also follow the failure of officials to cope with modern technology. "Thousands of passengers were stranded at Los Angeles," and others "scrambled" to make new travel plans; "for most, however, there were no alternate flights today." ABC correspondents filmed specific cases of disruption. For example, Edie Gruber could not "fly to Chicago on business" (on the following evening, May 30, ABC reported her finally about to depart). Another passenger lamented, "My wife is expecting me for our anniversary dinner tonight; I've got a problem, I've got to get home." (Viewers did not learn whether he did.)

The narrative of known cause, bureaucratic confusion, and human inconvenience took full form on ABC's newscast of May 30. "Less than twenty-four hours after the Federal Aviation Administration ordered all DC-10s grounded," reported anchor Frank Reynolds at the top of the telecast, "because of 'grave and potentially dangerous deficiencies' the same planes are back in the air today after inspections." Reynolds then introduced "a series of reports on this continuing and confusing situation." The first suggested that the airlines had moved quickly, "their fortunes in the balance." The report continued recounting, airline by airline, a series of inspections that produced "no problems." The implied question was, if so, why were there "disruptions for thousands of travelers"? Anchor Max Robinson reported O'Hare Field in Chicago "getting back to normal" after a "chaos of scheduling" produced by the groundings. "Just how bad it was" constituted the substance of this account. The third in the series of reports covered the success of Edie Gruber in Los Angeles. A fourth fixed the death count of Flight 191's crash at 274. The fifth returned to "the controversial bolt," this time about one which had been found missing and two damaged on a DC-10 owned by Japan Air Lines.

This, then, was the ABC narrative of the disaster of Flight 191. It was a tale of a cause more obvious to ABC than to officials, of bureaucratic mismanagement, and of human disruptions. That narrative did not end with the return of DC-10s to service. Over the course of the next week, ABC continued in the same vein. Although reporting that investigators had concluded that the "suspect bolt" did not cause the crash of Flight 191, the network still went on to reveal that a 1975 and a 1978 McDonnell Douglas memo pointed out possible weaknesses in mounting bolts; but the memos suggested courses of corrective action without requiring them. "Questions of safety are far from resolved," noted Max Robinson, introducing a report from Jules Bergman of a "basic defect" in the design of engine mounts. McDonnell Douglas, said Bergman, had "teams of designers behind closed doors trying to figure what went wrong and how to fix it." And, Bergman added, an official of the FAA said, "We still don't know what caused this; that's what scares me." Yet the FAA saw no reason to ground the DC-10 fleet.

But on June 6, ABC and other networks reported the third grounding of the DC-10s, along with a prohibition on any such aircraft of foreign airlines entering U. S. air space. Again, however, anchor Frank Reynolds found confusion. On the previous evening he had reported that a federal judge had issued an order grounding DC-10s, then held back to permit a rehearing so the FAA could argue against it. Now, twenty-four hours later "all 138 DC-10s operated by American air carriers have been grounded" (this time the correct number). The five reports which followed repeated the essential themes of the ABC narrative.

"The FAA went wrong from the moment of the crash itself," reported Jules Bergman, relying upon "top people" of the

National Transportation Safety Board as sources. Then all DC-10s should have been grounded. But there had been only "partial groundings." Bergman noted that inspection procedures—raising and lowering engines as complete units—might have caused pylon cracks, the discovery of which produced the latest groundings. McDonnell Douglas, reported Bergman, said so. Airlines, however, "fired right back" and denied using faulty inspection procedures. Fortunately, thought Bergman, the DC-10s would remain grounded while "the manufacturers and the airlines fight it out."

But manufacturers and airlines were not the basic source of the fact that "the DC-10 has had problems all along" (Bergman); it was the FAA. With the latest groundings, ABC did not hesitate to turn to the FAA. Langhorne Bond "admits his agency doesn't know what's causing the cracks." But "each new discovery of cracks in the jetliner's engine pylons has also left cracks in the FAA's credibility," reported correspondent Vic Ratner. "Why weren't the planes grounded as long as necessary at the first hint of trouble?" Ratner asked viewers. The plea by "a weary looking Administrator Bond" that the FAA acted only on evidence at hand did not seem to answer Ratner's query. Nor did FAA credibility rise, in ABC's view, when during a congressional investigation, Administrator Bond had to be handed "a copy of his own agency's memo" describing structural problems. There were calls that Bond be "fired," noted Frank Reynolds.

In addition, ABC invoked the problems of human disruption, "70,000 passengers scheduled to fly on DC-10s," said Max Robinson. It was "wall-to-wall people" at O'Hare Field. Nor were things better at ABC's other key site for originating stories of human disruption, Los Angeles. There too it took days to adjust again to disruptive conditions. By July 5, given the problems posed by the crash of Flight 191, repeated orders of groundings, unresolved matters of safety, and the fact that the FAA was "under fire," correspondent Charles Gibson posed the ultimate question on July 5: "Will people be willing to fly DC-10s again once they go back into service?"

A little more than a week later, Friday, July 13, ABC had an answer. Interviews with passengers at Chicago's O'Hare Field boarding the first flight of a DC-10 since the June 5 grounding, United Airlines Flight 338 to Baltimore, indicated confidence. Despite the earlier crash of Flight 191, and "a tragically confusing series of groundings, inspections, clearances to fly, and more groundings" (so summarized Jules Bergman of the 37 days since the crash), people boarded Flight 338. ABC personalized the event by noting that Mr. and Mrs. Richard Steininger were the "first to board a domestic DC-10 since their grounding." At 1:42 CDT the flight departed. Anchor Max Robinson, smiling, reported it to be a "routine flight, landing in Baltimore on time." Thus ended ABC's view of an aviation disaster.

NBC's Tale of Human Fallibility and Folly

If ABC uncovered a single technical cause for the disaster of American Airlines Flight 191 (a faulty bolt), a single political cause (FAA bungling), and single human consequence (passenger disruptions), NBC narrated a tale of multicausality, one emphasizing present and past contexts for events. NBC began with a longer (three minutes) and more detailed report of the crash. The number of the take-off runway, the distance between another runway and the crash, the distance of the crash from a mobile home park, weather conditions, a description of the flight of the craft and its condition—all these reported details put the event into the context of the moment. In addition, anchor John Chancellor gave a historical comparison of the severity of this crash with previous airline disasters. Like ABC, the *NBC Nightly News* confused the casualty count, reporting 279 dead. NBC also noted that O'Hare Airport was "filled with holiday travelers."

Although NBC carried additional details of the crash and of the memorial services for casualties on its next newscast, Sunday, May 27, it was not until the telecast on Memorial Day that thematic story lines began to emerge. The first is what can be labeled a "conversational" approach to interviews. Typically both ABC and CBS conduct interviews in the conventional fashion of having a correspondent ask questions of a source. Filmed interviews are then edited for substance and time requirements. Although NBC also carries such interviews in packaged reports, it is more typical of the network to film news sources interacting with one another, conversing with one another or chatting with a news correspondent. This rough approximation of *cinéma vérité* provides a different quality to NBC reports and furthers a sense of contextual background for events.

Thus, for instance, on the evening when the story of the first grounding of DC-10s broke, reporter Jim Cummins filed an account from Chicago's O'Hare. His voice-over-film described that "holiday travelers continued to ride DC-10s despite the crash," but "one passenger checked an airline guide for another flight before reluctantly boarding a DC-10" (the passenger appeared poring through the guide, then turning away). Then came the full conversational quality of the report. Film portrayed a passenger approaching a check-in attendant. The passenger asked, "Did you guys check the engine mounts on this?" "Not funny," was the attendant's reply. "I'm not being funny," said the passenger. "It's a serious question."

In its Memorial Day newscast NBC also reported the story of what ABC had made the key cause of the accident, the "missing," "fractured," or "suspect" bolt. There was, however, a difference. Anchor David Brinkley suggested that the reason for the groundings was an opportunity to check aircraft for "a set of bolts holding their engines to their wings." He reported that "federal authorities think but are not certain that a broken bolt caused the loss" of Flight 191's engine. The correspondent's report which followed noted—as with ABC, incorrectly—that there were 134 DC-10s in domestic service. That report too took note of a "three-inch bolt" but again stressed that it was only a "probable" cause of the accident.

In sum, to this point the NBC narrative had not placed absolute or sole responsibility in a bolt for the crash of Flight 191. Nor was NBC so prone to point a finger at the FAA. A packaged report depicted Langhorne Bond not as "admitting" blame but as talking about a "defeat for the FAA and for the designers and for the air carriers." Bond went on, "Somehow, somewhere along the way something wasn't done that should have been done. It is a personal loss to all of us." This longer, less edited version of a film clip which ABC had also run provides a sense of an administration characterized more by human fallibility and folly than culpability.

If fallibility and folly are, for NBC, part of the human condition, so too is perseverance. This message emerges from NBC's coverage of memorial services for the accident's casualties. Instead of a focus upon the tragic aspects of the loss of life, NBC correspondents spoke of a rebirth, of how "strangers shared their grief and sought consolation together," and how "people prayed, as they do every Sunday, to be spared such a tragedy."

Having developed a plot line that emphasizes the context, the human condition, and the human spirit, NBC carried this perspective into its reporting of the second grounding of the DC-10 on May 29. In a didactic introduction to the story, John Chancellor noted the "fact of grave and potentially dangerous deficiencies," then put the whole matter into context by reciting the number of casualties from the May 25th crash, the number of DC-10s in service ("more than a hundred"), the proportion of the passenger load borne by DC-10s ("twelve percent"), and the fact that keeping planes on the ground disrupted passenger traffic "from coast to coast."

Ensuing NBC reports on the broadcast listed a multiplicity of problems—not only bolts—that might have been the source of the crash of Flight 191. Again Langhorne Bond appeared, recognizing that "There is no question that somewhere along the way we didn't do it right." But rather than letting the report stop there, thus leaving Bond's admissions as the last point in viewers' minds, NBC continues by specifying each action being taken to insure thorough inspections. Again human error, not calculated insensitivity, appeared at issue.

As we noted in NBC's coverage of The People's Temple tragedy, there is room for heroic acts in the network's narration. The DC-10 crisis was no exception. In this case the heroes were two United Airline mechanics, Lorin Schluter and Ernie Gigliotti. For three evenings NBC filled in the details of the heroic acts that had uncovered the problems leading to the second grounding of DC-10s. An accident investigator told the story: "A very conscientious, old-time mechanic, who wasn't satisfied with the way an inspection plate was fitting, found this. I might have been flying it tonight," said the investigator, also an airline pilot himself. The "old-time mechanic" turned out to be two—Schluter and Gigliotti. In NBC conversational interviews the two mechanics discussed their discovery and how they decided to undertake a "detailed inspection":

SCHLUTER: "We felt that we needed to search real close, and I felt very bad when I found it."

CORRESPONDENT: "Were you shocked?"

BOTH MECHANICS, TOGETHER: "Yes."

GIGLIOTTI: "Very much so. The pylon would have separated from the wing."

SCHLUTER: "I feel it would have, eventually."

Correspondent Jim Cummins credited the mechanics with having discovered another possible accident cause. Bolts and cracked pylons were both at fault.

NBC also covered the story of passenger disruptions resulting from the second groundings. But it was a tale of a communal problem of human endurance told essentially through the conversational interview rather than one of individual travelers as victims of bureaucratic bungling or insensitivity. At the airport terminal in Los Angeles, NBC reported "hundreds of frustrated passengers" reacting to an airline employee's detailed explanation of scheduling problems. A few days later, June 6, when DC-10s had been cleared to fly, then grounded again, NBC took the same posture toward passengers' problems: namely, life goes on. In a packaged story from Newark airport, for instance, NBC showed airline officials rerouting passengers on aircraft, Amtrak, and by bus: "Don't worry. We'll get you there. And safely," says a travel agent to passengers in one film clip. "For now the grounding has caused more of an inconvenience than a crisis," concluded NBC correspondent Dianne Wildman.

Throughout the days of the events surrounding the DC-10,

NBC continued to put seemingly unrelated matters (what ABC termed "confusion" and "chaos") into context. This developed in two respects. As each event emerged—groundings, inspections, clearances—NBC anchor John Chancellor reviewed and repeated what had gone on before. That provided each event with a past.

But, as noted earlier, he placed events in a current context as well, with a marked didactic style and metaphors of the classroom. For example, on May 30 he reported that "Some DC-10s are back in the air today, having passed examinations to make sure their engines would not fall off." But, he continued, "other DC-10s flunked the exams and are still on the ground." The following evening he reported "more trouble for the DC-10," as though the aircraft were a student. There were defects in "27%" of such students. A day later, anchor David Brinkley kept the report-card motif alive, noting that "nearly half" of DC-10s had received "defective marks." John Hart, anchoring the Saturday edition of the *NBC Nightly News,* took account—again with the schoolteacher's metaphor—of a charge that the FAA "fell short of the mark" in dealing with the crisis.

As NBC coverage of the events surrounding the crash of Flight 191 continued, the theme of multiple causes was extended. To broken bolts and cracked pylons NBC added the possibilities of cracked engine mountings, faulty maintenance procedures, design defects, and even at one point—later rejected—pilot error. And, although the FAA remained the responsible agency for ferreting out causes, NBC coverage did not lay blame solely at its door. Indeed, in NBC's most critical account of the FAA's role in the crisis—a report on the evening of the third grounding, June 6, that reviewed previous FAA orders and clearances—the final charge was of a "built-in conflict of interest" rather than intentional wrongdoing. Thus NBC developed a story of a multiplicity of conflicting interests involved in the investigation just as it developed a narrative of multiplicity of factors contributing to the crash of Flight 191.

Unlike ABC and, as we shall see, CBS, the *Nightly News* narrative drama included numerous actors. In one or more reports devoted to each, NBC expressed the position of the following interests regarding what should, or should not, be done about the DC-10: the Federal Aviation Administration, National Transportation Safety Board, Airline Pilots Association, United Airlines mechanics, Airline Passenger Association, Association of Flight Attendants, several of the U.S. airlines, Laker Airlines, Air Alitalia, congressional subcommittees, federal judges, aviation consultants, McDonnell Douglas, and McDonnell Douglas employees ("I just hope, man, we don't get laid off, you know!").

NBC held to its contextual coverage of the DC-10 crisis to the end. Following the June groundings, John Chancellor provided a running series of reports providing reassuring background statistics on the airlines' "good safety record" (286 million passengers carried, 25 "mishaps," six fatalities in 1978). On five evenings following the third grounding, NBC reviewed the circumstances of the Flight 191 crash. And John Chancellor asked a troubling question one month after the third groundings of the DC-10s, "Will they ever fly again?" He gave a reassuring answer: "Yes, but there is work to be done before they do."

Finally, when United Airlines Flight 338, Chicago-Baltimore, was the first DC-10 to fly after the FAA's clearance on July 13, NBC continued its narration to the very end of the flight. Again the network showed films of the crash of Flight 191. All FAA recommendations, requirements, and orders were listed on the TV screen, true to a didactic style. Then came the boarding of Flight 338. Correspondent Roger O'Neill spoke with "nervous passengers" in conversational interviews. But, said one, "the plane's here and I'll go." Whereas ABC had followed the story until boarding, NBC went on—filming passengers in flight, conversing with one another, applauding when the plane touched down in Baltimore. And where ABC drew the moral that "people are quick to forget," the NBC correspondent concluded that "DC-10s are flying again, but it may be sometime before many passengers forget the aircraft's history."

Thus from beginning to middle to end, NBC narrated a drama of human fallibility, folly, and endurance told in both historical and contemporary context. A disaster, tragedy, and crisis there had been, but for NBC it could be understood within the context of a proper view of the human condition.

CBS: High Tech Detection and Correction

In content the report carried on the *CBS Evening News* on May 25, read solely by anchor Roger Mudd, differed little from the first report of the other networks. Certainly it did not foretell any story line that would distinguish it from its rivals, though Mudd's account did offer a few different details. For instance, CBS put the casualty count at 270 (it was, in fact, 273 at that point, the toll later rising to 275 when two more bodies were discovered.) Debris from the crash, not the aircraft itself, fell on a mobile home park, according to Mudd. An on-the-scene witness spoke of the plane coming down "perpendicular to the ground," a point not revealed in eyewitness accounts on other networks. And Mudd was precise in his description of effects on O'Hare, noting the airport was closed for but one hour (ABC made no mention of a closing, NBC no mention of a reopening).

In its telecast of the next evening, however, the basic outlines of what was to become the CBS real-fiction emerged. Each of three reports took a different stance on the accident from those airing on other networks. The first sounded the keynote of CBS coverage: an emphasis upon technical procedures in coping with crises. Correspondent Richard Roth, who figured prominently in CBS coverage over the course of the crisis, set the style for that coverage in his opening report.

Roth revealed that "two separate devices" being analyzed in Washington, D. C., by the National Transportation Safety Board might supply clues to the accident. One was a voice flight recorder and another "etched data such as speed and fuel supply on a thin metal tape." But "Safety Board Chairman James King said the tape was incomplete." King spoke of a loss of power to the cockpit and to the voice recorder "just after VR, that's rotation, when the front wheel comes off the ground."

Roth, using the King interview, made it clear that there might have been several causes for the loss of power. In any event, the only word heard after the loss was "Damn," for which King could cite no significance. Throughout Roth's packaged account, film rolled, showing recording equipment of the type allegedly aboard the aircraft. Roth noted that "computer analysis of data would take several days."

The second CBS report on May 26 concerned how "thousands of holiday travelers" were coping with the thought of flying DC-10s. The focus was upon those about to board that day's American Airlines Flight 191 bound from O'Hare to Los Angeles. Standard footage of interviews with passengers appeared—some anxious, some not. But what set the CBS report apart was film showing passengers avidly reading newspaper accounts of the disaster of the previous day, with headlines and portions of stories shown tightly on the screen. Anxious passengers or not, the CBS correspondent reported that Flight 191 turned out to be "routine."

CBS's final report on the evening of May 26 also differed from the type of accounts airing on other networks. The scene was Los Angeles. The subject was how families and friends of those on the crashed Flight 191 were reacting to the disaster. Only CBS covered such responses, and it did so in a distinctive way. Much of the report focused upon how those attending the American Bookseller's Convention grieved at the loss of "a number of writers and publishers bound for the event" who were "also on Flight 191." The convention gala planned for that evening at the Hugh Hefner mansion would now be cancelled because the managing editor of *Playboy* magazine was one of the crash victims.

These three reports originated the style that pervaded CBS coverage of the DC-10 crisis for the next two months, a narrative approach not characterizing rival networks. The first and most prominent theme of that narrative concerned the cause of the Flight 191 accident. Whereas ABC held doggedly to mounting bolts as the likely culprit and NBC stressed multicausality, CBS coverage placed less emphasis upon any actual cause(s) than upon the search for cause(s). CBS narrated a detective story, one in which experts pursued the task of discovery by marshalling all the technical devices at their command.

CBS exploited the "expert" theme early, first by originating its initial detailed report after the accident from Washington, D. C., containing interviews with the chairman of the National Transportation Safety Board (an expert), a pilot and spokesman of the Allied Pilot Association (also an expert), and a quotation from "one air safety expert." Thereafter, much in the fashion of the network's coverage of the crisis of The People's Temple, CBS anchor Walter Cronkite and network correspondents invoked "the experts" in reports. On both public sources and inside, unidentified sources, CBS bestowed the mantle of expertise.

This tendency to glorify the role of experts in its narrative led to a different portrayal of public officials in the drama than was the case with ABC or NBC. As we have seen, FAA Administrator Langhorne Bond was for ABC potentially one of the causes of DC-10 problems, a minor villain. For NBC, however, Bond was but another victim of the human condition. CBS did not treat Bond as a hero yet portrayed him in a far more commanding role than did the other networks. The dominant theme was that right or wrong, it's "Bond in charge." For CBS, Bond played the role of Chief Detective in solving, as Cronkite described it, "the mystery of the worst aviation disaster in U. S. history."

In covering Bond's role in the crisis, CBS used much the same film footage of his public statements as the rival networks. But there were two differences. One involved the camera shots taken of Bond. On CBS they were much tighter, often shot at a low or side angle rather than normal or high angle. Such camera work tends to suggest that the object of the picture is more powerful, or at least equal to, the viewer (see Jamieson & Campbell, 1983; Wurtzel, 1983). Second, CBS tended to use more of Bond's comments than the other networks. For example, on the evening of the first groundings of DC-10s, May 28, CBS carried, as did NBC but not ABC, Bond's comment that the O'Hare crash had been a "defeat" for FAA, manufacturer, and air carrier. But CBS did not stop there. Developing the mystery plot in which Bond was Chief Detective, CBS continued his remarks: "We take the attitude that nothing is unavoidable, there must have been a cause." Richard Roth's follow-up noted that "technicians at the Transportation Safety Board here today were continuing analysis," looking precisely for that cause. The implication was that FAA and NTSB detectives would work together to solve the mystery, not be in conflict as reported by ABC.

CBS wed technical expertise with technical gadgetry. On May 28 at the time of the first DC-10 grounding (CBS mentioned "grounding" but once, calling it instead a legally binding "airworthiness directive"), the network moved directly to explaining the state of the technical art. Richard Roth returned again to a description of how "flight data recorded on computer tape" was analyzed. This in turn introduced a report in which the CBS correspondent, using detailed film and an expert airline mechanic, demonstrated the various means for testing engine mounting bolts: inspection requiring a mirror ("there it is, about three inches long, 3/8 inch in diameter"), a special stress-producing wrench, or coating with a special liquid dye and testing magnetically (a procedure called "Magnaflux testing," according to the CBS reporter).

Two evenings later, following a second grounding for comprehensive inspections, CBS again stressed the highly technical aspects of ferreting out clues to the DC-10 mystery. Richard Roth described technical inspection reports dating back to 1971 "indexed in this computer printout," while portions of the printout rolled on the screen. That printout, according to "government sources," helped "federal authorities" realize that "problems were serious." Roth listed each incident making the DC-10 a "subject of safety questions and controversy" since being put into service in 1971: an engine part fell off a craft over Albuquerque, removing a cabin window and pulling a passenger "to his death"; a cargo door blew off a DC-10 in the same year, but the craft landed safely; the same thing happened to another DC-10 two years later, but the plane crashed, killing 346 people; in 1975 a DC-10 exploded during takeoff from New York City after a flock of birds were sucked into the engine; in 1978, tires on a DC-10 blew on takeoff and two passengers died.

Roth's contextual analysis approximated the NBC narrative style. However, in emphasizing the technical problems associated with each incident in the DC-10's history, Roth gave the report a distinctive flair. That high-tech flair continued in the next report of the evening, again on the inspection process. Using a rolling film, the correspondent described techniques of removing engines from planes, stress testing in place, and coating parts with a "liquid full of metal particles" in a dark room "under ultraviolet light and in a magnetic field." Other testing, the report continued, uses "high-frequency sound waves" and "X-rays." The report was just as detailed on corrective measures as on the detective ones, describing how "green aluminum strips" could be added to compensate for "slightly weakened aluminum underneath." With such a technical modification, concluded the report, there "was nothing really to worry about."

The high-tech search for the cause of DC-10 problems continued unabated in CBS reports. On May 31 the "broken bolt" theory was discarded, Cronkite reporting that the suspect bolt was actually a result of the accident of Flight 191, not the cause. The focus turned to cracked bulkheads instead. The search became more intense as the CBS newscast of June 6 reported the third—and what was to be the last in the crisis—grounding of the DC-10 "until the problem is found, analyzed, and cured" (Cronkite). Richard Roth, relying upon an FAA spokesman, described the seriousness of the cracks discovered on inspection. Langhorne Bond again appeared facing up to a hard decision, "acting responsibly and moving quickly." Once more CBS detailed inspection procedures, this time for examining pylons. "The cracks were barely visible to the naked eye but were confirmed by painting red dye over the suspect area; the crack then showed up as a tiny red scratch."

The CBS search did not end with the discovery of cracks. Of all the networks CBS was the only one to return to audio tapes recorded at the time of the accident for additional clues. This time they were air traffic control tapes. Richard Roth, reporting from Washington, D.C., described the content of the tapes as they were played, the printed content also being displayed on the screen. But no evidence of possible causes emerged. CBS also reported the possibility of pilot error, but, again using reports of expert testimony, dismissed the likelihood.

As other possible causes for the crash appeared—the warning system in the cockpit, wing slats, faulty maintenance—CBS reports examined each in technical detail. Finally, the network returned to the "aft pylon bulkhead" on July 6. Describing how "visual checks are to be supplemented with the use of sophisticated magnetic and soundwave tests," CBS suggested corrective action that "could signal the eventual return of the grounded DC-10s." Using a "ten-power magnifying tool" to discover "wear or cracks," experts found none.

When anchor Roger Mudd reported on July 13 that "the Federal Aviation Administration today unleashed the DC-10," thus returning them to service, it was very much the narrative of a successful technical search for sources of the aircraft's problems. The "aft pylon bulkhead" must be strengthened, according to the FAA. Langhorne Bond, still understood to be in charge in spite of congressional criticism and calls for his firing, announced the grounding lift.

A secondary story line accompanied the CBS search for technical problems and solutions. It was one of the impact of the DC-10's problems. However, aside from the network's first report, which narrated the consequences for the families and friends of victims of the crash of Flight 191, CBS devoted little time to tracing such an impact on the lives of travelers. The tale of inconvenienced passengers, so much a part of ABC and NBC coverage, took lower priority than another narrative, namely, the effects of DC-10 groundings on the airline industry. At the time of the May 29 groundings, for example, Walter Cronkite prophesied "troubled financial skies" for the airlines. A correspondent's report then spelled out—in statistical, economic detail—the place of the DC-10 in the industry. It all added up to economic woes and a "public relations nightmare," the report concluded.

Subsequent CBS reports enumerated the "confusion, cost,

and inconvenience" of repeated groundings. But confusion was reduced by the systematic, empirical search for causes. Inconvenience was dismissed or treated as not a paramount concern. Cost, however, was a problem. Where CBS emphasis lay is best illustrated by a report filed on June 6, the date of what was to be the most lengthy grounding. Walter Cronkite noted that "today's order grounding those planes changed flight plans for some, but it's the industry that is experiencing the worst turbulence."

Correspondent Ray Brady's following report contained a brief filmed interview with a woman whose flight had been cancelled because of the grounding. But interviews with airline executives added up to a report of cancelled routes, a loss of $7 million per day for the industry, financial crises for some airlines, and a loss on the airlines' "massive investment in those planes, one worth about $5.4 billion." Noting the drop in the value of McDonnell Douglas stock on Wall Street, Brady concluded that investors may feel "there is choppy flying weather ahead for the plane and its maker."

In subsequent days CBS returned to this theme of an industry in trouble. Besides manufacturers and airlines in trouble, the network reported the impact upon workers, filming one report with the president of an Aerospace Workers Union local. "Catastrophic circumstances" for all in the industry was the CBS emphasis.

In the main, however, the narrative of impacts was secondary to the mystery tale which CBS spun over the course of its coverage of the DC-10 crisis. And, for CBS, it was a story with a happy ending: the mystery had been solved. Expertise had triumphed.

Charting Techniques of Network Coverage

Although the plight of the DC-10 was primarily a studio story for TV news (Table 3.1), there were variations of locale between networks. These variations are not of statistical significance, yet they do conform to patterns detected in network coverage of other crises. ABC again concentrated its reporting efforts in network studios; moving outside the studio, ABC reverted to what it had done in reporting the crisis of The People's Temple, namely, utilizing private homes and offices as scenes for a developing narrative. CBS and NBC also employed studio locales but, as in the case of other crises, other dramatic settings as well. However, unlike its reporting of other crises, NBC turned to government offices as a primary nonstudio locale, as did CBS in this crisis and for TMI.

As might be expected in a crisis involving a government-regulated industry, public officials were the chief sources identified by all three networks, whether by names or simply as unnamed quoted sources. Also as might be expected, the principal means for obtaining official views came through either formal briefings or public statements. But unlike the crises of The People's Temple or of TMI, the networks relied considerably upon interest groups for information, although not necessarily going beyond statements of interest groups to conduct actual interviews with interest spokespersons. As noted in describing the NBC narrative of the DC-10 crisis, the network stated the position of a great variety of special interests. This, however, does not emerge in the data of Table 3.1 for the reason that although both ABC and CBS also identified interest groups as sources, they tended to rely upon the same groups repeatedly rather than looking to different interests. Hence, although the raw data used to compare network news sources might appear to say otherwise, NBC's focus upon the crisis was notably more pluralist than that of its rivals.

As we have seen in the case of other crises, there was no overriding visual distinctiveness between the networks in coverage of the DC-10 crisis. Talking heads, stand-uppers, and voice-overs typified the coverage of each network. As suggested by our analysis of each network's narrative, what makes a difference is not the quantity of graphics, stills, films, or interviews employed but which ones and how they are used to augment the messages of anchors and correspondents. A typical ABC graphic imposed on the screen a listing of crashes of DC-10 aircraft prior to Flight 191; that of CBS contained statistics on

Table 3.1
Newsgathering Modes for Flight 191 News Reports: by Network

Modes	ABC	CBS	NBC	Combined
Locale				
Network studio	40 (62%)	41 (56%)	31 (48%)	112 (55%)
Government office	9 (14%)	16 (22%)	18 (28%)	43 (21%)
Private home/office	15 (23%)	14 (19%)	14 (21%)	43 (21%)
Crisis site	1 (1%)	2 (3%)	2 (3%)	5 (3%)
Source (when identified)				
Public official	47 (56%)	54 (50%)	50 (59%)	160 (54%)
Technician/scientist	3 (3%)	6 (6%)	2 (2%)	11 (4%)
Interest group leader	20 (24%)	35 (32%)	31 (30%)	86 (29%)
Average citizen	14 (17%)	13 (12%)	13 (12%)	40 (13%)
Means				
Briefing by public official	22 (26%)	37 (34%)	28 (26%)	86 (29%)
Speech by public official	25 (30%)	18 (17%)	39 (36%)	82 (28%)
Interview with public official	9 (11%)	23 (21%)	13 (12%)	45 (15%)
Interview with interest group leader	3 (4%)	8 (8%)	2 (3%)	13 (5%)
Interview with average citizen	14 (17%)	13 (12%)	13 (12%)	40 (13%)
Reporter quoting a source	10 (12%)	9 (8%)	11 (31%)	31 (10%)
Source of reporter's quotations:				
Public official	8 (80%)	6 (75%)	8 (50%)	22 (65%)
Technician/scientist	0	0	2 (12%)	2 (6%)
Interest group leader	2 (20%)	2 (25%)	4 (25%)	8 (23%)
Average citizen	0	0	2 (13%)	2 (6%)

numbers of aircraft, flights, and passengers; and that of NBC a sketch of a pylon mount. Similarly, ABC filmed passengers in airline terminals with tight shots of persons standing in long lines, CBS used more open shots of passengers waiting their turns in orderly fashion, and NBC showed passengers talking with flight attendants.

One distinction between networks that proves of statistical significance does emerge from our visual data. Prominence scores ranged from 0–73 in coverage of the DC-10 crisis. Employing F-ratios to test for the significance of differences in network means (18 for ABC, 20 for CBS, and 23 for NBC), we find that with $p = .05$, NBC was the most visual in its presentation of the crisis, a finding coinciding with that derived from analysis of the crisis at Three Mile Island.

From the viewpoint of journalistic styles, the pattern detected in exploring coverage of Three Mile Island appeared again in

Table 3.2
Visual Elements in Flight 191 Stories: by Network

Visual elements of story	ABC	CBS	NBC	Combined
Anchor read story	81 (75%)	88 (73%)	65 (70%)	234 (73%)
Cut to packaged report(s)				
One or more, without interview	12 (11%)	15 (13%)	16 (17%)	43 (13%)
One or more, with interview	15 (14%)	17 (14%)	12 (13%)	34 (14%)
Graphic over anchor/reporter shoulder				
None	81 (75%)	82 (68%)	59 (63%)	222 (69%)
One	20 (18%)	27 (22%)	27 (29%)	74 (23%)
Two or more	7 (7%)	11 (10%)	7 (8%)	25 (8%)
Still picture/graphic on total screen				
None	95 (88%)	106 (88%)	76 (82%)	277 (86%)
One	5 (5%)	5 (4%)	5 (6%)	15 (5%)
Two or more	8 (7%)	9 (8%)	12 (12%)	29 (9%)
Film rolled during story				
None	73 (68%)	86 (72%)	67 (72%)	226 (70%)
Film, without interview	23 (21%)	32 (26%)	21 (23%)	76 (24%)
Film, with interview	12 (11%)	2 (2%)	5 (5%)	19 (6%)
Second film during story				
None	91 (84%)	93 (77%)	70 (75%)	254 (79%)
Film, without interview	12 (11%)	10 (9%)	11 (12%)	33 (10%)
Film, with interview	5 (5%)	17 (14%)	12 (13%)	34 (11%)

reports of events surrounding the crash of Flight 191. In several respects this is not surprising. Although lives were lost in the crash of Flight 191 as they were not at TMI, the two crises were similar. One accident had already occurred, and there was a threat that another might happen. No one knew the immediate cause of the accidents that involved something going wrong with high-technology equipment. And chief responsibility for dealing with matters resided in clearly defined government agencies: the FAA with respect to the DC-10, the NRC with TMI. Moreover, FAA Administrator Langhorne Bond, like NRC Chairman Joseph Hendrie for TMI, came under close press and congressional scrutiny for what was being done to assure the safety of the DC-10. Finally, it should be remembered that the two crises took place within only two months of each other. If networks do indeed have distinctive reporting styles, we might well anticipate that they woud remain consistent over such a brief period of time.

As Table 3.3 indicates, ABC was once again the network

Nightly Horrors: Television Network News

Table 3.3
Coverage Styles in Flight 191 Crisis:
by Networks, Anchors, Correspondents

Reports	ABC	CBS	NBC	Combined
Total number	65	73	65	203
Anchors	37 (57%)	41 (56%)	33 (51%)	111 (55%)
Correspondents	28 (43%)	32 (44%)	32 (49%)	92 (45%)
Style (by number of reports):				
Populist/sensationalist	37 (57%)	22 (30%)	22 (34%)	81 (40%)
Anchors	17	17	10	44
Correspondents	20	5	12	37
Elitist/factual	16 (25%)	42 (58%)	4 (6%)	62 (30%)
Anchors	14	19	4	37
Correspondents	2	23	0	25
Ignorant/didactic	2 (3%)	3 (4%)	14 (22%)	19 (10%)
Anchors	2	3	14	19
Correspondents	0	0	0	0
Pluralist/feature	10 (15%)	6 (8%)	25 (38%)	41 (20%)
Anchors	4	2	5	11
Correspondents	6	4	20	30
Total time of coverage (in minutes)	54	63	66	193
Anchors	15 (28%)	16 (25%)	11 (17%)	42 (22%)
Correspondents	39 (72%)	57 (75%)	55 (83%)	151 (78%)
Style duration (in minutes)				
Populist/sensationalist	34 (63%)	24 (33%)	25 (38%)	83 (43%)
Anchors	6	6	2	14
Correspondents	28	18	23	69
Factual/elitist	8 (15%)	38 (52%)	2 (2%)	48 (25%)
Anchors	5	9	2	16
Correspondents	3	29	0	32
Ignorant/didactic	2 (4%)	1 (3%)	5 (8%)	8 (4%)
Anchors	2	1	5	8
Correspondents	0	0	0	0
Pluralist/feature	10 (18%)	10 (14%)	34 (52%)	54 (28%)
Anchors	2	0	2	4
Correspondents	8	10	32	50

Significant differences are as follows:
1. Between networks for number of reports per style χ^2 = 69.740 with 6 df; p = .001.
2. Between networks for duration of reports per style χ^2 = 67.061 with 6 df; p = .001.
3. Between networks for number of anchor reports per style χ^2 = 27.498 with 6 df; p = .001.

emphasizing the human interest angle of the continuing DC-10 controversy. CBS treated the hard news associated with the elitist/factual style. NBC, as at TMI, divided the bulk of its reports between the didactic and the feature style, with anchors offering the former and field correspondents the latter. And it should be noted that CBS reverted to a form defined at the time of The People's Temple crisis: of the 30% of reports CBS undertook with a populist/sensationalist style, three-fourths came from anchors. Although this difference vanishes when we turn from numbers of reports to the elapsed air time devoted to them, it still remains noteworthy in light of earlier findings and of the significant difference between the networks' anchors in reporting styles. In short, we see again a pattern—chiefly attributable to Walter Cronkite—of CBS anchors using primarily the elitist/factual style, yet mixing in a sufficient number of human interest reports to "hype" what might for some viewers seem overly dry, factual, and statistical coverage.

The news content of reports, when examined for whether hard news, peripheral, or perspective values were dominant, displays an even distribution overall and across networks. If we combine categories in Table 3.4, for example, 27% of all reports were straight news, 37% were peripheral or contained peripheral material, and 36% involved some form of perspective material. The only marked break in the pattern—although not of statistical significance—comes from ABC (as had been a tendency in coverage of previous crises). Only 18% of ABC reports were straight news; the remainder were evenly divided between reports having either peripheral or perspective material.

Where ABC does emerge as distinctive in the content of its coverage is in the tenor of its reports. Overall, the majority of reports were neutral, and 80% of all network reports were neutral or reassuring. Only ABC broke from this general configuration in a significant way; almost one-half of the network's reports were alarming, a distribution in keeping with the ABC narrative of official failures to discover the single cause of the air disaster.

In the case of the crash and aftermath of Flight 191, then, the

Nightly Horrors: Television Network News

Table 3.4
News Content of Flight 191 Reports: by Network

Content Types	ABC	CBS	NBC	Combined
News value				
News	12 (18%)	24 (33%)	19 (29%)	55 (27%)
Peripheral	21 (32%)	22 (30%)	17 (26%)	60 (30%)
Perspective	17 (27%)	22 (30%)	16 (25%)	55 (27%)
News/peripheral	6 (9%)	2 (3%)	6 (9%)	14 (7%)
News/perspective	9 (14%)	3 (4%)	7 (11%)	19 (9%)
Emotional content				
Reassuring	4 (6%)	17 (23%)	16 (25%)	37 (18%)
Alarming	30 (46%)	11 (15%)	20 (3%)	61 (30%)
Neutral	31 (48%)	45 (62%)	29 (44%)	105 (52%)

$\chi^2 = 20.980$ with 4 df; $p = .001$.

three news networks evolved different real-fictions of events just as we argue they did in coverage of other crises. Moreover, although significance tests reveal few clearcut differences between networks, we find patterns emerging about the overall use of newsgathering devices by networks, distinctive journalistic styles, NBC's tendency to give more visual prominence to stories, and ABC's appeal to human anxieties during crises. These tendencies appeared to varying degrees in the human tragedy of Jonestown and two technological crises, TMI and Flight 191. We turn now to what tendencies, if any, network news coverage of a natural disaster reveals.

Chapter Four

The Mount St. Helens Eruptions: Network Coverage of a Natural Disaster

For 123 years Mount St. Helens, located in the Cascades chain in the state of Washington, stood dormant. Early in 1980 there had been signs of activity within the mountain, but nothing like the eruption that began at 8:39 a.m. on the Sunday morning of May 18. Lava poured down the sides of Mount St. Helens, volcanic ash and steam blew 10 miles into the air, mudslides poured into the adjoining valley, waves of water 30 feet high rushed down the Toutle River, forests were toppled, and Spirit Lake below was destroyed. Earthquakes shook the volcano as explosions that could be heard as far as 200 miles from the site continued.

The eruptions of May 18 were not to be the last at Mount St. Helens. The following Saturday another eruption blew ash 2,000 feet into the air; two weeks later another major explosion produced a plume of ash 50,000 feet high. In each case the clouds of volcanic ash spread throughout the surrounding region and, in the case of the major explosions, across the United States and around the globe.

By any standard the volcanic eruption of Mount St. Helens was a disaster. More than two dozen people were killed outright and another 40 were presumed dead. The economic damage was in excess of $2.7 billion. Communities in parts of Washington and Oregon were paralyzed by falling ashes and soot, transportation was halted, and schools were closed. Public officials were forced to call states of emergency, and the federal government, for purposes of providing financial relief, declared counties within the stricken region to be disaster areas.

Network coverage of Mount St. Helens focused, first, upon the explosions themselves, beginning with descriptions of the first major one on May 18. Drawing upon film shot by a freelance photographer, the nightly network newscasts were able to provide viewers with vivid pictures of what had taken place on that Sunday morning. Eyewitness accounts yielded descriptions of conditions at the time of the first eruption. The nature of the second and third eruptions, in late May and mid-June, received less televised coverage than had the first.

With coverage of actual eruptions concluded, the networks devoted most of their air time to what correspondents often referred to as the "aftermath" of the volcanic activity. Such aftermath reports fell into clear categories, estimated death tolls and the search for bodies of victims and survivors, physical damage, economic consequences, disruptions to cities and towns, official responses to the disaster, human interest vignettes, broader impacts of the disaster upon the nation, and speculation regarding the possibility of future volcanic activity.

In the six weeks following the May 18 eruption of Mount St. Helens, the three networks devoted just under three hours to coverage of the volcano's activity and its aftermath. The amount of emphasis placed upon these events was not evenly balanced. CBS and NBC offered equal coverage, 64 minutes each; ABC's coverage was limited to 45 minutes over the entire period. Differing amounts of coverage, however, were not the only contrasts between the networks.

CBS and the Facts of Life

Three motifs characterized the real-fiction that the *CBS Evening News* provided its viewers in covering the natural disaster of Mount St. Helens. The first, emphasis upon "expert" opinion regarding the course of events, we encountered in Chapter 1 and requires little additional comment. Since the crisis involved volcanic and earthquake activity understood almost solely by a small set of scientists, it is not surprising that a network would turn to experts for clarification.

What is noteworthy is CBS's handling of two themes. The network either included at least one identified expert in most of its reports—a geologist, specialist in air pollution control, meteorologist, forest service specialist, civil defense or law enforcement officer, agricultural expert, crop insurance specialist, volcanologist, or even public relations practitioner—or cited a generic group of experts. Of the latter, CBS reports incorporate a lengthy listing. "Geologists believe," "scientists say," "agricultural officials report," "volcanologists warned," "authorities won't even guess," "government scientists predicted," "scientists also know," "geologists calculated," and the inevitable "experts said today" were sprinkled liberally throughout the anchor reports of Walter Cronkite and Dan Rather and the packaged reports of field correspondents.

Of more interest is a second CBS technique, clearly related to the first: CBS coverage of events surrounding the Mount St. Helens eruptions was hyperfactual. The trend was set in correspondent Ken Woo's report filed on the network's May 18 newscast. Besides stating the precise time of the eruption, Woo reported that the mountain stands 9,677 feet above sea level, it was the greatest volcanic activity in 123 years for the mountain, the northwest flank of the mountain erupted, shooting smoke and ash 60,000 feet into the air, cities 200 miles away heard the explosions, and there were earthquakes measuring 5.0 on the Richter Scale. He also remarked on the number of a highway closed to traffic, the size of river waves, and the near-zero visibility levels from falling ash in Ellensberg, Washington.

Such devotion to factual detail continued the next evening as Dan Rather introduced the newscast by revealing that the eruptive "blast sheared 1,300 feet" from the mountain top. The single packaged report from the field indicated 14,000-foot plumes, a half-mile-wide crater, precise depths of fallen ash in specific cities, 3,000 persons evacuated, and 11 million salmon killed. The following evening's telecast added similarly to the store of statistical data: 10 patrol cars were out of commission in Ritzville, Washington, due to ash-clogged carburetors; Missoula, Montana, had one-eighth of an inch of ash, necessitating a speed limit of 15 miles per hour; and the air contained "19,000 micrograms of dust per cubic meter compared to a normal level of 75 micrograms."

Such attention to detail permitted CBS to lay to rest early in its coverage a speculation that its rival networks were reluctant to surrender. Dan Rather had introduced that speculation in his first report on the effects of the eruption on May 19: "As a vast volcanic cloud swept hundreds of miles east from Washington state's Mount St. Helens today, scientists speculated that it could slightly cool the world's temperature for a couple of years." The following evening Rather introduced a report with the remark that the volcano's eruption might "have an effect on everything from sunsets to snowfall." Correspondent Nelson Benton's report, however, punctured the speculation. Benton noted that "volcanic ash in the atmosphere can cause long-term cooling in the weather but not this time." From an interview with Dr. Ray Mitchell of the National Weather Service, Benton learned that the cooling effect would be "just a few tenths of one degree Fahrenheit, that's all it'll be, not enough to get very excited about." Striking sunsets and, at most, one more snowfall would be about all that would follow. Benton assured viewers that "except for those who live fairly near Mount St. Helens, the effects apparently will be small" for ash poses "no significant health hazard" and "except for the area within 500 miles of the mountain, agricultural experts were not alarmed."

Although Benton minimized the nationwide effects of the Mount St. Helens eruption, CBS did not thereby play down the newsworthiness of the event itself. On the evening of May 21 Dan Rather noted that "imponderables dust the air like volcanic ash," an introduction to an anchor report that recounted statistics of deaths, missing persons, and financial losses—"an event that defies superlatives." It might defy superlatives but not statistical comparisons. Noted Rather, citing "one geologist,"

"There is no record in geology in the last 4,000 years of anything like this happening before."

The CBS penchant for statistical detail continued unabated through the eruptions of May 24 and June 13. Viewers of the *Evening News* learned the exact temperature of the water in Spirit Lake (92° F), the weight of ash on highways in Washington (26,000 "tons"), the amount of ash removed from the Seattle airport (100,000 "tons"), the length of time that Mount St. Helens remained active following its eruption in the 19th century (30 years), timber losses ($250 million in national forests, $150 million outside national forests), highway repair costs ($40 million), dredging costs for the Columbia River ($32 million), shipping losses ($5 million per day), agricultural losses and unemployment benefit costs ($250 million each), the number of jobless as a result of the disaster (37,000), and much, much more. All in all, from an economic standpoint, this was "one of the half dozen biggest disasters of recent times," concluded one CBS report.

Recitation of dry statistics, whether relevant to narration or not, runs the risk of inundating viewers with information they may not be able to absorb. Whether for this reason or some other, CBS also adopted a secondary plot line. It consisted of a tale of life, one containing three facets. The first involved employing personification to speak of Mount St. Helens. The mountain was no inorganic hunk of rock for CBS but a living organism. The likeness was introduced early, in fact, on the opening evening of coverage on May 18. "Washington state's Mount St. Helens blew her top again," said anchor Morton Dean on the Sunday evening newscast ("again" was a reference to a minor display of activity a few days earlier). The phrase stuck; three days later correspondent Harold Dow also commented that the mountain "blew her top."

Anchor Dan Rather breathed even more life into the mountain. Taking note that two days after its first major eruption the volcano appeared serene, Rather cautioned it was but the "calm of a sleeping, still dangerous beast." Walter Cronkite by May 26 thought the mountain had finally "calmed down" but recanted two evenings later when he regarded the mountain as more of an agitated than a calm medical patient, one that must be studied with all the care of "doctors disputing an X-ray." One thing that made it so difficult to probe the mysterious ailment unsettling the patient was that the mountain wore a "shroud," that is, was covered with clouds. However, said correspondent Harold Dow on May 30, "the Lady of the Cascades removed her veil today," meaning that the clouds had moved away. Yet, five evenings later, even with veil removed, the mountain was giving a "veiled warning" of more volcanic activity. The warning grew more serious when the lady "put on another volcanic side-show" in mid-June. But after doing so she "seemed to simmer down," thought Cronkite.

Not everyone apparently agreed with Rather that the mountain, while a living being, was a beast. CBS, with other networks, celebrated Harry Truman, an 84-year-old caretaker of the Spirit Lake Lodge. CBS, in fact, labeled him "the old man of the mountain." Truman refused to leave the lodge area and as a result was killed with the first volcanic eruption. However, for Truman the mountain was an object of love, the meaning of his life. His death was contrasted with the continuing life of the mountain. Similarly, CBS dwelt on the story of the Seibold family who also died with the first eruption. "The mountain they loved so much brought death" to them, said correspondent Harold Dow in his report. Interviewing a surviving relative, Dow learned of "their love affair with Mount St. Helens." A friend spoke of them just as Harry Truman had talked of the mountain: "It was their home away from home; it would have been their choosing to have been there" (i.e., to be buried there).

There was life not only in the mountain but also among the people, even though "fallout fouled up life" with ash, said Dan Rather. Whether life was fouled up or not, the CBS version of how people were adjusting to their lives during and after Mount St. Helens "blew her top" was all upbeat. For CBS cameras a Spokane resident made light of "sleeping four in a Datsun"; tourists from Los Angeles who had traveled to Missoula, Montana, for the air joked that "it's worse than L. A."

Mount St. Helens

Films of people plagued with fallen ash depicted them as "in good spirits," sweeping walkways, driveways, and porches, washing their cars, and continuing their normal activities (even jogging) while wearing facemasks to protect against inhalation of the soot. In such spirits one motorist explained that he was able to travel unimpeded so long as he kept fluid in his windshield wiper-cleaner. Having run out of cleaning fluid, he said, he filled it with Coors beer instead.

The spirit of soldiering on that CBS implied was highlighted in a report from Toutle, Washington, about how residents were living in spite of the continuing threats of eruptions. "They still live in fear" but "are rugged people and quite self-sufficient" in their temporary tent encampment away from the mountain, reported the CBS correspondent. "It is trite to say this," the correspondent reported one resident of the tent city saying, "but life does go on." In the encampment life not only went on, however; a child was born and "life began for Michele Deckert the day Mount St. Helens blew, a day no one here will ever forget."

Life also went on in more ways than through grin-and-bear-it. On May 29, CBS featured a report from Portland, Oregon, concerning how people were profiting from sales of products exploiting the eruptions. This CBS called the "fallout of cash" and the "eruption of volcano products." The packaged film described all manner of baubles, trinkets, and toys—the Mount St. Helens ashtray, a pocket-sized version of Mount St. Helens that erupts with the aid of soda and vinegar; volcano tee-shirts, buttons, and frisbees. Vials of volcanic ash were alleged to be popular items. And "Captain Volcano," dressed in costume, was shown selling costume copies for anyone willing to buy.

The entrepreneurial life was matched in CBS reports by that of advertising and public relations. Aftermath stories from Portland and Spokane described the problems both cities were having in attracting tourists after the volcanic disaster. Interviews with officials in both cities led to the conclusion that there was more of a problem with public relations than with ash. So that life could return to normal, that is, in order to lure tourists again, the cities were undertaking advertising campaigns. These advertisements CBS reported in detail, including the presentation of one television ad in full about being "alive and well in Spokane."

CBS concluded its theme of the continuity of life later than it did its hyperfactual one. On June 22 reporter David Dow traveled to the volcano's mountainside. There he remarked, as anchor Morton Dean introduced the report, "life in the area reasserting itself." Films indicated "ferns poking up through the ash." And there were "fresh tracks of elks undaunted by the recent devastation." In fact, noted another report, "Some botanists even think the soil will eventually be enriched by the ash" and the post-disaster vegetation even more lush than before. Rather's slumbering beast, it seemed, had brought forth new, more abundant life.

NBC's *A*S*H*

From the viewpoint of style, NBC's coverage of the Mount St. Helens disaster contained many of the elements we encountered in the network's reports of other crises. To begin with, NBC relied upon a conversational approach, an informal style of reporting less strictly empirical than CBS in expression, less strident than ABC. This is not to say that the network eschewed facts, rather that it did not overpower the viewer with them nor report them without a familiar point of reference. For example, in reporting the first eruption on May 18, anchor Jessica Savitch provided distances from the mountain that both the explosion could be seen (50 miles) and tremors could be felt (200 miles). But these figures were secondary to the fact that the explosion could be seen in "Vancouver, Washington, to the south" and "tremors could be felt in Vancouver, British Columbia," to the north. In sum, data were placed in a familiar context.

NBC reporters pursued a conversational approach in a variety of ways. One involved the use of colloquialisms—the mountain "blew up with a bang," a car was "pelted with pea-sized mudballs," the lava dome beginning to form in June was "a stopper on the bottle,'' or, as John Chancellor said, ''the Mount St. Helens volcano is still at it today.''

A second technique consisted of what we have noted in NBC coverage of the crash of Flight 191 and of the TMI crisis—interviews involving one or more people simply talking in a relaxed, informal way, either to one another or to a correspondent. Examples abound: children conversing with one another in an evacuation camp, rescue workers talking to each other while in the cockpit of a flying helicopter, a conversation with a young man running to board a helicopter so that he can join a search party, an exchange with a rescue worker as he is preoccupied with washing down his aircraft, a woman describing how valuable her photo album is to her and how she has packed it carefully away in case she must evacuate quickly, or a mother conversing with her small child as she fits the offspring with a face mask.

Yet a third form that NBC informality takes is to roll film showing some objects or activities but with an oral report having nothing to do with the film. Thus, viewers see a line of helicopters sitting on the ground with rotary blades turning, but the voice-over describes families signing up for federal disaster aid. Or, as was often the case, filmed fly-overs of devastated areas provide a visual context within which largely unrelated topics are reported—costs of rescue missions, closed shipping ports, etc.

Finally, the conversational approach includes humor. On the evening of May 22, John Chancellor reported that Senator Mark Hatfield of Oregon had been caught in Spokane as a result of the fallout of volcanic ash. Unable to fly, he took a taxi to Seattle. Chancellor recognized that Hatfield would not soon forget the experience, but neither would the taxi driver. ''It's not often he gets a $450 fare,'' commented Chancellor.

Such a reporting style tends to minimize any state of urgency about a reported crisis, perhaps—although we do not know—providing a possible calming effect. So too does another stylistic characteristic of the *NBC Nightly News* we have noted earlier, namely, that of taking a long-range view of things, focusing upon historical context and multicausality. Aside from anchor Dan Rather's reference to eruptions at Mount Vesuvius and another CBS correspondent's remark about activity at Mount St. Helens in the 1800s, that network provided no historical background to current events, nor did it speak of causes for what was happening. ABC ignored such matters. But such contexts were key features of NBC coverage.

The first was on May 21. Like the other networks, NBC grew interested in potential weather changes resulting from volcanic eruptions. As we have mentioned, CBS set that question to rest during an interview in Washington, D.C., with an expert from the National Weather Service. The NBC report on the subject had several interesting facets. For one, it originated not from Washington, D.C., but from the National Center for Atmospheric Research in Boulder, Colorado. NBC ran films of "government scientists flying through the clouds of ash and smoke trying to find out what the volcano is putting into our atmosphere." The NBC correspondent quickly noted that "explosions like those at Krakatoa in 1883 cooled the entire world for as long as two years." But, unlike the CBS conclusion that such was unlikely in this case, NBC noted that researchers were "uncertain." As film rolled, showing people working with computers and checking instruments at a government observatory in Hawaii, the correspondent described how such researchers build models for purposes of projecting weather. Illustrative models then appeared for viewers. Concluded the correspondent, "They will be studying this eruption for years."

NBC again focused on the long view a week later. In a 4½ minute "Special Segment" report, NBC probed the "causes of the May 18 eruptions." NBC correspondent Robert Bazell took note that the volcanos in the Cascades chain had been formed "tens of millions of years ago." With diagrams he explained how the movements of "plates" one under another related to "magma" (molten rock) formation and eruptions—"it can be every 25 years or every 1,000 years, no one knows why." Bazell drew contrasts between eruptions of volcanos in Hawaii and that of Mount St. Helens, and why the latter was much more explosive. But "it could take years" to understand what happened, and research "will continue for decades."

The historical and causal emphasis continued to mark NBC coverage following later eruptions of Mount St. Helens. On June 1 viewers learned that "The Indians called it 'Fire Mountain' " and that there was a long-term concern with its potential danger. The NBC correspondent went on to read an excerpt from a diary of the editor of an Oregon newspaper written in "the mid-1800s, the last time Mount St. Helens erupted." It said "The mountain is struggling to be released. The mind of the beholder is impressed with the insignificance of the human power when compared with nature's God." Concluded the correspondent, "The same could be written today."

On the day of the June 13 eruption, NBC again put things into perspective. This time viewers were instructed in the relation of earth, moon, quakes, and eruptions. Correspondent Robert Bazell sought to find out if the most likely time for an eruption was the appearance of a new moon. Bazell noted that each eruption at Mount St. Helens had come close to the appearance of a full moon. Using graphics showing the relationship of earth, moon, and sun, Bazell described the role of "earth tide," or gravitational pulls between the three bodies. Bazell's interview with a geologist contributed the view that tidal forces might trigger, but not necessarily cause, eruptions. Similarly, Bazell probed the relationship of earthquakes and eruptions. Again he turned to historical record, pointing out that in 1857 there was one of the biggest earthquakes in California's history "when Mount St. Helens was last active." But, concluded Bazell, "The scientists say they are still a long way from making accurate predictions."

Such was the conversational and contextual approach of NBC coverage. Balanced against this calm, dispassionate style, however, was one thematic element suggesting that there was still danger in the Mount St. Helens eruptions. That was NBC's story of the fallout of volcanic ash. Both CBS and ABC carried reports on ash fallout, but far fewer than NBC and with a milder point. For those networks the ash was an inconvenience people had to endure; for NBC ash was a continuing threat.

Anchor Jessica Savitch first spoke of the problem on May 18 as "a poisonous gas cloud." She reported that "workers were being issued gas masks." The follow-up package report stated that the "volcano spewed out a huge cloud of ash two miles across and ten miles high." It was the ash cloud that blinded a pilot, resulting in his death in a crash. Ash produced dark skies and closed highways.

The ash problem was singled out for treatment again on the *NBC Nightly News* the next evening. Ash figured prominently in all four news reports. "Dust so thick some people wore gas masks" as far away as Portland, said the first. Describing it as a "fine, slippery, powdery ash," anchor David Brinkley charted the potential movement of the ash cloud through the area and "to the east coast." A follow-up report traced the movement through Wyoming and to Denver, leaving in its wake stalled cars, cancelled air flights, damaged windshields. "Scientists said this ash could be around for years," the NBC correspondent concluded.

Whether the substance would be around for years or not, NBC kept ash around in its news reports almost every evening thereafter. First was the narrative of what the "fine, powdery ash" does, "drifting for miles and destroying the landscape as it goes" (Brinkley). NBC blamed ash for destroying Spirit Lake, near Mount St. Helens, by turning it to mud. Brinkley listed what ash did elsewhere—"clogs automobile engines, is slippery to walk on and to drive on, dangerous to breathe," and creates "a set of problems never seen before." Those problems, shown in packaged reports, involved cars, trucks, and airports. "It's been like a midwest blizzard, except this stuff won't melt away," said an NBC reporter. But that was not all, for fallout threatened the Yakima Valley's fruit crops, as was demonstrated in a filmed report of fruitgrowers inspecting trees and washing them down with hoses.

In successive nights NBC stayed with the ash theme. Ash was smothering crops, threatening fish, making logging impossible. The ash might influence weather ("Nobody is sure," said Brinkley). President Jimmy Carter's visit to view the devastation was affected as "the dust kicked up by Air Force One was evidence of the problems to be faced for months to come." (In contrast, ABC news merely took note of "a little dust on the runway.")

On May 24, NBC news moved volcanic ash to even a higher order of threat. Now human health was threatened. Beginning his packaged report from Ritzville, Washington, an NBC correspondent said the city "now calls itself the ash capital of the world." Film showed National Guard troops cleaning roofs of ash to assure that they would not collapse if rains came. But, said the correspondent, "Hospital officials here and elsewhere are suddenly more worried about the roof falling in on the health of the community." The high silicone content of the ash might produce lung disease. But an interview with a local physician stated that "it would be a matter of years" before it was known for sure. He suggested that in the meantime people wear face masks for six months but doubted that the advice would be followed.

With the second eruption at Mount St. Helens, anchor Jessica Savitch reported the ash spreading toward the south and toward the Pacific. With the third eruption of June 13, the ash, said David Brinkley, "spread in all directions." In the case of these later ash flows, NBC identified other serious effects. Ash forced people off the roads and into motels; once there, they had to eat by candlelight because of power failures produced by the falling ash. "Seven hours of ash being blown up into the area," said John Chancellor, constituted danger. Stores sold out of facemasks, according to NBC reports, but even wearing them was no guarantee of avoiding health problems, since such masks did not screen out the smallest particles of dust.

And, reported NBC, falling ash was a threat to airlines. The network featured this danger after the June 13 eruption. So great was the problem that the Federal Aviation Administration, according to NBC, "was tracking the ash cloud and warning pilots to steer clear of it." Administrator Langhorne Bond, having weathered the fallout of the DC-10 crisis, had now to deal with ash fallout. "This stuff is terrible on airplanes," said Bond in an interview.

Rare was the evening when NBC did not feature the ash problem. When 73-year-old Ray Jennings was brought down from the southern side of Mount St. Helens after refusing to leave his cabin for 13 days, NBC made it clear that he would return "after the ash had cleared." When a local resident's chickens stopped laying eggs, her cows refused to eat, and "peas and beans would not come in as in the past," it was volcanic ash that NBC cited as the reason. So rare was it that NBC did not feature an ash report that, even if anchors found the volcano "quiet," that meant "no ash spewed forth today."

There is no doubt that ash was a major problem throughout the region surrounding Mount St. Helens. If, as Robert Bazell reported on May 27—even before the June 13 eruption—enough ash fell to amount to "a ton for each person on earth," a news network could scarcely discount the newsworthiness of it. What is noteworthy, however, is that ash dominated NBC's coverage. For that network, ash was the story of Mount St. Helens, not life as for CBS or death (as we shall see) for ABC.

On June 26 David Brinkley reported that residents in the area around Mount St. Helens "now see the eruptions as history." Said Washington Governor Dixy Lee Ray in an interview, "The impression's been created throughout the country that somehow we're all buried up to our armpits in ash. That is not true at all. Large areas of the state were not affected, of course. In those areas where the ash did fall, it's not a health hazard, it is a nuisance." Perhaps people who thought otherwise had been watching *NBC Nightly News*.

ABC's Tragic Melodrama

ABC's coverage of the eruptions of Mount St. Helens on *World News Tonight* was distinctive for its focus upon melodramatic features: the death of victims, the search for survivors, the spirit of heroes, and the plight of fools. "The Mount St. Helens volcano continues to darken the skies for hundreds of miles and slash a path of death and destruction across the ground," said anchor Frank Reynolds in the first ABC report on the disaster, aired on May 19. Max Robinson followed with the only set of statistics that ABC continued to emphasize in its coverage, the toll of dead and missing. The figures changed from newscast to newscast, but like NBC's focus on ash and CBS's on life, this feature provided a unifying theme for ABC coverage.

ABC took account of the essentials that rival networks had included in their first reports: the magnitude of the explosion, spewing steam and ash, mudslides, and walls of flood water. With respect to the ash, ABC noted that there were "special problems" (clogged auto engines), but "there is no special health hazard because it is volcanic ash." There would be "normal physiological reactions," ABC reported "officials" as saying. Anchor Max Robinson speculated that the ash cloud might have an impact on world weather patterns, but probably only if it concentrated over the North Pole.

Again the following evening the focus was on the toll of victims rather than other facets of the story. Frank Reynolds reported that "officials have now drastically revised their estimate of the death toll," up from five to six, with the number of missing persons rising from 21 to 100. "The great cloud of ash" that Reynolds reported drifting across the country was not causing "serious problems." For ABC it was the eruption itself that had been "devastating." The impact of ash in the atmosphere was, by comparison, "hardly a drop in the geological bucket."

But if ash was more inconvenience than threat, were there any other sources of future alarm? ABC found a few. One was the ever-changing toll of victims: ten lives lost as reported by the network on May 21, now 75 persons unaccounted for. And there was "still the threat that the mountain might erupt again," noted a packaged report that same evening. Finally, there was a report of an earthen dam "that might give way," threatening an area of 50,000 residents. Interviews with those residents, however, found them brave in the face of danger. Eleven-year-old Christine Cox, ABC reported, had a "newfound feeling of security." In an interview typical of ABC's human focus on popular response to crisis, she said, "Daddy's okay and our house is okay and puppy's okay and I'm not very worried."

As the crisis of Mount St. Helens grew, ABC shifted its focus slightly from "scenes of devastation" (as one correspondent called it) and death tolls to the search for survivors. By May 23, ABC had the count of missing at 88 persons. "Helicopter crews continue their search for survivors," said Frank Reynolds, "but today, as expected, they found more victims." Playing on this theme, ABC narrated tales of personal tragedy and irony. Cameras captured a Forest Service official relating "a scene of death and new life." The official told of how a tree had fallen on a man as he sought to rescue his dog. The dog had remained pinned by the tree for four days, but searchers found it alive and it had given birth to pups in the meantime.

Following the second eruption of the volcano, ABC stuck with its melodrama of searching for the dead. "Heavy clouds hampered search and rescue missions," reported Max Robinson on May 26 after the eruption of the preceding day. But, even though the ash from that second eruption spread across the region, again it was not viewed as an immediate or long-term danger. "Motorists concerned about the health of their engines" seemed unconcerned about any threat of this inconvenience to their own health. The following evening's narration once more focused on the death toll; rescue helicopters had by then recovered 21 bodies.

By the day of the third eruption, June 13, the search for victims of the first had ended. ABC noted there were no victims of the latest eruption, then turned to the possibility of a new threat: there was every likelihood of future eruptions "that could cause problems for a nuclear power plant only 30 miles from the volcano." But that was the sole mention of that possibility and, thereafter, ABC carried only two more reports on the volcano during the period under study. The final one returned, in passing, to the death scene. Taking account of all the destruction and death that had taken place "on the mountain," the ABC correspondent who had been allowed to fly there, felt good that "life has returned."

Sociologist Orrin Klapp (1962) has noted that any dramatistic analysis endeavors to identify the heroes, villains, and fools of the plot. And, if there are victims, those too enter into the account. In ABC's coverage of the natural disaster at Mount St.

Helens identification is not difficult. There were two types of victims: the dead who lost their lives at the time of the eruption and the living whose lives were seriously affected by the disaster. For ABC's *World News Tonight,* a typical example of the latter was Rodney Hudson, a farmer singled out by ABC to represent the fate of all farmers affected by the destruction. Hudson worried that fallen ash might have affected his crops and livestock. "Farmers have no idea how to deal with the ash," said the correspondent. But Hudson "would stick with it, no matter what." Said he, "It's a way of life you can't get rid of." The packaged report closed with a film of Hudson walking slowly up a farm path, followed by his dog.

Or there was "a man like Frank," an independent logger who suffered losses both from the eruption and from the ash fallout on his logging camp. With each minor kickup of dust, the ABC reporter said, the logger would have to shut down the camp. "Truckers can't haul logs because of the dust, and loggers can't log because of it, and people are scared to go close to the mountain; there's a lot of problems," said the logger.

ABC treated one group as acting in a foolish way during the crisis. A film crew led by Otto Sieber had violated restrictions on hiking into the Spirit Lake regions prior to the second eruption on May 25. When they were given the opportunity to be coptered out, they refused. Staying in the area, the five-man crew grew "hungry, exhausted, and cold," and were rescued by two army helicopter crews "who risked their lives to bring them out." The ABC correspondent commented, "Rescue officials were not pleased by their venture. The five would not have survived another day."

Of course we need not search far to discover the villain in the ABC melodrama—that was the mountain itself. But it was not the living "beast" of CBS, nor was the volcano simply a volcano as for NBC. Instead, Mount St. Helens was the sanctioning agent that made the whole drama possible, just as James Jones had made Guyana possible, nuclear technology had made TMI possible, and a "suspect bolt" had made the crash of Flight 191 possible. And just as there was speculation that Jones might still be alive, TMI still radioactive, and bolts escaping inspection, ABC's coverage did not suggest that the eruptions were growing less dangerous.

For the hero of the melodrama ABC fastened on the dramatis persona of Harry Truman, the caretaker of Spirit Lake Lodge. All three networks carried some comment on Truman. CBS made one reference to him, NBC two. But ABC gave Truman a role to play from the beginning and returned to him, even devoting one lengthy report solely to Truman. In its first report on May 19, ABC stated that 21 persons were missing after the first eruption, Harry Truman among them. Four days later, when ABC reported that 88 were now missing, the network correspondent again mentioned that Harry Truman was one of them. Then, on June 3, ABC devoted a three-minute report to the "crusty old man."

Whereas CBS had labeled Truman the "old man of the mountain," thus identifying his living being with that of the volcano, ABC focused upon Truman as the rugged individualist, a man who heroically lived and died for his beliefs. The ABC profile relied upon an interview with Truman filmed on March 30. Correspondent Stephen Geer stressed that Truman was 83 years of age although "he liked to claim 84," and had always said that if the volcano erupted he could row across Spirit Lake and escape. Moreover, said Geer, Truman had a cave with "a couple of cases of whiskey in it" as a precaution. But Geer added, "That wasn't true, and there was no escape." By the time of the explosion, Truman had "already become a legend." Would he leave the area? "When you've lived over fifty years in one place that's your home and you've built this god-damned place and pioneered this, and cut the trees out, and went through with what I went through, you think, well hell, I'm not goin' to leave. It'd kill me. If I left this place and left this home, I'd die in a week. I couldn't live. I couldn't stand it. So, I'm like that old captain. By God, I'm goin' down with the ship."

Geer went on with the report. "The legend of Harry Truman continues to grow." There followed a ballad about Harry being played on local radio stations, a ballad with the lines, "Oh, Harry Truman, your Spirit Lake is gone, but, Oh, Harry Truman, your spirit still lives on and on and on." Geer continued with film of a visit Truman had made to an elementary school in Salem, Oregon. Geer had visited the school for himself. He found "Harry's spirit was contagious." Said one schoolboy on film, "I wouldn't want to leave my home because of a silly old volcano." Geer closed with an interview of Harry's sister, Geraldine, who assured him that, for Harry, "It went just the way he wanted it."

There was one other facet of the real-fiction developed by ABC about the volcanic eruptions at Mount St. Helens. It was self-serving and cast ABC in heroic guise. The network correspondents informed viewers and reminded them that ABC had the first film crews to "go to the edge" of the crater, to "journey to the center" of the crater, and to "report the formation of a lava dome." The last report, like NBC's that residents "now see the eruptions as history," and CBS's "life returns to Mount St. Helens," was the conclusion of the drama. The tale of death, search, and destruction with real-life heroes, villains, victims, and fools had closed.

Mount St. Helens as an NBC Visual Feature

Looking back on coverage of other crises reported in this book, it is not an exaggeration to say that The People's Temple was an NBC story. The network broke the story, conducted a live satellite interview with its own field producer who was part of the story, and had by far the most extensive film coverage of events at Port Kaituma and Jonestown. ABC and CBS were left to cover the crisis from afar and in more indirect fashion. As technological tales, by contrast, TMI and DC-10 crises were more congenial to CBS's emphasis upon facts, experts, and official coping. With Mount St. Helens we encounter another made-for-NBC miniseries. That is apparent in the network's narrative of events. It is also apparent in how NBC distinguished itself from the other networks in gathering news and making visual presentations, in style, and in news content.

To begin with, Table 4.1 shows that to a significant degree

Nightly Horrors: Television Network News

Table 4.1
Newsgathering Modes for Mount St. Helens News Reports: by Network

Modes	ABC	CBS	NBC	Combined
Locale				
Network studio	24 (53%)	35 (54%)	36 (54%)	95 (54%)
Government office	3 (7%)	1 (1%)	1 (1%)	5 (2%)
Private home/office	15 (33%)	25 (39%)	16 (24%)	56 (32%)
Crisis site	3 (7%)	4 (6%)	14 (21%)	21 (12%)
χ^2 = 12.843 with 6 df; p = .05.				
Source (when identified)				
Public official	23 (45%)	37 (47%)	31 (38%)	91 (43%)
Technician/scientist	10 (20%)	17 (22%)	19 (23%)	46 (22%)
Interest group leader	3 (6%)	5 (4%)	10 (12%)	18 (8%)
Average citizen	15 (29%)	20 (25%)	21 (27%)	56 (27%)
Means				
Briefing by public official	18 (35%)	23 (28%)	27 (38%)	68 (35%)
Speech by public official	3 (6%)	5 (6%)	5 (7%)	13 (7%)
Interview with public official	5 (10%)	18 (22%)	7 (10%)	30 (16%)
Interview with interest group leader	9 (18%)	10 (13%)	15 (30%)	30 (16%)
Interview with average citizen	15 (29%)	20 (25%)	21 (30%)	46 (24%)
Reporter quoting a source	1 (2%)	5 (6%)	0	6 (2%)

NBC placed the setting of its coverage more at the crisis site than did its rivals. To a much lesser extent, this had also been so with the Jonestown crisis. Of course, the locale of most network coverage remained with the anchors, the resident storytellers, in network studios. And none of the networks stayed in government offices to tell what was happening at Mount St. Helens, although public officials and technicians or scientists were key sources of information for the news networks. Where NBC differed was in reliance on crisis site reporting while minimizing the nonstudio locale preferred by ABC and CBS, i.e., the private residence, office, or place of business.

NBC also was set apart in its coverage, although not to a significant degree, by the sources relied upon for information and how it came by that information. As with the DC-10 crisis, NBC turned to interest group spokespersons for information and interviewed such persons as a means of gathering news more than did competing networks in their coverage. Lumbering interests, fishing interests, recreational interests, chambers of commerce representatives—all provided opportunities for NBC correspondents to put the series of volcanic eruptions and their effects into a pluralist context more diverse than that emerging solely from basing news upon governing officials as informants. CBS, in contrast, stuck with tried-and-true network sources through briefings and interviews with public officials to a greater degree than did either NBC or ABC.

From the perspective of visual presentation, we again find as we turn to Table 4.2 no significant differences between networks in the use of alternative visual elements in their coverage. Close inspection does reveal, however, that when films were rolled during stories and when networks cut to packaged stories, NBC generally employed interviews in a higher proportion of its stories than did the other networks. The exception was when only one film was rolled during the story. Granted that such differences between NBC and the other networks in use of these visual elements are small, but that they do exist contributes overall to the fact that the *NBC Nightly News*—as in the case of TMI and DC-10 coverage—gave more visual emphasis to the Mount St. Helens crisis. Turning once again to visual prominence scores, we find the differences between networks significant. Scores ranged from 0–53. The mean scores of networks (ABC = 22, CBS = 20, NBC = 24) differed with F-ratios significant, $p = .01$.

The stylistic differences observed between networks in coverage of other crises continued in the case of the Mount St. Helens eruptions (Table 4.3). ABC again had populist stylistic leanings. Indeed, the heroic portrayal of Harry Truman was a prime example of the populist element in that overall stylistic tradition. CBS retained its more factually oriented style, as we noted in its narrative of the facts of life. But CBS anchors contributed two-thirds of such reports as the network carried that could be classified as populist/sensationalist in orientation. There is a point of minor interest here: Dan Rather, sitting in for Walter Cronkite, did much of his network's anchor work during the Mount St. Helens crisis. It is noteworthy that in the anchor role he performed in much the same fashion as Cronkite, i.e., with an occasional tendency to promote what viewers might

Nightly Horrors: Television Network News

Table 4.2
Visual Elements in Mount St. Helens Stories: by Network

Visual elements of story	ABC	CBS	NBC	Combined
Anchor read story	23 (52%)	37 (56%)	34 (53%)	94 (54%)
Cut to packaged report(s)				
One or more, without interview	7 (11%)	7 (7%)	2 (3%)	16 (6%)
One or more, with interview	14 (22%)	22 (22%)	28 (29%)	64 (25%)
Graphic over anchor/reporter shoulder				
None	44 (69%)	71 (72%)	70 (73%)	185 (71%)
One	16 (25%)	20 (20%)	25 (26%)	61 (24%)
Two or more	4 (6%)	8 (8%)	1 (1%)	13 (5%)
Still picture/graphic on total screen				
None	61 (94%)	90 (91%)	88 (92%)	239 (92%)
One	2 (4%)	2 (4%)	4 (4%)	8 (3%)
Two or more	1 (2%)	7 (7%)	4 (4%)	12 (5%)
Film rolled during story				
None	43 (67%)	69 (70%)	63 (66%)	175 (68%)
Film, without interview	11 (17%)	23 (23%)	22 (23%)	56 (22%)
Film, with interview	10 (16%)	7 (7%)	11 (11%)	28 (10%)
Second film during story				
None	50 (78%)	73 (74%)	67 (70%)	192 (74%)
Film, without interview	6 (9%)	8 (8%)	8 (10%)	23 (9%)
Film, with interview	8 (13%)	18 (18%)	20 (20%)	46 (17%)

otherwise find to be less interesting follow-up reports. Finally, it is also significant that of NBC's didactic reports all were from the network's anchors; of the network's features all but one came from correspondents.

The distribution of coverage across and between networks changes relatively little when length of coverage rather than number of reports becomes the measuring unit. One point, however, merits brief comment. It pertains to the total amount of time devoted by each of the three networks to the Mount St. Helens story. For ABC that was little more than three-quarters of an hour, for CBS and NBC an hour each. As with the other crises examined in these pages, ABC devoted less time to reports about Mount St. Helens than did other networks. A partial explanation is that ABC has but one weekend evening newscast. Even if that is taken into account, however, ABC devoted less coverage to the crises in question, perhaps because of the network's multianchor system. Since ABC has an overseas anchor who must be fitted into the evening newscast, it may

Table 4.3
Coverage Styles in Mount St. Helens Crisis:
by Networks, Anchors, Correspondents

Reports	ABC	CBS	NBC	Combined
Total number	45	65	67	177
Anchors	24 (53%)	39 (60%)	36 (54%)	95 (54%)
Correspondents	21 (47%)	26 (40%)	31 (46%)	82 (46%)
Style (by number of reports):				
Populist/sensationalist	31 (69%)	18 (28%)	9 (13%)	58 (33%)
Anchors	16	12	8	36
Correspondents	15	6	1	22
Elitist/factual	7 (16%)	43 (66%)	15 (22%)	65 (37%)
Anchors	7	22	12	41
Correspondents	0	21	3	24
Ignorant/didactic	2 (7%)	1 (1%)	15 (22%)	18 (11%)
Anchors	1	1	15	17
Correspondents	1	0	0	1
Pluralist/feature	4 (8%)	3 (5%)	28 (43%)	35 (19%)
Anchors	0	0	1	1
Correspondents	4	3	27	34
Total time of coverage (in minutes)	46	65	64	175
Anchors	9 (20%)	15 (23%)	12 (19%)	36 (20%)
Correspondents	37 (80%)	50 (77%)	52 (81%)	139 (80%)
Style duration (in minutes)				
Populist/sensationalist	33 (71%)	14 (22%)	4 (6%)	51 (29%)
Anchors	6	4	2	12
Correspondents	27	10	2	39
Factual/elitist	2 (4%)	44 (68%)	9 (14%)	55 (31%)
Anchors	2	10	4	16
Correspondents	0	34	5	39
Ignorant/didactic	3 (8%)	1 (1%)	5 (8%)	9 (6%)
Anchors	1	1	5	7
Correspondents	2	0	0	2
Pluralist/feature	8 (17%)	6 (9%)	46 (72%)	60 (34%)
Anchors	0	0	1	1
Correspondents	8	6	45	59

Significant differences are as follows:
1. Between networks for number of reports per style χ^2 = 93.443 with 6 df; p = .001.
2. Between networks for duration of reports per style χ^2 = 130.316 with 6 df; p = .001.
3. Between networks for number of anchor reports per style χ^2 = 32.695 with 6 df; p = .001.
4. Between networks for number of correspondent reports per style χ^2 = 78.244 with 6 df; p = .001.
5. Between networks for duration of anchor reports per style χ^2 = 13.828 with 6 df; p = .05.
6. Between networks for duration of correspondent reports per style χ^2 = 127.770 with 6 df; p = .001.

Nightly Horrors: Television Network News

Table 4.4
News Content of Mount St. Helens Reports: by Network

Content Types	ABC	CBS	NBC	Combined
News value				
News	6 (13%)	9 (14%)	20 (30%)	35 (20%)
Peripheral	28 (62%)	31 (48%)	22 (32%)	81 (46%)
Perspective	7 (16%)	13 (20%)	17 (26%)	37 (21%)
News/peripheral	4 (9%)	8 (12%)	6 (9%)	18 (10%)
News/perspective	0	4 (6%)	2 (3%)	6 (3%)
Emotional content				
Reassuring	9 (20%)	20 (31%)	31 (46%)	60 (34%)
Alarming	18 (40%)	26 (40%)	12 (18%)	56 (32%)
Neutral	18 (40%)	19 (19%)	24 (36%)	61 (34%)

$\chi^2 = 13.151$ with 4 df; p = .02.

have less time available for coverage of domestic crises. We will reconsider that possibility when we turn to the Iranian hostage crisis in Chapter 5.

Finally, NBC's coverage also emerges as distinctive when we consider the content of coverage from perspectives of news values and emotional content. As indicated in Table 4.4, the data concerning the distribution of news, peripheral, and perspective characteristics reveal no significant differences among networks. NBC appears to have had more straight news in its coverage and more perspective material placing the factual material into a larger context. That this would be in keeping with the heavy emphasis upon a pluralist/feature style by the network is suggested by data in Table 4.3. To test this possibility we recalculated the data in Table 4.4 by collapsing it into three categories: news, peripheral plus news/peripheral, and perspective plus news/perspective. When we do so, we get a χ^2 of 11.944 with 4 df; $p = .02$. The suspicion that NBC did differ from competing networks is plausible. NBC also had a significantly higher percentage of reassuring reports about Mount St. Helens and smaller percentage of alarming reports than did ABC or CBS, again setting its coverage off in a distinctive fashion.

In sum, then, we repeat that the crisis of Mount St. Helens was an NBC story, or at least the network in both dramatistic and journalistic ways went about covering the crisis in a way unlike either CBS or ABC. Let us now turn, then, to a crisis that many observers of TV network news asserted was basically one that helped ABC's *World News Tonight* reach parity and even surpass its rivals at some points in viewer popularity, the Iranian hostage crisis. Was it indeed an ABC story?

Chapter Five

Hostages in Iran: Television Coverage of a Political Crisis

The events comprising the 444 days of what the three television news networks labeled "The Hostage Crisis" defy brief description. Even a précis of the key scenes in the lengthy drama would constitute a bulky playbill. To list just a few:

- The U.S. Embassy in Teheran was seized on November 4, 1979. Sixty-six persons became prisoners—13 were released before the end of the month, another in July 1980, and the remainder, after complex negotiations, on January 20, 1981.
- In the first month of the crisis, the U.S. halted delivery of $300 million in military equipment to Iran, ordered that Iranian students illegally in the U.S. be deported, suspended oil imports from Iran, and froze all Iranian assets in U.S. banks and overseas branches.
- Also in the first month of the crisis Iran cancelled treaties with the U.S., tried to withdraw assets deposited in U.S. banks, and threatened to put the hostages on trial.
- The former Shah of Iran, who had fled into exile after the successful revolution led by Ayatollah Khomeini, flew to Panama, then Egypt. That the former Shah had been admitted into the U.S. for medical treatment on October 22, 1979, had been the justification for seizing the hostages. They would be

released, said Iran, when the former Shah was returned to Iran.

- In early 1980 six Americans working in the U.S. Embassy in Teheran, but sheltered secretly by the Canadian Embassy, returned safely to the U.S. "Thank You, Canada" was the reponse popularized in this nation's news media.
- Negotiations, sanctions, a review of events by a United Nations commission, and pleas by hostage family members, various emissaries, and celebrities marked efforts to free the hostages throughout early 1980, coinciding with the conduct of presidential primaries in the U.S.
- On April 25, 1980, a commando team aborted a rescue effort on orders of President Carter after equipment failures. In the aftermath Iranian leaders threatened death to the hostages should another effort be mounted and had a public display of bodies of U.S. servicemen killed in the attempt. U.S. Secretary of State Cyrus Vance resigned protesting the mission; he was replaced by U.S. Senator Edmund Muskie.
- In July 1980 the deposed Shah of Iran died in Cairo.
- In September 1980 Iran set terms for the hostages' release: the U.S. must yield the assets of the former Shah, cancel financial claims against Iran, release Iran's frozen assets, and promise no interference in Iran's internal affairs.
- In November 1980 a team of U.S. officials opened negotiations in Algeria, a nation acting as an intermediary, and accepted in principle Iranian terms "as a basis for resolution of the crisis." The team, led by Deputy Secretary of State Warren Christopher, continued negotiations into early 1981.
- On January 18, 1981, Behzad Nabavi, the chief Iranian negotiator, announced that an agreement had been reached "on resolving the issue of the hostages."
- At 12:25 p.m. (EST), after a series of complications and one-half hour after Jimmy Carter left office, the hostages boarded two Algerian aircraft and left Teheran. Departure of the planes from Iranian air space was the signal to consummate the final financial aspects of the negotiated settlement.
- Once the hostages had arrived in West Germany for medical

examinations and care, there were outcries from U.S. officials about reports of Iranian torture and brutality. The hostages returned to the U.S. on January 25. Two days later they were honored with a motorcade in Washington, D.C.

Such is the leanest of scenarios for the hostage crisis. Each act, and many more, both central and peripheral to the drama, played before nationwide television news audiences in what a former Under Secretary of State, George Ball, told *Newsweek* in an interview in 1980 was "the greatest soap opera of the year." Ball was not the only one to comment on televised news coverage of the hostage crisis. Journalists, television critics, and scholars have explored facets of what many concurred was "a TV story."

Peter Funt, for instance, writing in *Saturday Review* (1980), criticized television coverage for distorting the nightly images of anti-American protests from Teheran. Less than two blocks from where television films of demonstrations were originating, pictures giving a sense of a nation in turmoil, there was business as usual—vendors selling their wares, shoppers browsing casually, and people coming and going. Haynes Johnson of *The Washington Post* argued that television "made it almost impossible not to respond" to the hostages; thus the "hostage drama preoccupied, if not paralyzed, the public business of the nation as no other single episode in our history over a comparable length of time" (January 25, 1981, p. A3).

Edward Said (1981), after sifting through coverage of the hostage crisis in major newspapers, news magazines, and television, concluded that the news portrayed episodic attitudes toward events rather than a sense of long-term trends that might explain what was going on. Such episodes were more for the benefit of the "suspicious and frightened" than for understanding the background of class conflict, imperialism, religious disputes, and social patterns in Iran contributing to the crisis. Said cites the example of crowds in Teheran chanting "God is great," while ABC anchor Frank Reynolds' voice-over suggested their true intention was "hatred of America," as an instance of lack of understanding (p. 78).

Edward Diamond (1982) shares the view that the three nightly networks overplayed the hostage story and contributed to misunderstanding rather than understanding. His analysis suggests that the networks could have followed an alternative to their "crisis" scenario. By modulating their coverage, they could have avoided being used by the Iranian militants for self-serving purposes, such as staged media events and photo opportunities. Instead, networks' interests in viewer ratings coincided with demonstrators' interests in publicizing grievances. So, says Diamond, "early hostage coverage" was "the familiar pattern of the blockbuster story." First, the Big Event: John Lennon Shot Dead. Then, furious pursuit of that story until both it and audience are exhausted. "Then we want change, any change; there's been too much coverage" (p. 116).

Communications scientist David Altheide (1981a; 1981b; 1982) has compared the three major networks' nightly newscasts of portions of the hostage crisis. He argues that the formats, content, and potential effects of the three networks' coverage differed little. In format each network employed the anchor to introduce and summarize a story, an on-the-scene correspondent to report details, and various live, filmed, or taped visuals. Each network's content included pictures of demonstrating crowds, a pro-U.S. point of view, and negative world reaction to the hostage seizure while ignoring its background and context, especially the religious and revolutionary dimensions. Despite unprecedented coverage, noted Altheide, it was not true that "the more you watch the more you know," but, to the contrary, the probable effects are "well-informed ignorance" (1981b, p. 156).

Finally, rhetorical critic Ernest Bormann (1982), in a fantasy theme analysis of two breaking news events—the inauguration of President Ronald Reagan at the time of the release of the hostages from Iran—has demonstrated how televised news coverage contributed to the viewers sharing in a fantasy of "restoration." At the precise moment when Reagan's inaugural address was calling for the restoration of fundamental American values and, thereby, greatness, televised coverage of the release provided a drama of rebirth and recommitment underscoring the Reagan message. Day 1 of freedom for the hostages and

Day 1 of a new presidency combined in an overall fantasy of a restored nation.

As with televised coverage of the other crises explored in this book, our intention is to examine each network's unfolding narrative. However, we limit ourselves to three scenes in the drama: coverage of the seizure of the embassy in Teheran, the rescue attempt, and the release of the hostages. Are there differences between network narratives that transcend these three stories, are there different real-fictions for each event, or did the networks present consistent views of the hostage crisis?

ABC Asks Who Is in Charge, Finds Nobody

The State Department is doing what it can, but for the moment, at least, that doesn't appear to be much.

(Ted Koppel, November 4)

The U.S. does not have a great number of options in dealing with a very sensitive situation in which there is no central authority.

(Barry Dunsmore, November 5)

Since this crisis began, the U.S. government hasn't had a great deal of leverage in Iran. Now it has even less. So the U.S. government, deeply concerned about the welfare of those sixty-odd Americans inside the embassy compound, is reduced to announcing, in effect, that someone will be held responsible if anything happens to those people. (Ted Koppel, November 6)

Such were the pieces reported by ABC correspondents in the opening days of the hostage crisis, pieces that would be woven into the leading theme of the ABC real-fiction. It was a narrative that was to be associated with a rise in viewer ratings for ABC's *World News Tonight,* help spawn a successful late evening newscast for the network *(Nightline),* and mark ABC as a serious competitor in the race for advertising revenues generated by public affairs programming.

As the network with the only correspondent on the scene in Teheran for much of the first week of the breaking story, ABC got a jump on its rivals much as NBC did in coverage of The People's Temple crisis. ABC used its early advantage to present nightly reports from correspondent Bob Dyk accompanied by video films of fist-shaking demonstrators, the Ayatollah Khomeini, burning U.S. flags, armed "students" and "militants," effigy hangings, and blindfolded hostages. But neither Dyk's on-the-scene reports nor the provocative films alone distinguished the ABC narrative from those of the other networks (they too found ways to carry similar fare). Rather it was ABC's focus upon U.S. helplessness combined with its assertions that Iran had but a "phantom government" with which to negotiate that formed the unifying thread of its continuing narrative.

The network's initial report on November 4, 1979, stressed the two narrative elements. As films rolled of demonstrators and of blindfolded hostages "marched out on the U.S. Embassy's front steps," the ABC correspondent spoke of "revolutionary students" being in charge as "revolutionary guards and local police stood by and watched." The "takeover had the expressed blessing of the Ayatollah Khomeini," said the report. It concluded, "One fact is clear tonight, that for the second time in a year Khomeini demonstrators in Teheran have overrun the American Embassy and now appear in control of as many as 90 American lives."

Anchor Sam Donaldson's wrap-up of this initial report commented that the Ayatollah may or may not have ordered the takeover: "That is not clear." But, he said, "It does appear to have his blessing." That "adds to Washington's difficulty in trying to resolve this dangerous situation." State Department correspondent Ted Koppel followed, reporting there was not much the U.S. could do beyond setting up a special task force to study the situation. And, he observed, the State Department was making a particular point "to distinguish the Ayatollah Khomeini from the Iranian government."

Thus, the initial report from Teheran provided a picture of a nation whose government stood by during an embassy takeover that had Khomeini's blessing. Who was at the bottom of it, the government or the Ayatollah? Donaldson and Koppel implied the same question. And, of one thing there was no question, namely, that the U.S. was not yet in charge of the situation. These points were driven home on ABC's newscast of the next evening. Anchor Max Robinson's introduction to a report with "the only pictures" from Iran by any network made it clear that the Ayatollah Khomeini had given "full support" to the takeover. Dyk reported that "the youths" were still in control of the embassy compound; that Khomeini "endorsed" the takeover but the Ayatollah's son exerted "a moderating influence inside the compound." Barry Dunsmore's report from Washington emphasized again that the U.S. had few options and that Iran had "no central authority." Then Dunsmore summarized U.S. policy: "lean on the Iranian government as opposed to the Ayatollah Khomeini." But, opined Dunsmore, that might not put the U.S. in charge of the situation either, for "the Iranian government has little power, speaks with many voices, and is afraid to upset the mob."

A chaotic Iran. A helpless U.S. The next evening anchor Frank Reynolds touched upon both. "Here in Washington there is a growing sense of helplessness, as well as outrage," he commented, announcing that the "civilian government of Iran resigned today, and the students or whoever have seized the embassy have threatened to kill the hostages if the U.S. makes any military move to rescue them." Again Dyk reported from Teheran with an "exclusive account" (other networks not being there): "a sight to make any American here in Teheran feel insecure"—demonstrators calling for the death of President Carter, Carter hanging in effigy, a "student spokesman" threatening to kill the hostages, and "student activists" taking two more Americans as prisoners.

Again Ted Koppel reported from the State Department that the U.S. had less leverage now that the Iranian government had resigned; hence the U.S. had to negotiate "with what is almost a phantom government." And, "someone will be held responsible," but "the question of who is responsible awaits the formation of a new government," concluded Koppel. From Europe anchor Peter Jennings repeated the refrain: the resigned civilian government in Iran had been overruled repeatedly by Khomeini and "the Islamic Revolutionary Council," Teheran had been called "the city of a hundred sheriffs," and there was "widespread concern in Iran that the clergy is less than capable of running the government's machinery."

As ABC entered its fourth evening of coverage of the hostage crisis on November 7, Frank Reynolds reported that it "seems to have taken a turn for the worse." Khomeini refused to see Ramsey Clark, an emissary sent by President Carter to negotiate the hostages' release. Reporting from Teheran, Bob Dyk (with films rolling of fist-waving crowds and armed guards on the gates of the embassy compound) rephrased the question of who is in charge, again finding it not to be the U.S.: "The question here in Teheran tonight is how can Ramsey Clark's mission succeed when Iran's supreme ruler has refused to meet with the U.S. delegation?" Once more finding itself helpless, the U.S. was turning elsewhere, this time to the Palestinian Liberation Organization. "If, in fact, anyone has any influence with the Ayatollah Khomeini, it may just be the PLO," said Ted Koppel.

But not only was there no government in charge in Iran and no U.S. in charge of the situation, things were also getting out of hand at home. ABC reported anti-Iranian demonstrations—in Philadelphia, Pennsylvania; Columbus, Ohio; Houston, Texas; Los Angeles, California—and elsewhere there was "fear of violence." Moreover, in spite of House Speaker Tip O'Neill's efforts to restrain them, angry congressmen were calling for drastic action against Iran. Meanwhile, in New York City transport workers were taking things into their own hands by refusing to service Iranian airplanes landing at John F. Kennedy International Airport, while in Newark longshoremen walked off the job when unloading an Iranian ship.

ABC saw no one taking command in Iran for the remainder of its first week of coverage of the hostage crisis, unless it was "whoever" held the hostages in a land where America faced "a forest of hands, a torrent of abuse" (Dyk). Someone (unidentified) refused mediation efforts of the PLO. The U.S. sense of frustration mounted as blindfolded hostages were put on display (to shouts of "Yankee go home!") in order to "embarrass" the United States. Additional embarrassment came from a memo revealed by the "young Iranians" holding the embassy compound in Teheran: a U.S. State Department memo revealing that security at the embassy would require strengthening if the deposed Shah of Iran were allowed in the U.S. In short, a helpless U.S. had contributed to its own helplessness.

Ted Koppel's reports from the State Department contributed considerably to ABC's narrative of chaos and frustration. "U.S. diplomatic leverage in Iran seems to be diminishing by the hour," he reported on November 8. "Two of Washington's best hopes, the PLO delegation and the Ramsey Clark mission, seem to be stalled," he continued. And the U.S. might break relations "with a government that has shown itself unwilling or incapable of abiding by the most fundamental international practices." The following evening Koppel raised the same question he had asked about official U.S. action in the crisis of The People's Temple one year earlier, namely, whether "more could have been done" to assure the safety of Americans in Teheran. Koppel outlined what had been done but concluded that "help never came" to Americans in the Teheran embassy on November 4.

Nor did that help come on April 25, 1980, the date of the aborted rescue mission to free the hostages. Although it was a different act in ABC's dramatic narration of the hostage crisis, an act coming five months after the hostage seizure, the theme of a helpless America still prevailed. So too did the theme of chaos in Iran. "We tried, we failed, and we have paid a price," said anchor Frank Reynolds at the top of the newscast. He continued, "The bodies of eight young Americans still lie in the Iranian desert, the victims of a tragic end to a daring and dangerous attempt to rescue the hostages in Iran." But "the hostages remain in captivity."

Emphasizing the helplessness of it all, the ABC correspondent, reporting "how the attempt was made and why it failed," recounted a litany of mishaps: a helicopter forced down with engine problems, another lost in a sand storm, a hydraulic failure in a third, a bus filled with Iranians arriving at the secret staging site in the desert, a collision between a helicopter and a transport plane while on the desert floor, the bodies of eight crewmen left on the scene. The U.S. was still clearly not in control of events.

Again ABC posed the possibilities that no one might be in control in Iran or in the U.S. either. Picking up on President Carter's remark that one reason for the rescue effort was a "steady unraveling of authority in Iran," ABC continued its real-fiction of a nation ungoverned. Bob Dyk reported from Teheran (once more with films of demonstrating Iranians) that the Ayatollah Khomeini had warned that "If the American government tries another rescue attempt like the last one he, Khomeini, might not be able to control the militants inside the embassy." Two evenings later, ABC news reported the "continuing fallout" of the rescue attempt, stressing that "contrary to what President Bani-Sadr said yesterday," other "powerful Iranian officials" reported that the bodies of servicemen killed in Iran would not be returned to the U.S. soon or easily. And Bob Dyk reported that "no one except the militants" (including Iranian government officials) now knew the whereabouts of the hostages.

But ABC gave no assurance that there was anyone in charge of U.S. policy either. Reporting on the resignation of U.S. Secretary of State Cyrus Vance, Sam Donaldson called it "clearly the darkest moment of Jimmy Carter's presidency." Carter's handling of the rescue failure had played to mixed reviews, according to ABC. In network-filmed reports congressional leaders questioned why they had not been informed of the mission in advance. But the question of who was in charge did not arise in such reports. Correspondent Jack Smith summed up the situation thus: "The President's political future demands he get the hostages out, but physical realities on the ground now in Iran appear to preclude this. The President would appear to be caught between a rock and a hard place."

However, with the resignation of Vance, ABC resumed its theme of a government in disarray and helpless, suggested by Donaldson's "darkest moment" comment. Vance's resignation, said Frank Reynolds, "has brought into the open for all the world to see a major disagreement at the highest level of the government of the United States." Subsequent ABC reports continued the theme; the President was in trouble and hence no one seemed in charge. "It was a bad day for the President on Capitol Hill, too," said the network's congressional correspondent as he outlined criticism of Carter over Vance's resignation. Peter Jennings reported that allies of the U.S. had "concern over what's been happening in Washington." The allies have "deep misgivings"; the failed hostage rescue "raises many questions" about whether the U.S. can adequately defend Europe. Perhaps European allies might need to take charge.

The final act in the ABC narrative, the release of the hostages, was no more reassuring about there being political order and hope than earlier accounts had been. Of the agreement reached to free the hostages, Sam Donaldson announced, "It's done!" on the January 18 newscast. It was "a day of more ups than downs," reported Peter Jennings. But field correspondents kept noting that there had been no "formal announcement of an agreement." Reporting from Algiers that "trivial details had not been overcome," the ABC correspondent commented, "So, yet one more day has passed and no one is quite sure whether this is just a delay or another tragic deception." It was not, as another correspondent said, the "final day of anguish and uncertainty."

So America was still helpless, still not in charge of the situation. "They're not out yet," proclaimed Frank Reynolds on January 19. Why? The reasons were "still unclear," for "once again" there was "another batch of confusing and contradictory reports from Iran." Peter Jennings reported agreement, but "either side can change its mind." Sam Donaldson noted that "nothing is absolutely guaranteed" and that unless the hostages were freed prior to Ronald Reagan's inauguration, any agreement binding the Carter administration might no longer apply. Donaldson spoke of "an undercurrent of worry that the deal could still come unstuck." And, Barry Dunsmore reported that "there was still work to be done," apparently by "the negotiators in Algiers."

Finally, on January 20, 1981, the day of the hostages' release, ABC found that someone actually had been in charge. Ironically, it was the man who had been out of office, hence no longer in charge, for almost six hours: Jimmy Carter. After the hostage release Frank Reynolds remarked on events of the day that "before this happy day had dawned there were more anxious hours during the long night in this country." But, he went on, "The command post, as often in time of crisis" was "the Oval Office of the White House." Correspondent Barry Dunsmore, with film of Carter receiving "word" of negotiations via telephone, reported that "although there was always the nagging doubt," Carter "could relax even more." But, as Dunsmore concluded, there was to be a final irony: the hostages were released after he was no longer in charge. "The timing could hardly have been accidental," said Dunsmore.

Like the other networks, ABC devoted extensive coverage to how the crisis was being handled by families of the hostages. The network did so within the framework that the families, like the hostages, were victims of political disorder and helplessness. In an interview with one family member the evening before the release, an ABC correspondent asked, "How much more of this can you and the other families take?" The answer summed up the ABC plot line for its 444 days of crisis coverage: "I don't know, because we're just little folk sittin' here waitin' for the big people to do something." In other words, they too waited for someone to take charge.

CBS: Three Stories for Three Events

During its coverage of the hostage crisis, CBS joined the other two major networks as it included certain items that were virtually standardized. All networks carried lengthy accounts of how the families and relatives of the hostages were bearing up through the 444 day "ordeal." As other studies suggest, each also had an overall tone which implied that the U.S. was the wronged party in the crisis, Iran the aggressor. The three networks extended that view beyond the actual crisis itself, emphasizing, after the release of the hostages, the reports of brutal treatment they had received at the hands of their captors. And each network covered the celebrations taking place around the nation after the release and return of the hostages to America.

But these were not the basic story lines of any single network. Because they viewed the crisis from a dramatic perspective, each network told a different story. During the three weeks of coverage included in this study, CBS, unlike ABC, told three stories, one for each critical turn in the hostage scenario. This is not to say that CBS ignored features emphasized by ABC— disarray in Iran, a helpless America. CBS too carried such accounts. But in the case of Iranian disarray, only one report—a commentary by Rod MacLeish—had a message identical to that of ABC: "The basic problem in Iran is that there's no one to negotiate with!" As for American helplessness, CBS took the view that the U.S. might be down, but not out.

A "DIPLOMATIC POINT OF VIEW" OF THE HOSTAGE SEIZURE

In the first CBS accounts of the takeover of the U.S. Embassy in Teheran, aired November 5, Walter Cronkite provided a clue to what would become a focal point of later coverage. "The new trouble in Iran has presented the Carter administration with a diplomatic crisis at a time when it was hoping to mend fences with Teheran's Islamic government," said Cronkite. Contained in his statement, and developed at considerable length in later reports, is a view that (a) the Carter administration is in charge in the U.S., (b) a religiously based government is in charge in Iran, and (c) in diplomacy lies the solution. Cronkite displayed no confusion about who seized the embassy—"Moslem students spurred on by the Ayatollah Khomeini," who held not only the embassy in Teheran but also U.S. consulates in Tabriz and Shiraz (shown on a map above Cronkite's shoulder).

There then followed a verbal and pictorial frame familiar to close viewers of the *CBS Evening News*. It contained references to "the experts" (the first coming in Marvin Kalb's report from the U.S. State Department) in various forms—"senior department officials," "senior diplomats," "sources in the Carter administration." Reports were filled with factual material, such as statistics on oil imports, the precise distance (110 miles) Ayatollah Khomeini lived away from Teheran, details of treaties with Iran, kinds of military spare parts shipped to Iran, and a person-by-person listing (with backgrounds and photos) of each hostage. The CBS penchant for displaying documents on the TV screen was also conspicuous: exchanges of letters between officials, a copy of a letter sent by House Speaker Tip O'Neill to Khomeini, letters allegedly written by hostages, and even a printout of the words spoken by a "Mr. X" in a telephone conversation made by a CBS radio affiliate to the Teheran embassy on November 8. Finally, CBS relied considerably on still photographs rather than filmed reports to tell its stories. In part, this was in keeping with a device employed by the network in covering other crises. It also reflected that CBS had no film crew in Teheran during most of the crisis. For example, during the first week of the crisis while ABC nightly was rolling film of angry demonstrators, CBS had filmed coverage only twice, the first of those (November 6) consisting of film from a West German crew with voice-over narration originating in London.

CBS adopted its diplomatic narrative early. From the State Department Kalb reported that "the experts digested the details and faced the stark, depressing reality that the U.S. had so few options to play for getting the Americans released." To make matters worse, Kalb continued, "one official said there's chaos, a form of anarchy in Teheran, and no official here would be surprised if the government [of Iran] now collapsed." Hence, concluded Kalb, "the administration is now emphasizing diplomacy," for "we don't have The Shadow or Superman in our employ was the way one official put it." And "if diplomacy does not work" there are military contingency plans, but Kalb implied diplomacy was the key. In his wrap-up of Kalb's report, Cronkite added another diplomatic feature by reporting, as ABC had not, that Iran was cancelling treaties with the U.S. and U.S.S.R., giving those countries the right to intervene in Iran during time of crisis.

That was on November 5. One evening later Cronkite emphasized that "Washington's response to the turmoil" in Iran was "cautious." Again Kalb spoke of "options terribly limited," particularly since the civil government of Iran had fallen. Yet diplomacy remained viable nonetheless as the U.S. used intermediaries to urge "the Ayatollah Khomeini to recognize his responsibility under international law." Kalb cast some doubt, however, since "diplomacy isn't getting them out yet."

But successful or not, diplomacy remained the centerpiece of the CBS narrative. On November 7, taking note that the Ayatollah had refused to negotiate with the team led by Ramsey Clark, Kalb reported a "perceptible increase in tension" at the State Department. "Officials were acknowledging that the American hostages were being pushed around, abused, intimidated, and mishandled." All this, however, only magnified the necessity of holding to diplomatic means. "The Administration is using every diplomatic channel to get the hostages released" even if "at the moment things look very grim."

CBS followed the story of diplomacy closely. In detailed reports the network described the attempted use of the PLO as intermediaries, first noting that Khomeini would talk with the PLO, then that there had been the first "official contact" between the U.S. and the PLO, and finally, that the "Moslem students" holding the hostages had refused negotiation unless the deposed Shah were returned. By the fourth evening of CBS coverage, Walter Cronkite had boiled the crisis down to a "diplomatic dilemma." Kalb responded from the State Department, detailing the missions of Clark and the PLO. Featuring a statement by Secretary of State Vance ("It is a time not for rhetoric but for quiet, careful, firm diplomacy."), CBS rounded out the nature of its diplomatic narrative. "What the administration is trying to do desperately," said Kalb, "is to head off inflammatory comments." Instead, "The hope here at the moment is to string out the talk with anyone, anywhere."

This definition of the diplomatic situation (apparently picked up from Carter spokesmen) provided CBS with the context for covering side stories. Anti-Iranian demonstrations in the U.S., for instance, were reported by CBS as troubling "officials," for such outbursts might interrupt "restrained" diplomatic efforts. Congressional officials remonstrating against the administration, according to CBS reports of administration views, should restrain themselves so as not to interfere with "quiet diplomacy." When the White House requested, in a meeting with network executives, that TV news show maximum restraint in covering demonstrations, CBS noted the possible clash between diplomatic necessities and freedom of the press. And, in reporting that Iranian military personnel train in the U.S. and that Iran maintains a storage base in the U.S. for spare parts purchased here to be shipped to Iran, those accounts too were reported from a diplomatic perspective, namely, how halting either would affect possible negotiations to end the crisis. ("We wouldn't want to do anything to upset the Ayatollah," the CBS correspondent quoted an "official" as saying.)

As CBS concluded its first week of coverage of the crisis, the diplomatic narrative was pervasive. On November 9 Walter Cronkite reported that "In Washington the Carter administration was moving ahead with its policy of calm negotiation." Marvin Kalb, quoting "senior officials," noted an "intensification of diplomatic activity": a fresh contact in Teheran with the new acting foreign minister, direct approaches to Khomeini, and a diplomatic overture from the Pope. The following evening Marvin Kalb was more positive than ever about the value of "patience" even if there were no immediate solution to the "heart of the stalemate," the return of the former Shah to Iran. Speaking of "officials," Kalb said, "They continue to press on with all diplomatic approaches," despite there being "from a diplomatic point of view" no assurance of success.

In addition to the hostage seizure, there was a side story emphasized by CBS: oil. ABC had but one report on whether the oil flow from Iran to the U.S. would be interrupted by the crisis. CBS had eight reports during the same week. Cronkite speculated on the problem the first evening: once early in his broadcast, noting that four percent of U.S. oil imports were from Iran; then later in the newscast, saying "experts differ" over the impact of the crisis on oil flow. The next evening CBS devoted four reports totalling four minutes to the oil connection, detailing amounts of oil imported from Iran, "draconian measures" to conserve as a precaution, the destinations of Iranian oil supplies, and a report from Rotterdam on the "spot oil market." The message of "Don't do anything to upset the Ayatollah" had more to it than a concern for the safety of the hostages.

A TECHNICAL SCENARIO OF "THE BEST LAID PLANS"

The CBS narrative of the failed rescue effort on April 24–25, 1980, concentrated on the plan, background, execution, and rationale of the mission. In a lengthy (six minutes) filmed report, Walter Cronkite narrated the detailed, factual account of how the "174th day of captivity" had witnessed "a startling and tragic turn of events." Cronkite recounted each movement in the mission, the numbers and types of helicopters used, the numbers and types of transport craft, the terrain of the staging area where training was conducted for the mission, each step in the malfunctioning of helicopters, the arrival of the busload of Iranians, the details of the accident that killed eight servicemen, and the conclusion of the mission. Throughout the narration graphics, films, and statistics flashed across the TV screen.

But the Cronkite narrative was only the beginning of what CBS was to continue to report as a highly complex, technical, brave, and daring effort which was carefully planned but failed out of "bad luck" (according to a majority of those interviewed in a CBS poll). Reports of criticism, from the CBS view, raised problems not about the plan itself but because the "President faces personal reelection fallout" and the failure created "a new and potentially divisive confrontation with the Congress," as CBS correspondent Phil Jones summed it up.

Since the CBS scenario emphasized the plan and operation of the rescue rather than the consequences, reports concerning it had the same detail as that provided by Cronkite in the network's first account. Those reports touched upon all manner of items dealing with the plan: how and when it originated and when the "go ahead" was given; whether the effort was a "rescue mission" or "military operation"; the "many questions" about the nature of the plan (all technical questions and all answered positively by CBS correspondent Ike Pappas, who concluded of the failure, "It was just bad luck"); the equipment and modifications on equipment required before execution; and a profile of Colonel Charles Beckwith, the officer who trained the commandos and led the mission.

Within this context, accounts of the resignation of Secretary of State Cyrus Vance as a protest against the mission received secondary emphasis by CBS. Announcing the resignation on the nightly newscast of April 28, Dan Rather observed that the rescue attempt had "claimed another victim." But it was the choice of "that military move" over diplomacy that fueled Vance's protest, not details of the move itself. Marvin Kalb, again at the State Department, picked up the account. Showing on the screen Vance's letter of resignation and President Carter's letter of acceptance, Kalb took account of Vance's belief that the rescue plan was "misconceived" but concentrated his report instead on the possibility that Vance had been "sandbagged" because the Secretary of State was "instinctively repelled by the military option."

Contrasting with ABC's focus upon the reaction to Vance's resignation as a sign that no one had control of U.S. policymaking, CBS reports devoted minimal coverage to such reaction. That coverage consisted of filmed laudatory comments on Vance as a statesman and nothing regarding presidential candidates, congressional officials, and foreign leaders who thought Vance's judgment of the rescue effort was correct. Thus a view of a well laid plan persisted. Bad luck, not faulty decision-making, was the culprit.

THE RELEASE: "YOU CAN BANK ON IT"

In reporting the approach of the release of the hostages, CBS made clear that there were problems, snags, ups and downs. But unlike ABC's accounts, CBS did not suggest that the unexpected disappointments of the last few days of the crisis were due to a failure of leadership or to deception. Instead, CBS kept its focus upon the nature of the complex "process" of negotiating an agreement, particularly the complexities of the financial arrangements worked out through international banking circles.

In CBS's first report (January 17, 1981) on the possibility of an agreement, correspondent Robert Pierpoint assured viewers that the "process is still on track, but you never know you've got a deal until the last details are nailed down." Over the course of the next three days, CBS kept viewers abreast of the details of "excruciating negotiations." The character of the CBS narrative is best illustrated in reports by correspondent Steve Young, charged with exploring the financial transactions involved in the negotiations.

On January 17 Young reported details of two "theories" informing the negotiations: the "Big Mullah" and the "Black Hole Setoff." These theories applied to disposition of loans to Iran from U.S. banks. When Iranian assets in the U.S. were frozen, one bank, the Chase Manhattan (with a loan of $500 million through "an eleven-bank consortium") declared Iran in default on the loan. By allowing U.S. banks holding Iranian assets in foreign branches to "set off" Iranian loans, the U.S. Department of the Treasury made it possible for those banks to use monies equivalent to some Iranian frozen assets during the crisis. But U.S. banks set off $4 billion more than they were owed, with "untested legal theories conceived to fit the circumstances," i.e., "Big Mullah" and "Black Hole." By these rationales U.S. banks had, in effect, taken control of Iranian money. The problem was getting the banks to release that control, a demand made by Iran as a condition to the release of the hostages.

In follow-up reports on successive evenings, Young discussed the negotiations leading to an agreement so that Iran could re-obtain its $8 billion in assets. Moreover, other correspondents described the resolution of additional "mechanical and technical difficulties." These difficulties included not only "money details" but the number of planes that would fly the hostages from Iran and their destination; the status of military equipment purchased by Iran; the procedures for initialing agreements; and technical plans for receiving the hostages once they were released. Throughout, CBS was meticulous in listing technical considerations on the TV screen for benefit of the viewer. And, instead of making too much of these considerations as "problems," CBS treated them as "trivial matters" in negotiating the "implementation of an agreement, not an agreement itself."

For CBS the 444 days of captivity ended, characteristically, at a specific time and by a specific means: "Forty-one minutes after Ronald Reagan was sworn in as this country's 40th President, the American hostages began their flight to freedom," announced Walter Cronkite. Then, he continued, "It was a little more than an hour after the Americans took off from Teheran that they literally put Iran behind them, crossing into Turkish airspace."

Early in the crisis, on November 9, 1979, CBS correspondent Charles Osgood devoted a four-minute report to detailing the identity and backgrounds of individual hostages. After describing the lives and families of each—displaying photographs as well while he perched on the corner of a desktop—he concluded that "Americans are angry and frustrated tonight. It all seems so complicated: diplomacy, economics, geopolitics, religion, conflicting ideologies. And those two explosives, oil and pride."

NBC's Narrated Montage

On its broadcast of January 20, 1981, the day of the hostage release, *NBC Nightly News* closed with a three-minute film montage of events that had taken place over the past four days: galas in honor of a President soon to be inaugurated, President Carter's announcement that an agreement had been reached to free the hostages, preparations for the inaugural ceremonies, officials closeted in negotiations, Ronald Reagan taking the Oath of Office, Jimmy Carter departing for Plains, Georgia, the hostages freed, Reagan's announcement to that effect, singing of the National Anthem, fireworks before the nation's Capitol. Correspondent Linda Ellerbee in introducing the montage said, "The events of the past few days were related, but exactly how is probably best determined by our own minds and hearts. Let's just say the inauguration of a President and the release of the hostages shared the same time. And let's begin, arbitrarily, last Saturday night."

Ellerbee's comments and the film that followed illustrate NBC's overall coverage of the hostage crisis: related events left for the viewer to interpret. For the distinguishing characteristic of NBC coverage was that there was no discernible pattern as such, only muted emphases. In the content of its coverage, NBC news covered everything, giving overriding priority to no detectable themes, providing viewers with a sense that all events are created equal.

There were, however, minor exceptions to NBC's pluralist coverage. Three are worthy of mention. First, NBC introduced, but did not pursue, a basic theme of ABC's coverage, namely, that Iran was a land of chaos and anarchy. But for NBC such conditions did not mean that no one was in charge, that no one ruled. Instead, NBC implied, creating chaos and a semblance of anarchy was a technique for ruling. Who rules? For NBC it was the Ayatollah Khomeini.

Jessica Savitch introduced NBC's November 4 report: "The American Embassy in Teheran is in the hands of Moslem students tonight spurred on by an anti-American speech by the Ayatollah Khomeini." NBC was the only network to mention the speech. A report which followed, originating at an unidentified location and displaying films whose source also was unidentified, made much of the Khomeini speech. Reporting essentially the same details of the takeover as other networks, the NBC correspondent added, "Earlier today the Ayatollah Khomeini publicly criticized the U.S. for providing refuge for the Shah. This speech was viewed as a signal for the Moslem students to attack the embassy." The correspondent went on to report that the occupation of the embassy had Khomeini's "personal support."

It was the next evening that NBC suggested the full import of all this. John Chancellor introduced coverage, again implying that the Ayatollah was lending support to the "mob." The report that followed (from a different correspondent than that of the previous evening but once more from an unidentified location and using films of unidentified origins) hit hard on the Ayatollah connection. "The occupation of the embassy and the seizure of the hostages was carefully stage-managed," it began. Revolutionary guards and police did nothing to interfere. The students, the report continued, "were among the most fanatical supporters of the Ayatollah Khomeini." But the students had grown frustrated in the ten months since the revolution, blaming the U.S. for the failure of Iran to solve its problems. Then came a point of view not carried by the other networks: "The occupation of the embassy is part of a much more important power struggle between the Iranian government, headed by Prime Minister Bazergan, and the man the students support, the Ayatollah." The report concluded, "The real issue behind the occupation of the embassy may well be who is to have final authority over the chaos in Iran."

With the resignation of the Bazergan government the next day, NBC pressed the view that Khomeini was in charge, using the "Moslem students" and the embassy takeover for his own purposes. On November 6 (no location for the report, no source for films) NBC indicated that the resignation of the civil government of Iran left "the Ayatollah in total command." With the power struggle settled, NBC had a figure to hold responsible for decisions. "The Ayatollah says 'No!' " were the words John Chancellor used to open the *Nightly News* on November 7. The "No" was to any meeting with the negotiating team led by Ramsey Clark, "No" until the deposed Shah was returned.

Unlike ABC, which was unable to find anyone in charge, NBC (like CBS) found Khomeini. Emphasizing Khomeini's power, an NBC correspondent translated the shouts of demonstrators in Teheran as "We are the soldiers of Khomeini, we will follow him anywhere." NBC's interpretation of Khomeini's power led it to differ from CBS by downplaying the role diplomacy could take in the crisis. On November 9, when CBS reported "intensified diplomatic activity" as a positive response, NBC observed that "all the activity can be effective only if it influences one man, the Ayatollah Khomeini."

Emphasis on one diplomatic angle that intrigued NBC is the second characteristic that differentiates the network's coverage from that of its rivals. That angle was the role of the PLO. Although other networks reported the possible use of the PLO as intermediaries, then the failure of that hope, NBC dwelled on it. John Chancellor introduced the possibility on November 7, reporting that Yassir Arafat, head of the PLO, had sent an emissary to Teheran. Chancellor said "an American official" considered the action "fine with him." Later in the same telecast, NBC reported that a U.S. congressman had also proposed that solution.

By the next evening the story had taken on larger proportions. John Chancellor opened the telecast with a report that the PLO was talking with Khomeini about the hostages with "the approval of the American government." The NBC State Department correspondent reported official uncertainty as to what the PLO could or would do. A filmed statement from a PLO spokesman indicated that the PLO would not do much to "safeguard and protect American lives in danger as a result of miscalculation and misconception in American foreign policy."

The dampening of hopes by the PLO spokesman, however, did not deter NBC. On November 9 a report from Teheran began with the idea that "If there is one man in the world Ayatollah Khomeini will listen to, it's Yassir Arafat." There followed a recounting of the support Arafat had given Khomeini's revolution; in appreciation the Iranian had named a street after Arafat. John Chancellor confirmed, in a follow-up, that Arafat had "been in direct touch by telephone with the authorities in Teheran." Finally, closing its first week of coverage of the hostage crisis, NBC's Jessica Savitch reported on November 10 that PLO representatives had negotiated with the "Iranian students" and made no progress. Yet "one PLO official" said "we will continue to exert utmost effort." So although other networks had by this point dismissed the viability of the PLO connection, NBC kept it alive.

The third news item that NBC emphasized and its competitors did not involved what John Chancellor introduced on April 25, 1980, as "The Story of the Mission that Failed." Standing in front of a world map almost the size of the entire *NBC Nightly News* set, Chancellor instructed viewers in details of the failed rescue mission. Three points are noteworthy in NBC's treatment of this story. First, descriptive accounts of the background and actual conduct of the mission occupied much less of NBC's coverage than of CBS's (about one half) but the same as ABC's. Instead, NBC focused more on "reaction reports" from Congress, foreign allies, the U.S.S.R., hostage families, and Iranian officials. (So did the other networks, but not to the degree of NBC.) Second, for NBC this was a mission that failed, and there was thus no effort to go on and detail the technical complexities of its design that typified CBS accounts.

Third, however, NBC did stress one feature of the failed effort not covered by the other networks: i.e., what was to happen if the rescue effort had not been aborted. In a report on April 26, NBC's Pentagon correspondent, Hilary Brown, carefully outlined the step-by-step plan to be followed had the staging of aircraft and commandos at "Desert One" been successful. In addition to the fact that NBC undertook such speculation, there is one other noteworthy point. During the first week of the crisis, on November 9, NBC had aired almost precisely the same scenario. In that report, however, the thrust was that "the use of force was almost impossible" and "a logistical nightmare." For all the reasons outlined on November 9 (repeated on April 26), NBC quoted "U.S. officers" in its earlier report as saying "a rescue operation to Teheran probably could not succeed."

To say that NBC covered every item that the other networks covered—but without particular emphases—as well as adding minor angles of its own, is not to say that NBC's pluralist coverage merely combined characteristics of the other networks. What distinguished NBC's approach to the hostage crisis was not what was covered but how. The style of NBC coverage, made up of devices we have encountered in NBC's narratives of other crises, provided a distinctive tone.

Foremost was an emphasis, as we have seen before, upon putting news items in a broader context. The effort to place seizure of the American embassy in the context of internal Iranian power struggles is but one example; there are many others. The report mentioned above about the hazards of any military rescue effort, for instance, described as historical precedent the Israeli raid on Entebbe to rescue passengers from a hijacked airliner. And, relying on a correspondent from the British Broadcasting Corporation ("who also works for NBC") and BBC film, the network probed the context of Iranian fears that the U.S. was plotting a counterrevolution, concluding that

the Iranians were "not paranoid." Correspondent Linda Ellerbee gave a lengthy contextual account of how the deposed Shah
could (as like other patients just as ill) be moved from the
hospital without problems. A final example: on the evening of
the resignation of Secretary of State Cyrus Vance, NBC (unlike
other networks) profiled Vance's career, accomplishments,
personality, and even health (John Chancellor reporting that
Vance took his wife with him on trips to help tie his shoes when
he could not bend over because of a "troubling bad back").

As in reporting other crises, NBC incorporated numerous
colloquialisms. Here is but a sampling: for the hostage families
"things are pretty tough"; "while the families worry, Congress
frets"; "Congress was in a deporting mood"; "the situation in
Iran is causing some tempers to rise"; of Cyrus Vance, "He
never left any footprints"; of the rescue mission there was "the
tricky part"; implementation of the release agreement "hit last
minute snags"; and oil cutoffs would be an "inconvenience."

We have noted before that such colloquialisms lend a low-
key, quieting sense to news accounts. So too does the use of
rhetorical questions—questions that introduce slow-paced,
didactic explanations of complexities. For example, after John
Chancellor's "The Ayatollah says 'No!' " introduction of
November 7, which he called a "tough statement," he asked,
"How did the Clark mission get off the track? Is it permanently
delayed?" Three reports, each on the Clark mission, followed.
Each report contained the same information with respect to
Chancellor's questions, a device by which NBC carries its
pluralistic approach to reporting specific events as well as larger
stories.

NBC's conversational approach to interviews, which we
have remarked upon earlier, marked coverage of the hostage
crisis. It was particularly well adapted to coverage of stories of
how the hostage families were faring—frequently capturing
family members in discussions with one another. As with other
crises, NBC featured officials, private citizens, simply unidentified persons in many cases, on telephones—sometimes saying
things pertinent to a report, frequently not saying anything, only
listening. Although NBC employs a high number of visuals in

reports, these interviews might as well be on radio, for the voice-overs frequently have little to do with the report at hand. Context, colloquialisms, rhetorical questions, plural reports, a conversational model—all made up the NBC approach to the hostage crisis. With such a multifaceted coverage, both didactic and feature-oriented, it was fitting that of all the networks NBC was the only one to offer the montage review of the days preceding the hostage's release. It was even more fitting that NBC followed that the next evening with a montage placing the entire 444 days of the hostage crisis in context. John Chancellor introduced it as "The 444 Lost Days for the Hostages," an unusually long six-minute report. With films rolling that were taken on each day mentioned, the NBC correspondent went through, in sequence, selected days of the crisis: "The day before Day 1," "Day 1," "Day 3," "Day 6," etc., until eleven days' news events of the crisis had been recounted, ending with "Day 252." That, however, was not the end. The report continued, returning to "Day 57," describing other things that had happened on selected days: "Day 77," "Day 97," "Day 174," "Day 279" (a film of the eruption of Mount St. Helens), "Day 407" (mourning for John Lennon), through "Day 444, the day the nation stopped counting and started rejoicing the end of a long, harrowing, and frustrating ordeal."

Different Networks
Different Foci in the Hostage Crisis

Unlike the coverage of other crises examined thus far, in which there were relatively few statistically significant differences between the networks, the Iranian hostage crisis produced key variations. To examine these we have tabulated quantitative data in accordance with the three periods of the crisis for which we have already described network narratives: the seizure, the rescue attempt, and the release. As in considering the other crises, we turn first to newsgathering modes (Table 5.1). For the seizure there were only minimal differences between the networks in locales of coverage. The seizure was

Table 5.1
Newsgathering Modes for Hostage News Reports: by Network

Modes	ABC	CBS	NBC	Combined
	Seizure			
Locale				
Network studio	28 (51%)	33 (58%)	30 (53%)	91 (54%)
Government office	15 (27%)	14 (25%)	15 (27%)	44 (26%)
Private home/office	6 (11%)	8 (14%)	6 (10%)	20 (12%)
Crisis site	6 (11%)	2 (3%)	6 (10%)	14 (8%)
Source (when identified)				
Public official	52 (62%)	50 (55%)	41 (57%)	143 (58%)
Technician/scientist	1 (1%)	8 (9%)	1 (2%)	10 (4%)
Interest group leader	16 (19%)	13 (14%)	0	29 (12%)
Average citizen	15 (18%)	20 (22%)	29 (41%)	64 (26%)
χ^2 = 29.634 with 6 df; p = .001.				
Means				
Briefing by public official	31 (37%)	8 (22%)	5 (7%)	44 (22%)
Speech by public official	17 (20%)	15 (40%)	4 (5%)	36 (18%)
Interview with public official	12 (14%)	4 (11%)	7 (9%)	23 (12%)
Interview with average citizen	16 (19%)	8 (22%)	18 (24%)	42 (22%)
Reporter quoting a source	8 (10%)	2 (5%)	41 (55%)	51 (26%)
χ^2 = 72.950 with 8 df; p = .001.				
Source of reporter's quotations				
Public official	8 (100%)	2 (100%)	25 (61%)	35 (69%)
Average citizen	0	0	16 (39%)	16 (31%)
	Rescue attempt			
Locale				
Network studio	20 (56%)	32 (56%)	26 (62%)	78 (46%)
Government office	6 (17%)	13 (23%)	13 (31%)	35 (20%)
Private home/office	8 (22%)	12 (21%)	3 (7%)	23 (14%)
Crisis site	2 (5%)	0	0	2 (1%)
Source (when identified)				
Public official	45 (88%)	54 (69%)	55 (79%)	154 (77%)
Technician/scientist	0	3 (5%)	0	3 (2%)
Interest group leader	3 (6%)	5 (6%)	0	8 (4%)
Average citizen	3 (6%)	16 (20%)	15 (21%)	34 (17%)
χ^2 = 15.530 with 6 df; p = .01.				
Means				
Briefing by public official	12 (24%)	27 (35%)	1 (1%)	40 (20%)
Speech by public official	20 (39%)	8 (10%)	3 (4%)	31 (16%)
Interview with public official	6 (12%)	12 (15%)	7 (10%)	25 (12%)
Interview with interest group leader	0	2 (3%)	0	2 (1%)
Interview with average citizen	3 (5%)	15 (19%)	6 (8%)	24 (12%)
Reporter quoting a source	10 (20%)	14 (18%)	53 (77%)	77 (39%)
χ^2 = 93.960 with 10 df; p = .001.				

Continued on next page

Table 5.1 Continued

Modes	ABC	CBS	NBC	Combined
Source of reporter's quotations				
Public official	9 (90%)	12 (86%)	43 (83%)	64 (84%)
Technician/scientist	0	1 (7%)	0	1 (1%)
Interest group leader	1 (10%)	0	0	1 (1%)
Average citizen	0	1 (7%)	9 (17%)	10 (14%)
$\chi^2 = 13.468$ with 6 df; p = .05.				
	Release			
Locale				
Network studio	46 (60%)	45 (55%)	45 (59%)	136 (57%)
Government office	12 (16%)	24 (29%)	22 (29%)	58 (24%)
Private home/office	18 (23%)	7 (9%)	5 (7%)	33 (14%)
Crisis site	1 (1%)	6 (7%)	4 (5%)	11 (5%)
$\chi^2 = 21.573$ with 8 df; p = .01.				
Source (when identified)				
Public official	51 (53%)	52 (52%)	54 (58%)	157 (54%)
Technician/scientist	4 (5%)	0	1 (1%)	5 (2%)
Interest group leader	6 (6%)	0	0	6 (2%)
Average citizen	35 (36%)	47 (48%)	38 (41%)	120 (42%)
$\chi^2 = 18.981$ with 6 df; p = .01.				
Means				
Briefing by public official	23 (24%)	2 (2%)	3 (3%)	28 (10%)
Speech by public official	16 (17%)	4 (5%)	4 (5%)	24 (8%)
Interview with public official	11 (11%)	13 (13%)	9 (10%)	33 (11%)
Interview with interest group leader	4 (4%)	0	0	4 (1%)
Interview with average citizen	36 (38%)	32 (32%)	32 (30%)	98 (34%)
Reporter quoting a source	6 (6%)	48 (48%)	50 (50%)	104 (36%)
$\chi^2 = 85.264$ with 10 df; p = .001.				
Source of reporter's quotations				
Public official	5 (83%)	32 (68%)	39 (83%)	76 (76%)
Interest group leader	1 (17%)	0	0	1 (1%)
Average citizen	0	15 (32%)	8 (17%)	23 (23%)

covered by all networks as primarily a studio story with packaged reports deriving mainly from government offices, princi-
pally the Department of State. Coverage of the rescue attempt
had the same emphases, the principal difference being that the
Department of Defense vied with the Department of State as the
secondary setting of narratives for each network. But, as the
data in Table 5.1 illustrate, with the hostage release there are
significant network differences. ABC, in keeping with its narrative that the hostage families were as much victims of a leader-
less U.S. government as a disorderly Iran, turned to the private
homes of family members as coverage locales in a greater frequency than did CBS or NBC. Both those networks continued
to use government offices as common settings of their narratives, second only to the studio.

Across all three periods of the crisis, the networks differed in
the persons selected as news sources. The major difference was
in NBC's tendency to rely upon average citizens as a greater
fraction of their news sources during the seizure and rescue
attempt periods than did either other network and for CBS to do
the same during coverage of the hostage release. For NBC this
did not necessarily mean hostage families but also included
sampling the views of demonstrators, longshoremen refusing to
off-load Iranian ships, mechanics refusing to maintain Iranian
aircraft in the U.S., former residents of Iran, etc. For CBS,
however, focus upon the average citizen was actually limited to
the network's newscast on the last Sunday evening of the crisis.
On that night CBS devoted a lengthy report to a family-by-
family survey of how relatives of the hostages were reacting, a
concern which otherwise never was a principal one of CBS
narratives.

Nightly newscasts of the three major TV networks differed
with respect to how news was acquired as well as who provided
it. One would expect that official news channels, such as briefings, statements, speeches, and interviews, would be the pre-
dominant sources for all networks. This was generally the case
for ABC, even though the substance of reports reflected doubts
regarding what, if anything, could be done to resolve the crisis.
Only during the week of the hostage release did interviews with

average citizens (members of hostage families) become a major means of gathering news for ABC. And CBS coverage reflected a similar pattern. Coverage by NBC differed, however. A reporter quoting an unnamed source constituted a higher portion of the network's news techniques than was the case for ABC or CBS. Usually the source turned out to be an unnamed government official, yet it is noteworthy that throughout the three periods of the crisis NBC news personnel were reluctant to specify precisely from whom the network was obtaining its information.

From the standpoint of visual coverage as measured by the variables listed in Table 5.2, the networks differed relatively little. Anchor-read stories were the network norm. Although ABC had the only network correspondent in Teheran at the beginning of the crisis, the percentage of packaged reports it used during the seizure period was in fact lower than that of NBC. This may come as a surprise to viewers who recall the week of November 4, 1979, when ABC each night showed scenes of mobs waving their fists in Teheran, hanging President Carter in effigy, and burning U.S. flags. Frequently, however, these films rolled during anchor-read stories, whether originating at a U.S. studio or the network's London desk.

What appeared to be a continuing story in which ABC took quick visual command was actually one in which no network was clearly more visual than another. Visual prominence scores for the seizure period (ranging from 0–55) were not significantly different from network to network. By the period of the rescue attempt, however, this had changed. Significant differences appear between networks on the visual prominence measure. Scores ranged from 0–57, and the ABC mean of 23 had a significant F-ratio (p = .01) over the CBS mean of 18 and NBC's mean of 21. Again ABC was most visual in coverage of the release. Scores ranged from 0–59, with ABC's mean (23) being significantly higher than that of CBS (20) and NBC (16) at the .01 level.

Modal journalistic styles for each of the news networks, which on the basis of previous crises one might expect to guess, were not consistent across the three periods of the Iranian hostage crisis. During the seizure, patterns revealed by other

Nightly Horrors: Television Network News

Table 5.2
Visual Elements in Hostage Stories: by Network

Visual elements of story	ABC	CBS	NBC	Combined
Seizure				
Anchor read story	65 (72%)	69 (76%)	52 (64%)	188 (71%)
Cut to packaged report(s)				
One or more, without interview	10 (11%)	5 (5%)	13 (16%)	28 (11%)
One or more, with interview	15 (17%)	17 (19%)	16 (20%)	48 (18%)
Graphic over anchor/reporter shoulder				
None	69 (77%)	73 (78%)	64 (79%)	206 (78%)
One	13 (14%)	12 (13%)	14 (17%)	39 (15%)
Two or more	8 (9%)	8 (3%)	3 (4%)	19 (7%)
Still picture/graphic on total screen				
None	85 (94%)	87 (94%)	73 (90%)	245 (93%)
One	3 (4%)	3 (3%)	3 (4%)	9 (3%)
Two or more	2 (4%)	3 (3%)	5 (6%)	10 (4%)
Film rolled during story				
None	60 (67%)	71 (76%)	51 (63%)	182 (69%)
Film, without interview	21 (23%)	12 (13%)	21 (26%)	54 (20%)
Film, with interview	9 (10%)	10 (11%)	9 (11%)	28 (11%)
Second film during story				
None	73 (81%)	76 (82%)	65 (80%)	214 (81%)
Film, without interview	7 (8%)	4 (4%)	4 (5%)	15 (6%)
Film, with interview	10 (11%)	13 (14%)	12 (15%)	35 (13%)
Rescue Attempt				
Anchor read story	44 (70%)	70 (73%)	80 (78%)	186 (71%)
Cut to packaged report(s)				
One or more, without interview	5 (8%)	10 (10%)	11 (6%)	26 (10%)
One or more, with interview	14 (22%)	16 (17%)	17 (16%)	47 (19%)
Graphic over anchor/reporter shoulder				
None	49 (78%)	68 (71%)	80 (78%)	197 (75%)
One	8 (13%)	20 (21%)	18 (18%)	46 (18%)
Two or more	6 (9%)	8 (8%)	4 (4%)	18 (7%)
Still picture/graphic on total screen				
None	54 (86%)	86 (90%)	94 (92%)	234 (90%)
One	1 (2%)	4 (4%)	4 (4%)	9 (3%)
Two or more	8 (12%)	6 (6%)	4 (4%)	18 (7%)
Film rolled during story				
None	30 (57%)	69 (72%)	77 (75%)	186 (71%)
Film, without interview	11 (20%)	17 (18%)	14 (14%)	42 (16%)
Film, with interview	12 (23%)	10 (10%)	11 (11%)	33 (13%)
Second film during story				
None	50 (79%)	78 (81%)	92 (90%)	220 (84%)
Film, without interview	3 (5%)	3 (3%)	2 (2%)	8 (3%)
Film, with interview	10 (16%)	15 (16%)	8 (8%)	33 (13%)

Continued on next page

Table 5.2 Continued

Visual elements of story	ABC	CBS	NBC	Combined
	Release			
Anchor read story	61 (68%)	96 (73%)	79 (69%)	236 (70%)
Cut to packaged report(s)				
One or more. without interview	7 (8%)	12 (9%)	13 (6%)	32 (10%)
One or more. with interview	22 (24%)	24 (18%)	22 (25%)	68 (20%)
$\chi^2 = 30.272$ with 2 df (anchor/packaged); p = .001.				
Graphic over anchor/reporter shoulder				
None	74 (82%)	96 (73%)	85 (75%)	255 (76%)
One	13 (14%)	21 (16%)	27 (24%)	61 (18%)
Two or more	3 (4%)	15 (11%)	2 (1%)	18 (5%)
Still picture/graphic on total screen				
None	79 (88%)	126 (95%)	106 (93%)	311 (93%)
One	3 (3%)	6 (5%)	6 (5%)	15 (5%)
Two or more	8 (9%)	0	2 (2%)	10 (1%)
Film rolled during story				
None	59 (66%)	99 (75%)	79 (69%)	237 (71%)
Film. without interview	18 (20%)	18 (14%)	16 (14%)	52 (15%)
Film. with interview	13 (14%)	15 (11%)	19 (17%)	47 (14%)
Second film during story				
None	72 (80%)	110 (83%)	90 (79%)	272 (81%)
Film. without interview	5 (6%)	7 (6%)	13 (11%)	25 (7%)
Film. with interview	13 (14%)	15 (11%)	11 (10%)	39 (13%)

crises did not reappear with previous emphases. Heretofore the principal style of ABC reports was the populist/sensationalist, yet in this case fully one-third of the ABC reports were classified as elitist/factual. A majority of NBC coverage consisted of the elitist/factual style rather than being oriented toward the didactic or feature as has been the dominant NBC stylistic pattern. CBS was the only network to remain true to form. But again, even though a majority of CBS reports were elitist in orientation, factual in content, fully 40% were of the populist/sensationalist style. Again, however, human interest was primarily a style of CBS anchors, not correspondents.

Turning to the period of the aborted rescue attempt, we find another pattern in journalistic styles. ABC, normally the network with a populist/sensationalist bent, turned away from human interest accounts to more factual, officially based reports. In all, 61% of ABC reports and 72% of timed coverage

Table 5.3
Coverage Styles in Hostage Seizure:
by Networks, Anchors, Correspondents

Reports	ABC	CBS	NBC	Combined
Total number	55	57	57	169
Anchors	30 (54%)	32 (56%)	29 (51%)	91 (54%)
Correspondents	25 (46%)	25 (44%)	28 (49%)	78 (46%)
Style (by number of reports)				
Populist/sensationalist	26 (47%)	23 (40%)	11 (19%)	60 (36%)
Anchors	13	16	7	36
Correspondents	13	7	4	24
Elitist/factual	18 (33%)	30 (53%)	29 (51%)	77 (46%)
Anchors	12	16	15	43
Correspondents	6	14	14	34
Ignorant/didactic	2 (4%)	0	7 (12%)	9 (5%)
Anchors	2	0	6	8
Correspondents	0	0	1	1
Pluralist/feature	9 (16%)	4 (7%)	10 (18%)	23 (13%)
Anchors	3	0	1	4
Correspondents	6	4	9	19
Total time of coverage (in minutes)	56	60	52	168
Anchors	17 (30%)	23 (38%)	14 (27%)	46 (27%)
Correspondents	39 (70%)	37 (62%)	38 (73%)	122 (73%)
Style duration (in minutes)				
Populist/sensationalist	28 (50%)	18 (30%)	9 (17%)	55 (33%)
Anchors	9	6	3	18
Correspondents	19	12	6	37
Factual/elitist	15 (27%)	34 (57%)	27 (52%)	76 (45%)
Anchors	6	9	7	22
Correspondents	9	25	20	54
Ignorant/didactic	1 (2%)	0	4 (8%)	5 (3%)
Anchors	1	0	3	4
Correspondents	0	0	1	1
Pluralist/feature	12 (21%)	8 (13%)	12 (23%)	32 (19%)
Anchors	1	0	1	2
Correspondents	11	8	11	30

Significant differences are as follows:
1. Between networks for number of reports per style $\chi^2 = 20.989$ with 6 df; p = .01.
2. Between networks for duration of reports per style $\chi^2 = 23.054$ with 6 df; p = .001.
3. Between networks for number of anchor reports per style $\chi^2 = 20.989$ with 6 df; p = .01.
4. Between networks for number of correspondent reports per style $\chi^2 = 12.746$ with 6 df; p = .05.
5. Between networks for duration of correspondent reports per style $\chi^2 = 16.609$ with 6 df; p = .02.

was in the elitist/factual style. This conforms to the network's newsgathering habits revealed in Table 5.1 about the rescue attempt. Interviews with average citizens, usually a staple of ABC coverage, played only a small role, tempering the network's populist appeal. Although CBS devoted the highest percentage of its reports and the majority of its time to elitist/factual reporting, the style did not occupy so high a proportion of CBS coverage as it did of ABC. Finally, for NBC as well, the modal style was elitist/factual; the network devoted the smallest percentage of its coverage to what we have come to expect as the NBC norm, teaching and feature reporting.

Coverage of the period of the hostages' release did not restore stylistic patterns discovered in earlier crises. ABC did return to its populist orientation, primarily in its narrative that something could always go wrong when government officials are not truly in charge and when they are insensitive to the needs of the people. And although CBS's narrative of the release focused upon the technical and process aspects of the release agreement, by turning more to how relatives and friends of the hostages were reacting than it had during the seizure or rescue periods, the network had the highest proportion of its coverage in the populist/sensationalist style as well. As for the number of reports, NBC undertook almost one-half of its coverage in the elitist/factual style normally associated with CBS. But from the standpoint of time devoted to coverage, NBC reverted to its established style of feature reporting.

It is noteworthy that network differences in reporting styles did not conform to the pattern revealed by an examination of coverage of other crises. Dramatistic analysis suggests that each network did narrate a tale of the hostage crisis in keeping with overall story and plot lines used in reporting other crises, a point to which we shall return in Chapter 6. So although stylistic shifts occurred, real-fictions did not change. We suspect that the reason for the stylistic patterns in hostage crisis coverage, greater elitist/factual reporting by all three networks, derived from how the networks were forced to cover it. Not having access to the principals involved, namely, the hostages, all networks were forced to focus upon either the official actors in

Table 5.4
Coverage Styles in Hostage Rescue Attempt:
by Networks, Anchors, Correspondents

Reports	ABC	CBS	NBC	Combined
Total number	36	57	49	142
Anchors	20 (56%)	22 (38%)	26 (53%)	78 (55%)
Correspondents	16 (44%)	35 (62%)	23 (27%)	64 (45%)
Style (by number of reports):				
Populist/sensationalist	11 (30%)	13 (23%)	17 (35%)	41 (29%)
Anchors	10	10	9	29
Correspondents	1	3	8	12
Elitist/factual	22 (61%)	28 (49%)	20 (41%)	70 (45%)
Anchors	10	18	10	38
Correspondents	12	10	10	32
Ignorant/didactic	0	1 (2%)	1 (2%)	2 (2%)
Anchors	0	0	1	1
Correspondents	0	1	0	1
Pluralist/feature	3 (9%)	15 (32%)	11 (22%)	29 (20%)
Anchors	0	4	6	10
Correspondents	3	11	5	19
Total time of coverage (in minutes)	40	67	51	158
Anchors	9 (22%)	22 (38%)	18 (35%)	49 (31%)
Correspondents	31 (78%)	45 (62%)	33 (65%)	109 (69%)
Style duration (in minutes)				
Populist/sensationalist	5 (13%)	8 (12%)	18 (35%)	31 (20%)
Anchors	4	4	4	12
Correspondents	1	4	14	19
Factual/elitist	29 (72%)	34 (51%)	20 (39%)	83 (52%)
Anchors	5	16	8	29
Correspondents	24	18	12	54
Ignorant/didactic	0	3 (4%)	2 (1%)	5 (2%)
Anchors	0	0	2	2
Correspondents	0	3	0	3
Pluralist/feature	6 (15%)	22 (33%)	13 (25%)	41 (26%)
Anchors	0	2	6	8
Correspondents	6	20	7	33

Significant differences are as follows:
1. Between networks for duration of reports per style $\chi^2 = 21.383$ with 6 df; p = .01.
2. Between networks for duration of correspondent reports per style $\chi^2 = 33.512$ with 6 df; p = .001.

Table 5.5
Coverage Styles in Hostage Release:
by Networks, Anchors, Correspondents

Reports	ABC	CBS	NBC	Combined
Total number	77	82	76	235
Anchors	46 (60%)	45 (55%)	43 (56%)	134 (57%)
Correspondents	31 (40%)	37 (45%)	33 (44%)	101 (43%)
Style (by number of reports):				
Populist/sensationalist	40 (52%)	35 (43%)	10 (13%)	85 (36%)
Anchors	27	21	10	58
Correspondents	13	14	0	27
Elitist/factual	28 (36%)	29 (35%)	37 (49%)	94 (40%)
Anchors	16	12	20	48
Correspondents	12	17	17	46
Ignorant/didactic	3 (4%)	13 (16%)	7 (9%)	23 (10%)
Anchors	2	10	6	18
Correspondents	1	3	1	5
Pluralist/feature	6 (8%)	5 (6%)	22 (29%)	33 (14%)
Anchors	1	2	7	10
Correspondents	5	3	15	23
Total time of coverage (in minutes)	78	91	85	248
Anchors	21 (27%)	24 (26%)	22 (26%)	67 (27%)
Correspondents	57 (73%)	67 (74%)	63 (74%)	181 (73%)
Style duration (in minutes)				
Populist/sensationalist	35 (45%)	37 (44%)	6 (7%)	78 (31%)
Anchors	11	11	6	28
Correspondents	24	26	0	50
Factual/elitist	23 (29%)	32 (38%)	35 (41%)	90 (36%)
Anchors	5	6	8	19
Correspondents	18	26	27	71
Ignorant/didactic	5 (7%)	11 (13%)	5 (6%)	21 (8%)
Anchors	4	6	3	13
Correspondents	1	5	2	8
Pluralist/feature	15 (19%)	5 (5%)	39 (46%)	59 (25%)
Anchors	1	1	5	7
Correspondents	14	4	34	52

Significant differences are as follows:
1. Between networks for number of reports per style χ^2 = 43.207 with 6 df; p = .001.
2. Between networks for duration of reports per style χ^2 = 58.733 with 6 df; p = .001.
3. Between networks for number of anchor reports per style χ^2 = 21.242 with 6 df; p = .01.
4. Between networks for number of correspondent reports per style χ^2 = 26.514 with 6 df; p = .001.
5. Between networks for duration of correspondent reports per style χ^2 = 55.796 with 6 df; p = .001.

the drama or the only "little people" available, families of the hostages or of those servicemen killed in the rescue attempt. During the week of the hostage seizure, there were relatively few family stories. What was going on in Iran, what the U. S. was or was not doing, what could or could not be done—these were accounts of official action/inaction which lend themselves to coverage in an elitist/factual style. With the rescue attempt there was once more a focus upon officialdom, not the little people. This too provoked a high proportion of elitist/factual coverage. And the negotiation of the hostage release during the final week of the crisis meant basically that again public officials would be the dramatis personae of narratives, contributing to elitist/factual accounts. But ABC was dubious that officials would bring it off, a populist orientation. NBC accepted what seemed to be happening, a pluralist style. CBS narrated a story of elitist management but injected a concern for hostage families not displayed during the previous periods, thus providing its populist style at the end.

As the data in Table 5.6 suggest, neither the news nor emotional content of network coverage of the hostage seizure differed markedly. NBC relied upon a smaller proportion of peripheral reports in its overall coverage of the seizure than did other networks, but to no significant degree. This changed with reports of the rescue attempt. ABC served as the channel of straight news accounts, while NBC resorted to a high proportion of reports either peripheral to the essentials of the attempt or combining news with peripheral information. Straight news over peripheral and perspective concerns was also the order of the day in ABC coverage of the release. CBS and NBC presented viewers with peripheral accounts along with the news or, especially in the case of NBC, endeavored to add perspective to breaking events.

Overall, the percentage of network reports on the hostage crisis became more reassuring in the movement from seizure to rescue attempt to release. NBC aired a higher proportion of alarming reports during the seizure and rescue attempt but, with prospects of a release, turned to reassurance. CBS, with half of its reports neutral during the seizure and rescue attempt

Table 5.6
News Content of Hostage Reports: by Network

Content Types	ABC	CBS	NBC	Combined
	Seizure			
News Value				
News	8 (14%)	17 (30%)	18 (31%)	33 (21%)
Peripheral	23 (42%)	20 (35%)	11 (19%)	54 (34%)
Perspective	8 (14%)	4 (7%)	12 (22%)	24 (15%)
News/peripheral	9 (16%)	5 (9%)	5 (9%)	19 (12%)
News/perspective	7 (14%)	11 (19%)	11 (19%)	29 (18%)
Emotional content				
Reassuring	9 (16%)	8 (14%)	9 (16%)	26 (15%)
Alarming	19 (35%)	20 (35%)	24 (42%)	63 (37%)
Neutral	27 (49%)	29 (51%)	24 (42%)	80 (48%)
	Rescue attempt			
News Value				
News	13 (36%)	13 (23%)	5 (10%)	31 (22%)
Peripheral	14 (39%)	19 (33%)	24 (49%)	57 (40%)
Perspective	1 (3%)	13 (24%)	15 (31%)	29 (20%)
News/peripheral	5 (14%)	6 (10%)	1 (2%)	12 (9%)
News/perspective	3 (8%)	6 (10%)	4 (8%)	13 (9%)
$\chi^2 = 20.315$ with 8 df; p = .01.				
Emotional content				
Reassuring	5 (14%)	17 (30%)	6 (12%)	28 (20%)
Alarming	13 (36%)	12 (21%)	23 (47%)	48 (34%)
Neutral	18 (50%)	28 (49%)	20 (41%)	66 (46%)
$\chi^2 = 10.780$ with 4 df; p = .05.				
	Release			
News Value				
News	26 (34%)	15 (18%)	13 (17%)	54 (25%)
Peripheral	29 (38%)	30 (37%)	25 (33%)	64 (30%)
Perspective	13 (17%)	20 (24%)	14 (18%)	47 (22%)
News/peripheral	7 (9%)	8 (10%)	3 (4%)	18 (8%)
News/perspective	2 (2%)	9 (11%)	21 (28%)	32 (15%)
$\chi^2 = 27.644$ with 8 df; p = .001.				
Emotional content				
Reassuring	30 (39%)	33 (40%)	37 (49%)	100 (43%)
Alarming	13 (17%)	17 (21%)	9 (12%)	39 (16%)
Neutral	34 (44%)	32 (39%)	30 (39%)	96 (41%)

periods, also became reassuring toward the end. ABC's *World News Tonight* also followed the trend toward reassurance but not to the degree of the other networks. At the conclusion of the crisis, all three evening newscasts could report a happy ending not only to the crisis itself but to disparate journalistic narratives, newsgathering, and styles of coverage as well.

Chapter Six

The More Things Change, Do They Remain the Same?: Network Coverage of the Tylenol Poisonings

Three networks, three narratives, three styles, three real-fictions, perhaps three rhetorical visions. That is the burden of our findings after close examination of nightly news coverage of five different kinds of natural and manmade crises. We need not review the specific details of each network's narrative of each crisis here. Rather our intent is, first, to return to the dramatistic pentad introduced in the Introduction and employ its elements as the basis for comparing and contrasting overarching differences in network news coverage. Then we turn to the coverage of the events comprising the 1982 Tylenol crisis to see whether changes in news personnel fostered shifts in the basic narrative patterns that distinguish the networks. With that accomplished, we conclude our argument by describing what we think are the more encompassing rhetorical visions presented to viewers of network television news.

The Dramas of Crisis Coverage in TV News

The basics of Kenneth Burke's pentad (1966), mentioned in the Introduction, consist of the acts, actors (he calls them agents), agencies, scenes, and purposes in any drama. In the televised news coverage of five crises, we have identified the specifics of each of these elements for each network. Sometimes networks treated elements of the pentad in similar ways; sometimes they differed markedly. In the crisis of The People's Temple, for example, all three networks wove into their respective narratives the basic acts of that crisis, namely, the mass murders and suicides at the Jonestown compound. But when it came to another element of the pentad, scene, the networks differed. NBC, for reasons we outlined in Chapter 1, narrated basically a crisis site story, CBS emphasized locales far removed from Jonestown in its reports, and ABC extended the story to everywhere religious cults exist. The three networks also differed when they cast the leading roles in the drama of Three Mile Island: ABC pitted a monster-in-the-machine against helpless villagers, CBS provided experts and technicians acting on behalf of concerned citizens, and NBC showed a plurality of differing interests of equal prominence in the narrative.

Another way of utilizing Burke's dramatic pentad is to match its elements to the standardized basics of a news story: actors are the *who,* acts the *what,* scene the *when* and *where,* agency the *how,* and purpose the *why.* Looking back over the five crises examined in this study, we find that the networks did not, as conventional wisdom says (Dye & Ziegler, 1982, p. 133) "present identical news 'packages' each evening." We can summarize key differences by describing the basic trends in each network's treatment of the basic elements of a news story as they match Burke's pentad. There are, of course, slight variations from crisis to crisis, but the recurring patterns are clear.

For CBS, the *who,* or leading actors, in crisis stories consisted essentially of public officials, scientists, technicians—in short, insiders "in the know." They appeared in different roles from crisis to crisis: "government officials" in the Jonestown crisis, "experts" of one stripe or another dealing with TMI and Mount St. Helens, "regulators" coping with defective DC-10s, and "diplomats" seeking solutions to the hostage crisis. In any event, they were not America's ordinary citizens faced with unexpected dangers in everyday life. The actors, the *who,* typical of CBS narratives are members of America's establishment, its ruling elite.

The acts, the *what*, of a CBS drama are efforts at coping, managing, detecting, and otherwise responding to crisis. Even, as in Jonestown, when the crisis itself had already ended before news organizations had the story (that is, the murders and suicides were accomplished facts), CBS took a managerial point of view. Experts, in this case government officials and the military, had the task of identifying, processing, and returning bodies, as well as survivors, to the United States. Process was central to the Jonestown story just as detecting the cause of Flight 191's crash, a process, was crucial to that story; or diplomacy, again a process, was the only option in freeing the hostages.

CBS correspondents stand back and stand up. They stand back in the sense that, even though the network originates reports from crisis sites, it is the interpretive reports from official settings (often using interviews with "experts") that are the backbone of CBS narratives. They also stand back in another sense—not jumping on a story quickly, not being the network to break it. CBS came late to the crisis of The People's Temple, had TMI as its third story on the evening of March 28, 1979, and broke neither the Iranian hostage story nor Mount St. Helens. Correspondents stand up in the sense that the correspondent standing in front of a government building—Department of Energy, Nuclear Regulatory Commission, State Department, Federal Aviation Administration—is familiar to viewers of the *Evening News.*

The agency, the *how,* of CBS reporting is the fact. The pattern seldom varies: CBS narratives contain data, statistics, technical jargon, formulas, and official pronouncements. Viewers learn from CBS what they do not find elsewhere: the precise formula for the cyanide concoction used at Jonestown; exact distances between towns in Pennsylvania, Washington state, and even Iran. Facts are read by correspondents or shown on TV screens in the form of computer printouts, letters, documents, affidavits, regulations, even newspaper articles. It is a tradition of print, of wire service, journalism that pervades the style and character of CBS crisis coverage. Emphasis on data enters into both routine and nonroutine reports.

Finally, the purpose underlying everything that happens in a CBS narrative is to cope skillfully with the awesome. It is not to threaten or frighten, not to tell viewers to accept their fate. It is a message revealed in the style of interchange between anchor and correspondent. We have already seen many examples of that interchange: the anchor alerts people to danger, and correspondents report what is being done to avert disaster. It is what we choose to call a "Gee Whiz!" mode of TV journalism. The CBS anchor, usually Walter Cronkite in the cases examined, says, in effect, "Gee Whiz! Things are bad!" Correspondents, delivering their follow-up reports in painstaking detail and emphasizing how "the experts" respond, chorus that "Yes, things are bad. But don't panic, Walter. The experts, even in the worst of times, can and will manage." A much-relieved Cronkite then closes with "And that's the way it is."

The pattern is much different for ABC. Here actors are not cast in heroic roles of experts managing crises. Instead, the leading actors are the common folk, members of the populace with nothing to gain and everything to lose at the hands of public leaders. They are victims and, if there are heroes in ABC narratives, even they are merely specific victims: the Fansler family fleeing the cooling towers of TMI; the Sutton family who died in the crash of Flight 191, leaving a "collie named Charlie"; Harry Truman of Spirit Lake; or any one member of each of 52 hostage families.

If CBS portrays acts as fight, not flight, ABC takes the opposite tack: flight, not fight. The victims of Jonestown could not take flight, but ABC showed that there were others who could: members of The People's Temple in the U.S. whose lives were threatened by the Temple's "hit squad." The crisis of TMI was, for ABC, one of evacuation; of the DC-10, one of passengers fearful of boarding the aircraft; of Mount St. Helens, one of people victimized by ash fallout; and of Iran, a helpless giant, the U.S., unable to flee the grasp of the Ayatollah Khomeini.

ABC favors two scenes for crisis reporting, the studio and the crisis site. Being essentially scooped on the Jonestown story,

ABC had to cover it after the fact as a site story. But at TMI, O'Hare, Mount St. Helens, and Teheran, ABC took advantage of backdrops to relate appropriate narratives—cooling towers, charred runways, falling ash, and embassy gates. A sense of continuity flows from repeating the same on-site scenic background night after night. That continuity reinforces the narrative of how what happened did happen, the agency of the drama.

If CBS makes "The Experts" the sanctioning agent of its real-fictions, ABC makes it "The People." The People speak through specific persons, the actors described above. The means by which The People speak, and thus the means by which ABC tells its story of how things happened as they did, is the human interest interview. How things happened is not left to accounts by experts, but by average people—a farmer living across from the TMI plant, a relative of a victim of Jonestown, a friend of the Sutton family of Chicago, a sister of Harry Truman, a family member of one of the servicemen killed in the aborted hostage rescue attempt. The "how" story repeats itself: people in power ignoring the welfare of the little people cut corners, went too far, grasped too much. That's how things happen, always to the detriment of the populace.

The *how* and *why,* agency and purpose, of the news drama blend into an overriding message. Those in power are either insensitive to, or inimical to, the popular interest. That being the case, the message is "Don't trust anybody." This we call "Good Grief!" journalism. In effect, ABC anchors introduce a "series of reports" with a motif of "Good Grief! Things are bad. They could, probably will, get worse!" Correspondents' follow-up reports do little to relieve the anxiety. When the anchor wraps up the story, it is with a sense of heightened, not reduced concern, as for instance, in the last three words of this statement by anchor Frank Reynolds on April 4, 1979, after the crisis at TMI had subsided: "It was one week ago today that we first learned of what was then called an 'incident' at the Three Mile Island nuclear plant outside Harrisburg, Pennsylvania. The incident quickly became a crisis, then a possible catastrophe, and finally a disaster averted, or so we hope!" At ABC the genie never is put back in the bottle.

As we have seen, NBC news dramas have "a cast of thousands," to use a phrase once employed to promote Hollywood epics. Officials, scientists, technicians; ordinary people, living and dead; members of various private interest groups, inside and outside of power—all of these have a role to play in the *NBC Nightly News.* NBC confines itself to no particular source for its multiplicity of reports on a particular crisis but finds every angle possible: survivors of Jonestown talking with one another in a hotel room; elderly ladies in a backyard arguing the dangers of the TMI plant; diners in a darkened motel restaurant seeking shelter from falling ash; airline mechanics discussing how to muddle through; members of a hostage family discussing their disappointment at not being able to travel to Teheran after the aborted hostage rescue. Such reports aired only on NBC and gave the network coverage a distinctly pluralist, conversational character.

Neither fight nor flight constitutes the pattern of acts contained in NBC reports. Resignation is the byword. What happens, suggests NBC, is never unique. Each crisis has a long history and is embedded in a social, political, economic, religious, and human context. Granted that what happens has occurred for the first time to most of the people it directly involves—residents of Jonestown, Harrisburg, or Washington and Oregon; or airline passengers; or diplomatic officials and servicemen. And what happens is not good; indeed it is tragic. But in the larger scheme of things, a given crisis is but a crisis, not the end of the world.

NBC complements this sense of the larger scheme of things in ways that it portrays the scene, the *where* and *when,* and agencies describing how things happen. From the scenic standpoint NBC uses far more filmed, packaged reports in telling its stories than do rival networks. These are filmed everywhere—public and private offices, local businesses, homes, workshops, schools, churches, passenger compartments of airliners—in fact, anywhere that could have any conceivable bearing on the story. These filmed reports constitute a distinguishing characteristic of NBC reports: namely, they are feature stories of background and context. The anchors introducing these reports—and, indeed, many of the reports themselves—employ a didactic style. The result is a story of how things work, an account that removes the magic and the supernatural from the human condition. NBC says not that the genie can be returned to the bottle; that is CBS's view. Nor does it say, as ABC does, that the unbottled genie is free to roam and do mischief forever. NBC simply says that there is no genie.

The underlying message for NBC, based upon a view of dramatic purpose, is that, in the end, things don't really change much. The style is "Aw shucks" journalism. "Aw shucks," say NBC anchors, "It is a shame, but, as usual, something bad has happened. Let's see what and how and why." Correspondents, although presenting multiple reports, respond alike: "Ho hum, yes, things are bad, but they have been before, they will be again, so don't fret." There are no saints, no sinners, just people resigned to getting along the best they can once they have learned what things are really about. Life does go on.

The Bizarre Case of the Tylenol Poisonings

The beginning of the crisis that anchors on all three networks at one time or another labeled "bizarre" occurred on Thursday, September 30, 1982. At the time, the networks did not treat it as a Big Story. Only CBS led its evening newscast with the account, devoting slightly less that three minutes to it; NBC was nine minutes into its newscast before reporting on the Tylenol poisonings (the reports were only two minutes in length), and ABC did not get to the story for twelve minutes, giving only one minute and ten seconds to it.

The three networks not only placed different priorities on the story that first evening, they played it differently. Even though the locale of the poisonings was Chicago, home base of ABC co-anchor Max Robinson, the network reported little about them: Robinson reported three deaths from taking Extra-Strength Tylenol capsules laced with cyanide; the following report carried a film of a member of the medical examiner's office speculating that the deaths were homicides; a second physician remarked that the capsules had been contaminated in a manner similar to incidents of poisoned Halloween candies. The reference to Halloween introduced what was to become a prime motif of ABC's later coverage.

NBC's first report was more informative. Anchor Tom Brokaw began with the three Chicago deaths from cyanide-laced Tylenol and added the lot number of the capsules involved. The report that followed carried films of two physicians, one saying the capsules had been tampered with and the second explaining how, a feature always of interest to NBC. The report then identified the three victims, described the investigation of the deaths, and carried an official statement by a spokesman for the manufacturer of the pain reliever opining that the lacing did not occur at the plant, as well as a conversational statement by a woman on the telephone seeking a medical checkup. NBC's pluralist approach was intact: seven items in a two-minute report, four filmed statements.

CBS, too, stuck with the format typical of its coverage of other crises. Anchor Dan Rather sounded the alarm: there were deaths from cyanide-laced Tylenol in Chicago. The field correspondent's report, before reviewing details of the deaths themselves, outlined how authorities were conducting their investigation, a description including film of a police dispatcher broadcasting a public warning. So the alarm had been sounded and crisis management was underway. Then the report stated the number of deaths—using separate films of three physicians to emphasize CBS's interest in process—of sudden death from cyanide, of cyanide-lacing, and of distinguishing between normal and poisoned capsules. With alarm, management, and process covered, the report turned statistical as the lot number of contaminated capsules appeared on the screen with other data including the quantity of the product in that particular lot. The report closed with a mention of the possibility of a fourth victim. Repeating the lot number of the poisoned capsules, Rather then wrapped up the story. Later in the broadcast he confirmed a fourth death.

In short, the initial reports of the three networks ran true to

form: ABC went directly to a concern of the populace—fear—
by evoking Halloween comparisons; NBC pluralized its items
of information without a theme linking them; CBS alerted viewers to danger, reported a managerial response, emphasized
process, and cited statistics. Over the course of the next week,
both NBC and CBS continued the Tylenol poisonings as their
lead stories; ABC led with it on all but one evening. After that,
emphasis upon the case ebbed and flowed as newsworthy
events warranted. Overall, the month's long drama of the Tylenol poisonings (September 30 through October 31) consisted of
distinct scenarios. One included reports of the early Chicago
deaths. Another narrated the tale of the investigation of those
deaths and the search for suspects. A third was an account of
spreading danger as cases of other contaminated over-the-
counter products in other parts of the country developed. A
fourth was a story about packaging: namely, precautions to
prevent future poisonings. And the final act emphasized the
"Grinch who stole Halloween." In the end, however, there was
no clear resolution of the Tylenol crisis. The People's Temple
crisis ended with the return of victims' bodies; TMI when Walter Cronkite sounded the "All Clear"; the DC-10 crisis when
Roger Mudd "unleashed" the aircraft; Mount St. Helens when
NBC put a "stopper" (a dome) on the volcano; and the hostage
crisis with release and return. But in the Tylenol case, the *who*
and *why* of the poisonings has at this writing still not been
explained.

Each of the networks covered each of the scenarios outlined.
But each emphasized different ones to build its real-fiction.
NBC presented the most low-keyed narrative, a tale that an
ounce of prevention is worth a pound of cure. And prevention
requires knowing how things happen so as to avoid them in the
future. On the newscast of October 3, anchor John Hart introduced a report featuring an interview with the Attorney General
of Illinois, Tyrone Fahner. Hart remarked that police in Illinois
"know how but not who did it." He might have easily been
describing the underlying theme of NBC's narrative: i.e., since
how the poisonings occurred was clear but the search for the

identity and whereabouts of culprits was going nowhere, the appropriate response was to take precautions so that things like this would not happen again. This is not to say that NBC found any failure on the part of investigating officials. Attorney General Fahner's investigation NBC viewed as well-meaning, but—as other networks reported—lacking in tangible leads. Fahner was not villain or fool, just human, a not overly newsworthy story. Instead, NBC focused upon precaution. Two reports illustrate the tone of this emphasis, which is in keeping with NBC's overall approach to crisis coverage.

The first report, which aired on October 4, consisted of a detailed account, with appropriate film and graphics, of alternative methods for packaging over-the-counter drugs so as to reduce chances of intentional contamination. It "won't be easy," said a spokesman for a task force exploring ways to secure packages. In didactic fashion the report explained each remedy. But it did not end there. It went on to illustrate how, in each instance, the secure packaging could be tampered with (the "how to" instruction was thus as informative for would-be poisoners as for general viewers). Since there is "no obvious solution," the report concluded, consumer vigilance is the ultimate remedy. The second report exploited a format only recently coming into vogue in nightly network TV news: an extended live interview by the anchor. In an October studio interview with the president of Johnson & Johnson, parent company of Tylenol, Tom Brokaw explored in detail efforts to make packages tamper-resistant, concluding with questions of how people viewed over-the-counter drugs after the poisonings. The tone and content of the interview again stressed precautions as the best preventative for future cases.

NBC's didactic approach to the packaging story, as we have seen, was in keeping with its "show and tell" format. The network also continued its feature format in covering the poisonings. One report illustrates the pattern. On October 8 in a three-minute feature, correspondent James Polk reviewed the likely scenario of the previous Tylenol poisonings in Chicago, putting each death in context. All the victims had died on the same day, the report stressed. But there was one death not in context, that of Mary Reiner. This was much the same technique that the network's Robert Bazell had employed in putting the details of the workings of a nuclear reactor, a DC-10, a volcano, or a weather pattern into the larger scheme of things. The *CBS Evening News* also covered each of the acts of the Tylenol crisis. However, for that network the emphasis was on the investigation and search for culprits. What Tom Brokaw found a "bizarre mystery," Dan Rather labeled "bizarre and terrifying." But if, for NBC, precautions were the way to deal with the bizarre, detective work was the response for CBS (much like the CBS search for the cause of the crash of Flight 191). In fact, CBS envisioned itself contributing to the detective work. On October 18 Rather opened his newscast with a report of a "breakthrough" in the Tylenol murders investigation. That breakthrough turned out to be a photograph taken by a surveillance camera in a drugstore where one of the Tylenol victims shopped. The fuzzy and blurred photo showed the victim going through the checkout line. In the background was a man identified as the prime suspect in the investigation, a man labeled with several aliases. Using "technology to clear up the picture," CBS again displayed the "technically enhanced" photo to give viewers a better look at the suspect. The implication was that viewers should be on the lookout. Three evenings later CBS again used the photo in another report, this time detailing false arrests of persons resembling the suspect.

The photo of the alleged suspect and victim did not appear on rival networks until October 19, one day after CBS broke the story. Each played the account much differently from CBS. After showing the photo, NBC then reported that investigators could not agree that the man in the picture was the prime suspect being sought. And the suspect's landlord said in an interview that he did not think the man in the picture was the suspect. So much for CBS's detective work and scoop. ABC at first shared with CBS the view that the man in the photo was the suspect, even though it, too, ran film of the landlord expressing doubts. What made ABC's report distinctive were three things. First, the network put circles around both man and victim in the photo (each of the other networks had also pointed out with circles or arrows the two persons). But that was not enough. The circle around the man's face then moved toward the victim as though in pursuit. Second, ABC's Max Robinson noted that the breakthrough might be to no avail, since the suspect might have changed his appearance by now anyway. Third, Robinson closed by reporting that Attorney General Fahner was urging close parental supervision of Halloween activities to prevent "copycat" poisonings. By the next evening, October 20, Max Robinson reported that the man in the drugstore photo was probably not the suspect anyway.

By October 29, CBS also had some doubts about the way things were going. Perhaps there was a reason for the breakdown of managerial coping. The network identified a possibility. Attorney General Fahner might be using the investigation as part of his campaign for reelection (he lost). It was a role reversal for Fahner, from manager to politician. ABC's *World News Tonight* had no need for such reversals. The murders (which eventually totaled seven), spreading cases throughout the country of contaminated over-the-counter drugs (pain relievers, eyewashes, nose drops, mineral oil, etc.) and "no new leads" meant that, like the U.S. in the hostage crisis, investigators were helpless in "The Tylenol Scare" (Robinson). And the reason was again that another genie was out of the bottle. Like Jim Jones, nuclear power, missing bolts, volcanic activity, and the Ayatollah, the Tylenol murderer would never be found. What had first been thought to be an "isolated case of foul play" was turning into a real-life version of the Hollywood horror movie *Halloween,* wherein an unseen and deranged killer stalked his innocent victims.

That Halloween motif tied the ABC narrative together. Introduced in the network's first account of the breaking story, ABC returned to it in other newscasts. But as October 31 approached it further served as the whole meaning of "The Tylenol Scare." As in a horror movie, some unknown murderer was stalking victims everywhere for no apparent reason. On October 29, ABC reviewed all of the sites across the nation where poisoning incidents had occurred, illustrating them on a map in precisely the same fashion the network had used during the TMI crisis to pinpoint the location of each nuclear plant built by Babcock & Wilcox. After that review a second correspondent, using a screen listing, noted all cases of tampered Halloween goodies, such as Demoral in a brownie in New Hampshire. "America is fighting fears about Halloween," said one correspondent. But if the genie can't be returned to the bottle, what can be done? The answer was what communities were doing: banning trick-or-treat. But who would be the innocent victims of these bans? The children who, because of forces unknown to them, were being robbed of a magical childhood experience. Yet there was no choice, for children were "scared of eating anything." And to summarize, ABC had Charles Schulz, creator of the *Peanuts* comic strip and animated cartoons—many of which employ the Halloween motif, albeit differently from ABC—comment on the loss.

These, then, were the narratives of the Tylenol scare. They differed between networks in ways that we would have been led to expect from our previous dramatistic analysis of crisis coverage by the three networks. In that sense, the more things changed at the networks (i.e., personnel changes), the more things remained the same. But what of technical aspects of the Tylenol coverage? Here some things remained the same, but not all. First, as noted in Table 6.1, there were no significant differences in newsgathering modes for the networks. (Because there were such a limited number of sources in the Tylenol crisis and the networks did not differ in sources, we omit that listing from Table 6.1). Yet old habits are apparently hard to break, even in the absence of significant differences. ABC remained in the studio more than other networks; CBS went to government offices; NBC did a little of everything. As in other crises, CBS interviewed technicians and scientists along with governmental "experts." Although the difference was slight, ABC turned more to interest group spokespersons than in other crises, and NBC shifted the highest proportion of its newsgathering to interviews with average citizens.

From the standpoint of visual prominence, something else happened. One of Van Gordon Sauter's aims after assuming the executive producer's role of the *CBS Evening News* was to make the newscast more visual. Graphics and technical gim-

Nightly Horrors: Television Network News

Table 6.1
Newsgathering Modes for Tylenol News Reports: by Network

Modes	ABC	CBS	NBC	Combined
Locale				
Network studio	27 (68%)	30 (54%)	39 (58%)	96 (59%)
Government office	10 (25%)	18 (32%)	17 (26%)	45 (28%)
Private home/office	3 (7%)	8 (14%)	10 (15%)	21 (12%)
Crisis site	0	0	1 (1%)	1 (1%)
Means				
Briefing by public official	4 (8%)	7 (13%)	21 (36%)	32 (20%)
Interview with public official	16 (31%)	13 (25%)	7 (12%)	36 (21%)
Interview with technician/ scientist	3 (6%)	7 (13%)	6 (10%)	16 (10%)
Interview with average citizen	13 (25%)	17 (32%)	23 (39%)	53 (32%)
Interview with interest group leader	6 (11%)	3 (6%)	2 (3%)	11 (6%)
Reporter quoting a source	10 (19%)	6 (11%)	0	16 (10%)

micks were his speciality (Kitner, 1982). Over at NBC there was a new anchor team of Tom Brokaw and Roger Mudd. Since each was being paid handsomely in hopes of elevating the *Nightly News* in viewing ratings, it was natural that the two star anchors would be featured in the nightly newscasts. As the data in Table 6.2 demonstrate, these changes had effects. There are significant differences between networks in anchor versus packaged stories (all packaged stories had interviews). The difference between CBS and its rivals (a lower ratio of anchor to packaged stories) is significant. And CBS joined ABC in using stills in a greater proportion of stories than did NBC. And all three networks in rolling films normally included interviews within the film clips.

There is evidence that CBS became a more visually prominent news network than its rivals, at least in coverage of the Tylenol crisis. Visual prominence scores ranged from 0–57, with the CBS mean 27, ABC 25, and NBC 20. The differences have F-ratios significant at the .05 level, making CBS the most visual, NBC the least, in Tylenol coverage. In short, visual promotion at CBS and anchor promotion at NBC did make a difference.

Stylistic emphases of the three networks remained the same as in previous cases of crisis coverage. Yet there were some variations on old themes. ABC remained the network of popu-

The Tylenol Poisonings

Table 6.2
Visual Elements in Tylenol Stories: by Network

Visual elements of story	ABC	CBS	NBC	Combined
Anchor read story	60 (77%)	61 (68%)	98 (78%)	294 (74%)
Cut to packaged report(s)				
One or more, with interviews	18 (23%)	29 (32%)	28 (22%)	75 (26%)
χ^2 = 36.103 with 2 df (anchor/packaged); p = .001.				
Graphic over anchor/reporter shoulder				
None	52 (67%)	72 (80%)	94 (74%)	218 (74%)
One	18 (23%)	18 (20%)	29 (24%)	65 (22%)
Two or more	8 (10%)	0	3 (2%)	11 (4%)
Still picture/graphic on total screen				
None	57 (73%)	72 (80%)	114 (90%)	243 (83%)
One	6 (8%)	9 (10%)	4 (3%)	19 (6%)
Two or more	15 (19%)	9 (10%)	8 (7%)	32 (11%)
Film rolled during story				
None	53 (68%)	58 (64%)	92 (73%)	203 (69%)
Film, without interview	1 (1%)	2 (3%)	2 (2%)	5 (2%)
Film, with interview	24 (31%)	30 (33%)	32 (25%)	86 (29%)
Second film during story				
None	57 (73%)	66 (73%)	98 (78%)	221 (75%)
Film, without interview	1 (1%)	1 (1%)	3 (2%)	5 (2%)
Film, with interview	20 (26%)	23 (26%)	25 (20%)	68 (23%)
on still pictures χ^2 = 14.773 with 6 df; p = .05.				

list/sensationalist style but with a considerable increase in the proportion of number and duration of pluralist/feature stories. CBS remained elitist/factual and, again in its populist/sensationalist reports the anchor (Dan Rather) contributed more than correspondents by almost a 2:1 ratio. NBC, as its narrative indicated, continued as a feature-oriented network.

Finally, in news content no significant differences emerged between networks. Nor do we observe clear-cut changes in earlier network patterns. NBC remained the news program offering perspective as its leading motif; CBS did not depart from its basic news format (although peripheral matters were the highest percentage of CBS stories); but ABC worked some degree of perspective into more than a third of its news accounts, a shift away from its more common inclusion of peripheral materials in past crisis coverage. None of the networks stressed reassurance, but no significant differences existed between them in proportions of alarming to reassuring stories.

Thus changes did occur within the networks between the

Nightly Horrors: Television Network News

Table 6.3
Coverage Styles in Tylenol Crisis:
by Networks, Anchors, Correspondents

Reports	ABC	CBS	NBC	Combined
Total number	40	56	67	163
Anchors	27 (68%)	30 (54%)	40 (60%)	97 (60%)
Correspondents	13 (32%)	26 (47%)	27 (40%)	66 (40%)
Style (by number of reports)				
Populist/sensationalist	21 (52%)	16 (29%)	13 (19%)	50 (31%)
Anchors	14	11	11	36
Correspondents	7	5	2	14
Elitist/factual	7 (18%)	30 (54%)	14 (21%)	51 (31%)
Anchors	6	16	12	34
Correspondents	1	14	2	17
Ignorant/didactic	3 (8%)	3 (5%)	12 (18%)	18 (11%)
Anchors	1	3	7	11
Correspondents	2	0	5	7
Pluralist/feature	9 (22%)	7 (12%)	28 (42%)	44 (27%)
Anchors	6	0	10	16
Correspondents	3	7	18	28
Total time of coverage (in minutes)	52	65	62	179
Anchors	35 (67%)	22 (34%)	24 (39%)	81 (45%)
Correspondents	17 (33%)	43 (66%)	38 (61%)	98 (55%)
Style duration (in minutes)				
Populist/sensationalist	26 (50%)	17 (26%)	9 (15%)	52 (29%)
Anchors	16	9	6	31
Correspondents	10	8	3	21
Elitist/factual	7 (13%)	34 (52%)	6 (10%)	47 (26%)
Anchors	6	11	4	21
Correspondents	1	23	2	26
Ignorant/didactic	3 (6%)	1 (2%)	10 (16%)	14 (8%)
Anchors	1	1	5	7
Correspondents	2	0	5	7
Pluralist/feature	16 (31%)	13 (20%)	37 (59%)	66 (37%)
Anchors	12	1	9	22
Correspondents	4	12	28	44

Significant differences are as follows:
1. Between networks for number of reports per style $\chi^2 = 37.745$ with 6 df; p = .001.
2. Between networks for duration of reports per style $\chi^2 = 17.597$ with 6 df; p = .01.
3. Between networks for number of anchor reports per style $\chi^2 = 17.011$ with 6 df; p = .01.
4. Between networks for number of correspondent reports per style $\chi^2 = 23.681$ with 6 df; p = .001.
5. Between networks for duration of anchor reports per style $\chi^2 = 20.056$ with 6 df; p = .01.
6. Between networks for duration of correspondent reports per style $\chi^2 = 52.502$ with 6 df; p = .001.

Table 6.4
News Content of Tylenol Reports: by Network

Content Types	ABC	CBS	NBC	Combined
News value				
News	9 (23%)	11 (20%)	13 (19%)	33 (20%)
Peripheral	8 (20%)	22 (39%)	21 (31%)	51 (31%)
Perspective	4 (10%)	6 (11%)	15 (22%)	25 (15%)
News/peripheral	9 (22%)	9 (16%)	11 (16%)	29 (18%)
News/perspective	10 (25%)	8 (14%)	7 (12%)	25 (16%)
Emotional content				
Reassuring	1 (2%)	4 (7%)	6 (9%)	11 (7%)
Alarming	19 (48%)	20 (36%)	28 (42%)	67 (41%)
Neutral	20 (50%)	32 (57%)	33 (49%)	85 (52%)

period of the crises reported in Chapters 1–5 in this book and the Tylenol scare of 1982. But, as far as crisis coverage goes, it is apparent that changes in executive and anchor personnel contributed more to technical shifts in news coverage than to the tendencies of the respective networks to tell differing dramatic stories and, consequently, to provide viewers with contrasting real-fictions. This is not to say that over a longer period these technical shifts will not influence the stories the networks tell as well as how they tell them. But throughout the Tylenol crisis such does not seem to have been the case. This leads us to consider a final matter. If, as we argue, the nightly newscasts of the three major television networks do produce a variety of real-fictions, are there such transcendent patterns in these real-fictions as to suggest that the networks offer viewers markedly different rhetorical visions as well?

Rhetorical Visions in Crisis Coverage

Ernest Bormann (1972) has defined rhetorical visions as "the composite dramas which catch up large groups of people in a symbolic reality." For Bormann such visions are constructed from fantasies shared by large numbers of people. Without weighing the pros and cons of fantasy theme analysis as a method of rhetorical criticism (see Bormann 1972, 1982, and Mohrmann, 1982a, 1982b, for that debate), we can adapt the notion of rhetorical vision to conclude our discussion of crisis coverage by nightly network television news. As we noted in the Introduction, we consider rhetorical visions also to be composite dramas, but dramas in the form of journalistic real-fictions. In his seminal account of real-fictions, Fisher (1970) argues that they are produced in rhetorical compositions. Such compositions occur when communicators encounter situations in which they must act. Their discourse in those situations is influenced in part by the situation itself (say, a crisis) but just as much by the motives they carry into that situation. From the perspective we have taken in this book, we may apply those motives to the overall patterns of style and content television news networks impose upon critical events as they report them. These motives define the relationships between communicator, audience, time, and place. They offer a view of what things are all about, a thesis to describe them, and a value-oriented interpretation of the rhetorical situation, parts of the world, and the world at large.

This value-oriented image, suggests Fisher, implies conceptions or assumptions communicators make about situations and about their audiences. Fisher lists four types of motives that influence rhetorical situations, and hence, images of things. We think of these as four types of rhetorical visions of the world: "affirmation" gives birth to an image, "reaffirmation" revitalizes it, "purification" corrects flaws in an image, and "subversion" undermines an image. It is our contention that these motives underlie how television news reports crises to viewers. Behind *NBC Nightly News* stands a combined vision of affirmation and purification. At the heart of the *CBS Evening News* is a vision of reaffirmation. ABC's *World News Tonight* manifests a vision that is subversive in the rhetorical sense.

Affirmation occurs in academic situations. Things are judged valid not because of who said them (say, a person in authority) or because they are emotionally pleasing. Validity depends instead upon the sense of the situation. NBC's feature and contextual orientation defines situations as extensional (across space) and durational (across time). Any crisis is but a special case of something that has happened before and elsewhere in the larger scheme of things. In spite of dangers, calamities, threats, crises, disasters and countless other untoward events that are part of the human condition, life goes on.

This rhetorical vision of a primal assurance and affirmation that life will continue, no matter what, does not imply, at least in NBC's version, that people should sit idly by and do nothing in the face of danger. What they should do is learn. They should take complex, confusing, and overwhelming situations and both define and refine the essentials thereof in conformity with the simple ways of human life. This is the rhetoric of purification. So nuclear power plants are tea kettles and volcanic crater domes are stoppers. Thus purified, the complex and overwhelming features of life are stripped of all mystifying contradictions and confusions. Life is even more likely to continue. For if Socrates was correct in saying "the unexamined life is not worth living," NBC by demystifying crises demystifies life, thus examining it and making it worth living.

But sometimes the dangers threatening life are so awesome that an affirmed and purified vision of resignation is difficult to accept. Someone must move against danger, not simply try to understand it in simplified terms and take it as given. Here the CBS revitalization process enters. Life can go on, says this vision, only "if the system works." And the system does work for *CBS Evening News*. True, it is beset by crises—not just by those described in this book but by others such as energy crises, war, and corruptions in government. Yet in the end the system triumphs because the responsible, trustworthy elite that manages it relieves the danger. An orderly society is thus restored, and in a properly managed, orderly society, life can indeed go on.

For NBC the rhetorical vision thus suggests that reality is threatening but affirms that purified life will continue in spite of everything. CBS has a vision of threatening reality too, but ruling elites cope with the dangers and reaffirm that life can indeed continue. The ABC vision, too, is of a threatening reality. But why is life threatened? Because the system does not work. "Subversive rhetoric," writes Fisher, "is an anti-ethos rhetoric; that is, it invariably is an attempt to undermine the credibility of some person, idea, or institution" (1970, p. 138). The pattern of ABC news reports is consistent: those in charge of the system have rendered it helpless in the face of crisis. "The strategy is to make a man, idea, or institution consubstantial with Satanic attributes and intentions" (p. 138). Since politicians, economists, scientists, engineers, technocrats, bureaucrats, and others have in a Satanic way released uncontrollable forces, life is today always a crisis. Eventually the common folk will have to pay the price of their rulers' folly; life itself will end.

Fisher notes that there is "a nice relationship between affirmative and subversive rhetorics: to affirm an image is, in effect, to subvert an old one; to subvert an old one is, in effect, to affirm a new one" (p. 138). We cannot, of course, conclude from our evidence that the rhetorical vision of one network is dominant over another. Rather we see, at least in crisis coverage, three rhetorical visions competing for the attention of television news audiences: NBC's vision of affirmation and purification, CBS's vision of reaffirmation, and ABC's vision of subversion. And with the number of options for viewers increasing as a result of the formation of cable news networks, satellite feeds to local television news broadcasters, and other technical changes, other visions could also emerge.

In any event, as Ernest Bormann (1982, p. 300) has noted, the poet Robert Frost expressed a basic insight: "People can never figure things out for themselves: they have to see them acted out by actors." Whatever the rhetorical visions that may evolve and diminish, the role of television news in crisis coverage will remain that of storytelling, in keeping with Frost's advisory. Anchors and correspondents will continue as the griots[1] of our era, narrators of real-fictional tales of past and present, which people heed as they struggle to project the future, if—as one major network might warn—there is a future.

---

[1]Griots are carriers of history. They narrate the history of a tribe by recalling tales that have been passed from one generation to another, Griot to Griot. Alex Haley claimed to have learned his African roots from a Griot.

References

Adams, W. C., & Schreibman, F. (Eds.). (1978). *Television network news: Issues in content research*. Washington, DC: School of Public and International Affairs, George Washington University.

Adams, W. C. (Ed.). (1981). *Television coverage of the Middle East.* Norwood, NJ: Ablex.

Adams, W. C., & Joblove, M. (1982). The unnewsworthy holocaust: TV news and terror in Cambodia. In W. C. Adams (Ed.), *Television coverage of international affairs* (pp. 217–226). Norwood, NJ: Ablex.

Adams, W. C. (Ed.). (1982). *Television coverage of international affairs*. Norwood, NJ: Ablex.

Adams, W. C. (Ed.). (1983). *Television coverage of the 1980 presidential campaign*. Norwood, NJ: Ablex.

Altheide, D. L. (1976). *Creating reality*. Beverly Hills, CA: Sage.

Altheide, D. L. (1981a). Network news: Oversimplified and underexplained. *Washington Journalism Review, 3*, 28–29.

Altheide, D. L. (1981b). Iran vs. U.S. TV news: The hostage story out of context. In W. C. Adams (Ed.), *Television coverage of the Middle East* (pp. 128–157). Norwood, NJ: Ablex.

Altheide, D. L. (1982). Three-in-one news: Network coverage of Iran. *Journalism Quarterly, 59*, 482–486.

Altheide, D. L., & Snow, R. P. (1979). *Media logic*. Beverly Hills, CA: Sage.

Arterton, F. C. (1978). The media politics of presidential campaigns: A study of the Carter nomination drive. In J. D. Barber (Ed.), *Race for the presidency* (pp. 25–54). Englewood Cliffs, NJ: Prentice-Hall.

Ball, G. (1980, November 17). The hostages as "soap opera." *Newsweek*, p. 57.

Bantz, C. R. (1979). The critic and the computer: A multiple technique analysis of the ABC evening news. *Communication Monographs, 46*, 27–39.

Bargainnier, E. F. (1980). Hissing the villain, cheering the hero: The social function of melodrama. *Studies in Popular Culture, 3*, 47–56.

Berg, D. M. (1972). Rhetoric, reality, and mass media. *Quarterly Journal of Speech, 58,* 255–263.

Berger, A. A. (1981). Semiotics and TV. In R. P. Adler (Ed.), *Understanding Television* (pp. 91–114). New York: Praeger.

Bernays, E. L. (1979). Crisis communication failure: Three Mile Island. *Perspective, 1,* 4–8.

Blumler, J. G., & Katz, E. (Eds.). (1974). *The uses of mass communication.* Beverly Hills, CA: Sage.

Bogart, L. (1977). *How the public gets its news. The APME Red Book,* 75–89.

Bormann, E. G. (1972). Fantasy and rhetorical vision: The rhetorical criticism of social reality. *Quarterly Journal of Speech, 58,* 396–407.

Bormann, E. G. (May 1982a). A fantasy theme analysis of the television coverage of the hostage release and the Reagan inaugural. *Quarterly Journal of Speech, 68,* 133–145.

Bormann, E. G. (August 1982b). Fantasy and rhetorical vision: Ten years later. *Quarterly Journal of Speech, 68,* 288–305.

Braestrup, P. (1978). *Big Story.* Garden City, NY: Anchor Books.

Breen, M., & Corcoran, F. (1982). Myth in the television discourse. *Communication Monographs, 49,* 127–136.

Brock, B. L., & Scott, R. L. (Eds.). (1980). *Methods of rhetorical criticism* (2nd ed.). Detroit: Wayne State University Press.

Burke, K. (1966). *Language as symbolic action.* Berkeley: University of California Press.

Carey, J. W. (1969). The communications revolution and the professional communicator. In P. Halmos (Ed.), *The sociology of mass media communication* (pp. 23–38). Keele, Staffordshire, England: University of Keele.

Coleman, J. S. (1956). Statistical problems. In S. M. Lipset, M. Trow, and J. S. Coleman (Eds.), *Union Democracy* (pp. 427–432). Glencoe, IL: The Free Press.

Cragan, J. F., & Shields, D. C. (Eds.). (1981). *Applied communication research: a dramatistic approach.*Prospect Heights, IL: Waveland Press.

Darnton, R. (1975, September). Writing news and telling stories. *Daedalus, 104,* 175–194.

Diamond, E. (1975). *The tin kazoo.* Cambridge, MA: The M.I.T. Press.

Diamond, E. (1978). *Good news, bad news.* Cambridge, MA: The M.I.T. Press.

Diamond, E. (1982). *Sign off.* Cambridge, MA: The M.I.T. Press.

201
References

Doyle, P. K. (1982). *A descriptive study of bad-good news content in television newscasts.* Unpublished master's thesis, University of Tennessee, Knoxville.

Dye, T., & Ziegler, H. (1982). *American politics in the media age.* Belmont, CA: Wadsworth. 1982.

Efron, E. (1971). *The news twisters.* Los Angeles: Nash Publishing.

Entman, R. M., & Paletz, D. L. (1982). The war in Southeast Asia: Tunnel vision in television. In W. C. Adams (Ed.), *Television coverage of international affairs* (pp. 181–204). Norwood, NJ: Ablex.

Epstein, E. J. (1973). *News from nowhere.* New York: Vintage Books.

Farrell, T. B., & Goodnight, G. T. (1981). Accidental rhetoric: The root metaphors of Three Mile Island. *Communication Monographs, 48,* 271–300.

Fisher, W. R. (1970). A motive view of communication. *Quarterly Journal of Speech, 56,* 132–139.

Fisher, W. R. (1980). Rhetorical fiction and the presidency. *Quarterly Journal of Speech, 66,* 119–126.

Frank, R. S. (1973). *Message dimensions of television news.* Lexington, MA: Lexington Books.

Friedman, S. M. (1981). Blueprint for breakdown: Three Mile Island and the media before the accident. *Journal of Communication, 31,* 116–128.

Fritz, C. E. 1961. Disasters. In R. K. Merton & R. Nisbet (Eds.), *Contemporary social problems* (pp. 651–694). New York: Harcourt, Brace and World.

Funt, P. (1980, November). Television news: Seeing isn't believing. *Saturday Review,* pp. 30–32.

Gans, H. J. (1979). *Deciding what's news.* New York: Vintage Books.

Glaser, B. G. (1978). *Theoretical sensitivity.* Mill Valley, CA.: The Sociology Press.

Glaser, B. G., & Strauss, A. L. (1967). *The discovery of grounded theory.* Chicago: Aldine.

Graber, D. (1980). *Mass media and American politics.* Washington, DC: Congressional Quarterly Press.

Hawkins, R. P., & Pingree, S. (1981). Using television to construct social reality. *Journal of Broadcasting, 25,* 347–364.

Herzog, A. (1973). *The B.S. factor: The theory and technique of faking it in America.* Baltimore: Penguin Books.

Hofstetter, C. R. (1976). *Bias in the news: Network television news coverage of the 1972 election campaign.* Columbus, OH: Ohio State University Press.

Holsti, O. R. (1969a). *Content analysis for the social sciences and humanities*. Reading, MA: Addison-Wesley.

Holsti, O. R. (1969b). Content analysis. In G. Lindzey & E. Aronson (Eds.), *The handbook of social psychology* Vol. II (pp. 596–602). Reading, MA: Addison-Wesley.

Iyengar, S., Peters, M. D., & Kinder, D. R. (1982). Experimental demonstrations of the "Not-So-Minimal" consequences of television news programs. *American Political Science Review, 76*, 848–858.

Jamieson, K. H., & Campbell, K. K. (1983). *The interplay of influence: Mass media and their publics in news, advertising, politics*. Belmont CA.: Wadsworth.

Johnson, H. (1981, January 25). The reassuring truth of genuinely caring about individuals. *The Washington Post*, p. A3.

Karp, W. (1982). The networks from left to right. *Channels, 2*, 23–27, 56.

Kish, L. (1959). Some statistical problems in research design. *American Sociological Review, 24*, 328, 338.

Kitner, M. (1982, November). Profile: Van Gordon Sauter. *Washington Journalism Review, 4*, 26–32.

Klapp. O. (1962). *Heroes, villains and fools*. Englewood Cliffs, NJ: Prentice-Hall.

Klapper, J. T. (1960). *The effects of mass communication*. Glencoe, IL: The Free Press.

Knight, G., & Dean, T. (1982). Myth and the structure of the news. *Journal of Communication, 32*, 144–161.

Krause, C. A. (1978). *Guyana massacre: The eyewitness account*. New York: Berkeley.

Krebs, G. A. (1980). Research needs and policy issues on mass media disaster reporting. In A. Kreimer (Ed.), *Disasters and the mass media* (pp.35–74). Washington, DC: National Academy of Sciences.

Kreimer, A. (Ed.). (1980). *Disasters and the mass media*. Washington, DC: National Academy of Sciences.

Krippendorff, K. (1980). *Content analysis*. Beverly Hills, CA: Sage.

Lang, G. E., & Lang, K. (1980). Newspapers and TV archives: Some thoughts about research on disaster news. In A. Kreimer (Ed.), *Disasters and the mass media* (pp.269–80). Washington, D.C.: National Academy of Sciences.

Lang, G. E., & Lang, K. (1983). *The battle for public opinion*. New York: Columbia University Press.

Lang, K., & Lang, G. E. (1968). *Politics and television*. Chicago: Quadrangle Books.

References

Larson, J. F. (1980). A review of the state of the art in mass media disaster reporting. In A. Kreimer (Ed.), *Disasters and the mass media*. Washington, DC: National Academy of Sciences.

Lawrence, J. S., & Timberg, B. (1979). News and mythic selectivity: Mayaguez, Entebbe, Mogadishu. *Journal of American Culture, 2*, 224–234.

Lemert, J. B. (1981). *Does mass communication change public opinion after all?* Chicago: Nelson Hall.

Lichty, L. W. (1982). Video versus print. *The Wilson Quarterly, 6* (5): 49–58.

Lichty, L. W., & Bailey, G. A. (1978). Reading the wind: Reflections on content analysis of broadcast news. In W. C. Adams & F. Schreibman (Eds.), *Television network news* (pp.111–138). Washington, DC: George Washington University.

Lippmann, W. (1922). *Public opinion*. New York: Macmillan.

MacNeil, R. (1968). *The people machine*. New York: Harper & Row.

McLuhan, M. (1964). *Understanding media*. New York: Signet.

Mead, G. H. (1934). *Mind, self, and society*. Chicago: University of Chicago Press.

Mohrmann, G. P. (1982a, May). An essay on fantasy theme criticism. *Quarterly Journal of Speech, 68*, 109–132.

Mohrmann, G. P. (1982b, August). Fantasy theme criticism: A peroration. *Quarterly Journal of Speech, 68*, 306–313.

Muravchik, J. (1983). *TV news coverage of the Lebanon war*. New York: Heritage Foundation.

Paletz, D. L., & Entman, R. M. (1981). *Media power politics*. New York: The Free Press.

Patterson, T. E., & McClure, R. D. (1976). *The unseeing eye*. New York: G.P. Putnam's Sons.

Patterson, T. (1980). *The mass media election*. New York: Praeger.

Report of The President's Commission On The Accident at Three Mile Island. (1979). *The need for change: The legacy of TMI*. Washington, DC: U.S. Government Printing Office.

Robinson, M. J. (1976). Public affairs television and the growth of political malaise. *American Political Science Review, 70*, 409–32.

Robinson, M. J. (1981). A statesman is a dead politician: Candidate images on network news. In E. Abel (Ed.), *What's news* (pp.157–186). San Francisco: Institute for Contemporary Studies.

Robinson, M. J. (1981). Reflections on the nightly news. In R. P. Adler (Ed.), *Understanding television* (pp. 313–330). New York: Praeger.

Rollins, P. C. (1982). TV's battle of the Khe Sanh: Selective images of defeat. In W. C. Adams (Ed.), *Television coverage of international affairs* (pp. 203–216). Norwood, NJ: Ablex.

Roper, E. (1983). *Changing public attitudes toward television and other media 1959–1982*. New York: Roper Organization.

Roshco, B. (1975). *Newsmaking*. Chicago: University of Chicago Press.

Said, E. W. (1981). *Covering Islam: How the media and the experts determine how we see the rest of the world*. New York: Pantheon Books.

Saldich, A. R. (1979). *Electronic democracy*. New York: Praeger.

Sandman, P. M., & Paden, M. (1979). At Three Mile Island. *Columbia Journalism Review, 18*, 43–58.

Schudson, M. (1982). The politics of narrative form: The emergence of news conventions in print and television. *Daedalus, 3*, 97–112.

Schulman, M. A. (1979). The impact of Three Mile Island. *Public Opinion, 2*, 7–13.

Scott, W. A. (1955). Reliability of content analysis: The case of nominal scaling. *Public Opinion Quarterly, 19*, 321–325.

Selvin, H. C. (1957). A critique of tests of significance in survey research. *American Sociological Review, 22*, 519–527.

Selvin, H. C. (1960). *Statistical significance and social theory*. Berkeley: University of California Press.

Shaw, D. L., & McCombs, M. E. (1971). *The emergence of American political issues: The agenda-setting function of the press*. St. Paul, MN: West Publishing.

Sperry, S. (1981). Television news as narrative. In R.P. Adler (Ed.), *Understanding television* (pp.295–312). New York: Praeger.

Staff Report to the President's Commission on the Accident at Three Mile Island: Report of the public's right to information task force. (1979). Washington, DC: U.S. Government Printing Office.

Stephens, M., & Edison, N. G. (1982). News media coverage of issues during the accident at Three Mile Island. *Journalism Quarterly, 59*, 199–204.

Swanson, D. L. (1977). And that's the way it was? Television covers the 1976 presidential campaign. *Quarterly Journal of Speech, 63*, 239–248.

Theberge, L. J. (1979). *Television evening news covers nuclear energy: A ten year perspective*. Washington, DC: The Media Institute.

Theberge, L. J. (1982). *TV coverage of the oil crisis*. Washington, D.C.: The Media Institute.

Thomas, W. I. (1928). *The unadjusted girl*. Boston: Little, Brown.

Tuchman, G. (1978). *Making news*. New York: The Free Press.

Vogel, A. (1980). Three Mile Island attitudes. *Response Update on Energy* [occasional newsletter], 3.

References

Weaver, P. H. (1976). Captives of melodrama. *New York Times Magazine, 6,* 48, 50–51, 54, 56–57.

Westin, A. (1982). *Newswatch.* New York: Simon and Schuster.

Wurtzel, A. (1983). *Television production.* New York: McGraw-Hill.

Yardley, J. (1983, May 22). Hype and the manufacturing of news. *The Manchester Guardian Weekly, 128,* pp.7, 18.

Zettl, H. (1981). Television aesthetics. In R. P. Adler (Ed.), *Understanding television* (pp.115–142). New York: Praeger.

Index

Nightly Horrors has been composed on the Linotron 202N digital phototypesetter in ten point Times Roman with two points of spacing beween the lines. Bernhard Antique Bold Condensed was selected for display. The book was designed by Sandra Strother Hudson, typeset by Williams of Chattanooga, printed offset by Thomson-Shore, Inc., and bound by John H. Dekker & Sons. The book is printed on paper carrying acid-free characteristics designed for an effective shelf life of at least three hundred years.

The University of Tennessee Press : Knoxville